AA
Essential ✔ KU-218-911

explorer
CALIFORNIA

AA Publishing

Essential

Written by Mick Sinclair
Series Adviser: Ingrid Morgan
Series Editor: Nia Williams
Copy Editor: Diana Payne
Designer: KAG Design Ltd

Edited, designed, produced and distributed by AA Publishing, Fanum House, Basingstoke, Hampshire RG21 2EA.
© The Automobile Association 1993.
Maps © The Automobile Association 1993.

A catalogue record for this book is available from the British Library.

ISBN 0 7495 0561 3

This book was produced using QuarkXPress ™ , Aldus Freehand ™ and Microsoft Word ™ on Apple Macintosh ™ computers.

Colour origination by Fotographics Ltd
Printed and bound in Italy by Printer Trento S.r.l.

Published by AA Publishing.

Mick Sinclair is the author of *The Rough Guide to Florida* and *The Rough Guide to California*, and is a regular contributor to many travel magazines and newspapers.

The Chinese Theater, opened in LA by Sid Grauman in 1927

About this book

This book is divided into three principal sections.

The first part of the book discusses aspects of life today and in the past. Places to visit are then covered region by region, along with Focus on... and Close-up features, which highlight areas and subjects in more detail. Drives and walks are also suggested in this section of the book. Finally, day-to-day practical information for the visitor is given in the Travel Facts chapter, along with a selected Directory of hotels and restaurants.

The indoor 'Roman' swimming pool in Hearst Castle, San Simeon

Some of the places described in this book have been given a special rating:

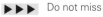 Do not miss

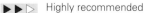 Highly recommended

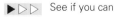 See if you can

General Contents

My California

by Pamela Bellwood-Wheeler

I finished 132 miles in a four-wheel drive vehicle, camping along the Mojave Desert Trail with my husband and older son. We returned home for a few hours to change gear and head off again to ski the snow-covered mountains of Mammoth. As we left, I recalled a sneering description I once heard on the East Coast: 'A Californian is someone who rises in the morning, has his orange juice, takes a swim in his pool, lies down in the sun, and when he wakes up, he's 84'.

Wrong. California is not a place of physical boredom, consistency or complacency. It has a manic terrain, one of vast contrast. The highest and lowest points in the continental US are just an hour apart. It has droughts and floods, crowds and quiet, dense forests and barren deserts, endless sunshine and days of fog, and the ability to improvise its seasons. The undisciplined sprawl that is Los Angeles, with its many suburbs in search of a city, is controlled anarchy.

When I left the East Coast, the words of HL Menken rang in my ears: 'When the earth tilts, everything not nailed down slides and lands in California.' Californians re-invent themselves daily; their homes are fronted by walled façades with windows facing rear. Is this a symbolic way of denying the past and looking only ahead?

I've now lived here for 15 years. This is where I met my husband. Our children were born here. We spend our summers in Europe. But when we return each Fall, the physical optimism of California's terrific space excites me. There is a clarity in its light, and a freshness in familiar sights, despite the smog.

Perhaps one day we'll move on. It's an undemanding place, easy to leave. If we do, it might seem that we were here for only a moment – but it will have been a colourful moment. A period that will leave my children confident in their abilities, with the potential to realize them...like the limitless boundaries of the California landscape.

A view of Sierra Nevada from Route 395

Pamela Bellwood-Wheeler was born and raised on the East Coast, where she attended college and acting school. She appeared on Broadway before moving to Los Angeles, where she is best known for her television role in the series *Dynasty*. She currently lives in Los Angeles with her husband, photographer Nik Wheeler, and their children, Adam, Kerry and Cristian.

My California

by Ray Riegert

To visit California for the first time is to experience *déja vu*. My introduction to the state occurred when I was 18 years old, hitch-hiking down the coast to Mexico. My entire life had been spent on the outskirts of New York City, within 20 miles of the Atlantic Ocean. But as a child of the television age, I had come to believe that major cities were lined with palm trees. Hundreds of movies and television shows had convinced me that the Wild West began in the Mojave Desert, and that all oceans resembled the Pacific.

A view from the 17-Mile Scenic Drive, Monterey Peninsula

To American kids like me, the architecture of California represented the building styles of the world, and the people of the Golden State portrayed populations everywhere. I was hitch-hiking along Memory Lane.

For that kid on his way to college, California was a picture in the mind. Just as for all of us, California already existed, through the medium of film, somewhere in my psyche. To visit it was to go back through my own past, to locations not quite real, yet already behind me.

Today, over 20 years later, I realize that in my immature eyes Hollywood had elevated California to a metaphor for the good life. The attributes that initially attracted movie-makers to the state, and that Hollywood still projects around the globe – California's Italian climate, diverse geography and leisurely pace – were precisely the features that lured me here.

To me, the beauty of California is that after two decades the myth has become reality. I came in search of an address that existed only in celluloid, but found a land where I could forge my own life. My California is Yosemite Valley and the Golden Gate Bridge, the coast of Big Sur and Los Angeles at night. But it also means the woman I married, who grew up in the shadow of Hollywood, the publishing company I started here and a nine-year-old son and five-year-old daughter who, unlike that starry-eyed hitch-hiker, were born and bred west of the Sierra Nevada mountains.

Ray Riegert is the president of Ulysses Press, a publishing company based in Berkeley, California. He is the author of four books on California, including *Hidden Coast of California* and *California: The Ultimate Guidebook*. His most popular work, *Hidden Hawaii*, won the Lowell Thomas Award and Hawaii Visitors Bureau Award for Best Guidebook.

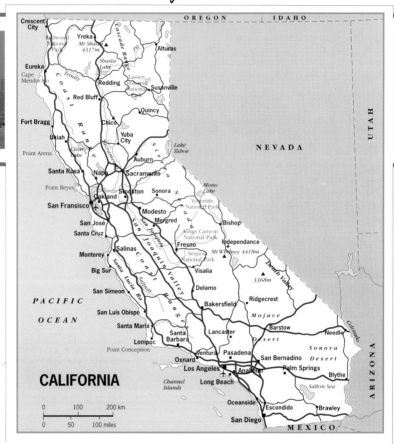

CALIFORNIA

■   **Rarely has a region captured the imagination for as long or as strongly as California. Spanish explorers, the forty-niners, would-be film stars, and millions of tourists have all arrived in anticipation of finding America's promised land. Few of them have been disappointed, although California is never quite what people expect it to be. .....■**

This state is far too diverse and complex – socially, geographically and politically – to be defined by a single, simple image. Of nearly 30 million Californians, surprisingly few were born in the state and barely half fit the traditional Anglo-American stereotype.

California is a land of golden beaches only along the most southerly quarter of its 1,000-mile coastline; the rest is typified by bracing, pristine bluffs lashed by crashing ocean waves.

Inland California embraces parched deserts and snow-capped mountains, but also finds room for the lush valleys of the wine country and the lava landscapes of the far north.

California's two major cities are poles apart. San Francisco is small, visually attractive and it exudes a warm, cultured atmosphere. By contrast, brash Los Angeles, while never dull, struggles to justify its glamorous image and gives new meaning to the word 'sprawl'.

A flourishing New Age movement strengthens California's anything-goes reputation, while increased environmental protection is a product of many years of left- leaning legislation. Yet California has plenty of conservatives and Ronald Reagan's eight-year reign as state governor was far from unrepresentative of the state's political mind.

Part of California's golden coast: a beach to the north of Malibu

state motto
  eureka (I have found it)

state song *I love you, California*

state mineral gold

state flower golden poppy

state animal grizzly bear

state bird valley quail

state fish golden trout

state reptile desert tortoise

state insect dog-face butterfly

state mammal grey whale

state fossil sabre-toothed tiger

■ **Even before its European settlement, California was thought to harbour treasures beyond man's wildest dreams. The discovery of gold compounded this belief and set the state on the road to becoming a financial superpower, with a handful of key industries forming the bedrock of an economy that would make today's California – if it were a country – the seventh richest in the world. .....■**

Despite the benefits of a place on the increasingly important Pacific Rim, a question mark hangs over California's future. A shifting world order, national recession, demographic changes, and pressing social and environmental issues, are all placing a strain on the state's resources – and are beginning to make Californian poverty every bit as conspicuous as Californian wealth.

The aerospace industry From modest beginnings in Los Angeles in the early 1900s, aircraft manufacturing escalated into a vast aerospace industry with companies such as Hughes Aircraft, Lockheed and McDonnell Douglas, between them employing more than half a million Californians.
Lately, the end of the cold war has signalled a drop in the government-funded defence projects that traditionally bolstered the industry and has been a contributing factor to many giant companies leaving California for the lower taxes and cheaper work-forces offered in other states.

Agriculture: a boon or a threat?

Silicon Valley From the 1970s, the development of the silicon chip turned computer whiz-kids into millionaire corporate executives overnight and made so-called Silicon Valley – a region south of San Francisco, long at the forefront of electronics research and the state's fastest-growing area.
Silicon Valley's fall has been as spectacular as its rise. The stabilising of the computer industry left too many companies competing for the same market while government-funded projects were being axed. Socially, too, Silicon Valley is paying for its short-lived boom years, with its traffic creating the worst smog outside Los Angeles.

<< Discovered in the 1860s, California's oil reserves continue to be lucrative. There are major wells in Los Angeles and in the Central Valley, although exploitation of offshore deposits was curtailed after a huge spill off Santa Barbara in 1969 caused widespread environmental damage. >>

Agriculture California's most reliable commodity is not film stars but farm produce. The Imperial and Central valleys produce half the fruit, nuts and vegetables grown in the US, a crop that is worth around $16,000 million annually. Yet even here there is controversy surrounding the over-use of chemicals and the long-term ecological upsets caused by the conversion of desert to farmland.

■ **The price of more than a century of unrestrained growth has been a wrecking of California's ecosystems by the diverting of rivers and the decimation of forests, factors that have wrought havoc on the state's wildlife and created the worst air pollution in the US. From the founding of the Sierra Club in 1892 to the anti-pollution initiatives of the 1970s, California has led the country in encouraging environmental protection but the greening of the Golden State is a far from settled issue: state bureaucrats, conservationists and commercial interests, regularly do battle in the courts. .....■**

Air pollution Twenty-five million vehicles and a cruel combination of geography and climate make smog a major Californian headache. Infamously bad in Los Angeles, smog also affects many southern areas and Silicon Valley in the north. Catalytic converters and the use of unleaded petrol has had some effect, but attempts to encourage car pooling (employees sharing vehicles) have been less successful. A multi-million dollar public transport programme in Los Angeles hopes to have weaned 8 million drivers off their cars by the year 2000.

Danger to habitats Half a million people settle annually in California and the demand for new homes causes fragile coastal and desert regions to disappear beneath tract housing and shopping malls. In some areas, residents have voted for higher taxes to ensure undeveloped land stays that way, and to maintain protected wildlife areas.
A stimulus to southern California's growth and the productivity of the Central Valley farmlands was the diverting of water from the state's northern rivers. Consequently, the Sacramento delta, the confluence of rivers from the Sierra Nevada mountains, and the San Francisco Bay underwent profound changes, adversely affecting migratory birds and fish stocks, and leaving inhabited land prone to flooding. Legal arguments rage over water rights and droughts have led to rationing.

Forests Ninety per cent of California's redwood and Douglas fir trees have been chopped down since the gold rush. Even the federal protection of some strands of coastal

<< California has more endangered, rare or threatened species than any other state: 283 at the last count. >>

redwoods and giant sequoias does not guarantee the big trees' survival, as the felling of the forest leaves them exposed to erosion.

LA: centre of car dependency

■ There is precious little evidence of it as yet on the state's governing bodies, but in 1990 only 57 per cent of Californians were white Anglo-Americans. By the year 2000, there is expected to be no ethnic majority at all in the state, just several large ethnic minorities. .....■

Military conflicts and eased entry restrictions brought substantial increases in Asian immigration into California from the 1950s, and the state's already established Hispanic population has expanded by over 70 per cent in the last 10 years. Of 7 million new arrivals and births in California during the 1980s, 85 per cent were Asian or Hispanic. Among whites, however, a declining birth rate and a disillusionment with the quality of life (and, for some, a fear of the multiracial and multilingual California of tomorrow) have brought a fall in numbers, with around half a million whites departing California each year, many settling in Arizona or the states of the Pacific northwest.

Variety is the spice of California: Melrose Avenue, LA

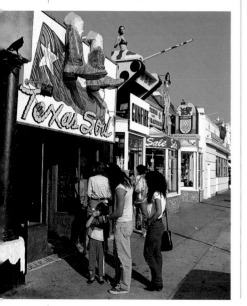

Native Americans Enduring removal from their ancestral lands since the time of the Spanish missions and with few recognised rights until the 1960s, California's native Americans increased in number during the 1970s and 1980s and there are now around 250,000 living in the state. Despite being indigenous residents, native Americans are the least conspicuous of all California's ethnic communities, not least the (approximately) 20 per cent of them living on reservations.

<< More people live in California than in Canada. >>

Black Americans Blacks of African descent were a significant element in some of California's earliest Spanish-run settlements, though the state's black population underwent its biggest expansion during the 1940s when wartime heavy industry attracted labour from the ailing rural economies of the Deep South. Subsequently, sheer weight of numbers provided the electoral clout to put blacks into important positions in Californian political life, but failed to impinge upon the entrenched racism of many whites or provide the economic power to escape from – or regenerate – the cheaply built housing projects which evolved into inner-city ghettos. In some instances, the recent arrival of Asians into black neighbourhoods has caused resentment and violence among already established communities. Simultaneously, California's uncertain job market is tempting some Californian blacks back to the Deep South.

Pictures of a diverse and lively culture from the Hispanic Mission District in San Francisco

Hispanics California's Spanish history is echoed by its place names and street names while its Spanish-speaking present is evident in the TV and radio stations catering to a Hispanic population now accounting for one in six of the state's inhabitants.

As early as 1945, Los Angeles had the biggest Mexican community outside Mexico and many more crossed the border between 1951 and 1964, when the US government encouraged the import of agricultural labour. Since then, the depressed Mexican economy, and trouble and strife throughout Central and (to a lesser extent) South America, has contributed, along with a comparatively high birth rate, to the constant expansion – legal and otherwise – of California's Hispanic numbers.

Asians Thirty-five per cent of the Asian population of the US lives in California where they make up one in ten of the state's inhabitants. This grew by 127 per cent during the 1980s.

California's earliest Asians were Chinese arrivals at the time of the gold rush. Many became labourers, some became merchants, and all experienced the racism which caused them to band together in Chinatown districts. Chinese numbers did not significantly change until the repeal of anti-Asian immigration laws in 1965. After that year many new arrivals left the traditional Chinatown bases as soon as they could afford to in favour of middle-class homes in the suburbs. Those left behind tended to be the poor and elderly, least able to integrate into US society.

Following on the heels of the first Chinese, Japanese labourers and farmers settled in California and laid the foundations of the state's prosperous agricultural industry. After the Japanese attack on Pearl Harbour in 1941, their internment devastated an entire generation of Japanese Americans, but among their children, increasingly adept at balancing two cultures, are success stories spanning most walks of Californian life.

15

> **<<** If immigration to California stopped tomorrow, the state would still have 4 million more people by the year 2000. **>>**

Koreans became a strong presence in parts of Los Angeles from the 1950s; in the 1970s, following the fall of Saigon, 100,000 Vietnamese, Cambodians and Laotians arrived in California.

In San Francisco, the Laotians and Vietnamese have been evident in regenerating the Tenderloin district. Less happily, teenage Cambodians in Long Beach's 'Little Phnom Penh' are integrating into American society by joining in the battles of black and Hispanic street gangs.

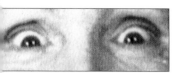

■ From Marxist logging colonies to the rag-bag of beliefs of the New Age movement, cults have been a mainstay of California life for decades and show no signs of abating. .....■

Idealistic co-operative communities appeared as early as the 1880s, the largest being the 400-strong Kaweah Colony, who followed a Marxist plan for self-sufficiency which included a potentially devastating project to scythe down all the state's giant sequoia trees.

Oriental mysticism and arcane magic had stolen the cult spotlight from utopian politics by the 1920s, when the Krishnamurti Foundation was founded in Ojai and the Rosicrucian Order built a home in San José, both of which still exist. In Los Angeles, inspired by a visit by English occultist Aleister Crowley, the Builders of the Adytum formed; their tarot-decorated temple continues to explore the mysteries of the Kabbala. One place with more than its share is Mount Shasta, thought by some to be inhabited by Lemurians, a race of highly advanced beings from a lost city of the Pacific.

In 1930, one G W Ballard claimed he had quenched his thirst while hiking on the mountain with what turned out be the Elixir of Life, handed to him by a youth who proceeded to reveal the secrets of the universe. Ballard responded by forming the I AM Foundation of Youth which, by the 1950s, was attracting 3,000 brightly robed believers to its ceremonies.

While Ballard was being enlightened on Shasta's slopes, mining engineer W Warren Shufelt was producing a map of tunnels beneath Downtown Los Angeles which, he thought, were the home of an ancient race of 'Lizard People', mentioned in Hopi Indian legends. Nothing came of Shufelt's investigations, although building work later revealed a series of mysterious tunnels beneath the modern city.

> **<<** Tales of 'glowing humanoids' and three-fingered aliens buying supplies in local grocery stores have convinced some Californians that the Joshua Tree National Monument is a UFO landing site. **>>**

In 1969, the Charles Manson 'family' (see page 33) committed gruesome murders; in the 1970s, Synanon, a drug rehabilitation unit, was accused of brainwashing its patients; and Jim Jones's People's Temple, which began in Ukiah in 1965 and later moved to San Francisco, finished up in Guyana with Jones and his 900 followers committing mass suicide.

Have aliens gathered at Joshua Tree National Monument?

■ **In August 1987, thousands of Californians participated in a 'Harmonic Convergence' gathering at Mount Shasta – one of the world's designated 'energy points' to usher in the Age of Aquarius, or the New Age. Growing partly from updated hippie beliefs and partly to provide something to aspire to for those Californians who are so wealthy they have nothing left to achieve on the material plane, the New Age is a catch-all term which encompasses a wide range of esoteric beliefs and practices, broadly aimed at getting one's life and life-style in tune with the infinite and away from the negativity of the material world. .....■**

New lines of business California's New Age is also big business, with shamans, rebirthers, reflexolgists, aromatherapists and many more, advertising their services from the pages of innumerable New Age publications and appearing at a seemingly endless round of expositions, gatherings and seminars.

Many of the ideas connected with the New Age have been tested at the Esalen Institute in Big Sur; founded in 1962 by Michael Murphy and Richard Price, the Institute made a name for itself during the '60s and '70s as a centre of the 'human potential' movement, and still holds workshops, conferences and meetings.

Although the likes of astrology, tarot reading and dream interpretation all have a place in the New Age, they will seem distinctly old hat to any psychically adventurous visitor, who might be more stimulated by one of the following.

Channelling Conducted in one-to-one or group sessions, channelling brings a non-corporal entity – native American sages and extra-terrestrials are popular, though you are likely to learn from your personal spirit guide – to talk through a 'channeller', or medium. Most channelling sessions allow participants to question the entity.

Crystals Thought to affect the human energy field, crystal power can be used by consuming a crystal dissolved in water although it is more common for a crystal to be carried somewhere on the person or placed in a particular room. Different types of crystals have different properties and uses. Amethyst, for example, can relieve stress and headaches, and remove negative energies from rooms; rose quartz can improve sleep; clear quartz can be used in healing and in

>> A 1991 survey revealed 25,000 people claiming to be pagans or wiccans (practitioners of witchcraft) in San Francisco and the Bay Area. >>

generally enhancing the user's passage through life, according to those who have faith in the crystals' powers..

Smart drugs A newer New Age phenomenon are cognitive enhancers, or smart drugs. These act on the brain and are claimed by some to increase memory and intelligence. Smart drugs (legally manufactured by major pharmaceutical companies) are being consumed socially in a growing number of smart bars and nightclubs.

■ **For creature comforts they are among the world's most pampered people, but driven by a society that worships physical perfection and a climate that drags all except the most confirmed couch potato into the open air, Californians typically fill their leisure time with sweat-inducing exercise and do not stop until they are radiating health and vitality.** .....■

With hills to be hiked and rivers to be rafted, physical culture in northern California usually amounts to getting and staying fit enough to enjoy the great outdoors. In the more image-conscious and less scenic Los Angeles (and in southern California generally), however, getting healthy can also mean being seen to get healthy by the right people in the right places.

Health clubs In LA, health clubs and gyms are two a penny and each is equipped with a mind- (and body-) boggling array of weights, gravity machines and floating floors, and instructors conversing in the vogue words of kinesiology. The clubs in demand, however, are those with a celebrity or two among the membership and a reputation for business deals being clinched beneath their barbells.

<< Few of California's professional sports teams have roots in the state: the LA Rams moved west from Cleveland in 1946; the LA Dodgers arrived from Brooklyn in 1958; the LA Lakers were based in Minneapolis until 1960; the Oakland A's played in Kansas City until 1968. >>

Jogging Likewise jogging, though practised all over the state on a fabulous assortment of landscaped routes, is subject to regional interpretation. In the north of the state you can jog dressed like a tramp; in the south, jogging resembles a fast-moving fashion parade with *haute couture* tracksuits, leg warmers, designer-label trainers, a (preferably CD) Walkman and a Swiss watch (for accurate timing of performance), being essential accessories.

Once you have dodged (or joined) the joggers, beware skateboarders and roller skaters – armies of both weave enthusiastically, if not always legally, along beachside paths and pavements.

Watch out, too, for blade skaters. Unlike traditional roller skates that have wheels arranged in pairs, blade (or 'in-line') skates have five wheels set in a single row. Originally developed for ice hockey players to practise without ice, blade skates can achieve speeds of up to 30mph – which means stopping in a hurry is often a problem – and also, costing the earth, are a statement of the owner's level of disposable income.

A Muscle Beach-boy, LA

Ocean sports Although it may seem the most Californian of all the state's participant sports, surfing arrived from Hawaii in 1907 and did not capture the Californian imagination until the invention of lightweight surfboards in the 1950s.

Subsequently mythologised by the songs of the Beach Boys and the beach-blanket films of the early 1960s, surfing became a lasting symbol of the sun-kissed Californian beach life.

From the masses gathered at San Diego's Mission Beach to the hardy loners spotted off the rocky Central Coast, surfing is still widely popular and has evolved into a subculture with its own barely penetrable language (see panel) and customs. In some areas, local surfers are known to actively deter outsiders from encroaching on the breakers they consider to be theirs.

If exploring beneath the waves holds more appeal than riding on top of them, scuba-diving and snorkelling provide an alternative ocean sport in numerous locations, especially along the Central Coast.

Beach sports Back on the sand, beach volleyball nets line many southern California beaches and 'pick-up' games (those made up of anyone who fancies a game) are common. If you join in, do not expect a gentle knockabout – sand quickly saps the leg muscles. You will soon appreciate the stamina of those Californians who play beach volleyball professionally – they are the big-earning stars of televised tournaments held each summer. If none of the above appeal and you still want to pose as a Californian on the beach, buy a frisbee and fling it.

Winter sports During the winter, many coast-dwelling Californians head inland. The holding of the 1960 Winter Olympics at Squaw Valley (near Lake Tahoe) was the first inkling for many residents that the state offered some of the US's best skiing. This is not an activity which comes cheap, of course, and for some it presents a social as much as a physical challenge, the swankier ski resorts of Lake Tahoe and Mammoth Lakes being (unofficially) graded according to their social cache as much as by the difficulty level of their slopes.

Surfing at Hermosa Beach

<< *Some surfing slang:*
beddie
male term for a female

bogus
calm waters; no waves

grind
to eat

grommets
adolescent surfers

pouch grovel
to stay home with one's beddie even when the surf's good. >>

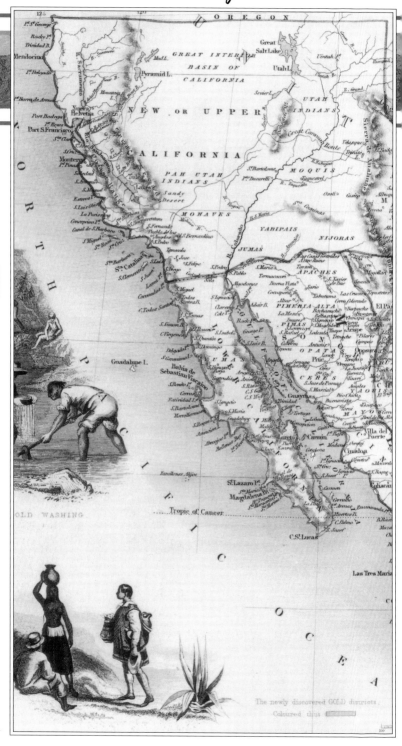

OREGON

GREAT INTERIOR
BASIN OF
CALIFORNIA

Great Salt Lake

NEW OR UPPER

CALIFORNIA

PAH UTAH
INDIANS

MOHAVES

YABIPAIS

NIJORAS

APACHES

OLD WASHING

Tropic of Cancer

The newly discovered GOLD districts.
Coloured thus

20

■ **The area now filled by California was consumed 200 million years ago by the Pacific Ocean with the western edge of North America being defined by the mountains of what is now known as Nevada. ....■**

Geology Around this time, two of the 20 tectonic plates which form the earth's crust – the Pacific plate and the North American plate – began moving. The heavier ocean plate slid beneath the continental plate and caused buckling, which eventually created undersea mountain ranges.

Mountains One mountain group would become California's coastal ranges, another group, further east, would become the Sierra Nevada mountains. The latter formed along an east-west geological fault line which caused the northern section to move slowly 60 miles west, becoming what are now the Klamath Mountains.
Pressure within the earth forced the mountains continually upwards, and they broke surface 25 million years ago.

Plains Owing to the movement of the Klamaths, the Pacific Ocean continued to cover northeastern California until its sediments created a plain. As high temperatures in the earth's mantle forced the plain to fracture, lava flowed to the surface through fissures and solidified to become the Modoc Plateau.
The Coastal Ranges and the Sierra Nevada mountains had also trapped a section of the Pacific between them. This too filled with sediment and became the Central Valley.

Desert Sixteen million years ago, the Sierra Nevada mountains became tall enough (though well short of their present height) to influence the weather. Blocking the passage of rain from the ocean, the mountains caused the land on their eastern side to become arid and evolve into deserts.

Over several ice ages, the most recent finishing 30,000 years ago, glaciers smoothed the Sierra's granite peaks and carved great U-shaped valleys, one such being Yosemite.

<< The first Europeans to experience a Californian earthquake were the members of the Portolá expedition of 1769. At the time, they were encamped by the Santa Ana River in what was to become Orange County. >>

The San Andreas fault California's immensely varied landscapes lie on one of the world's most geologically active zones, part of the 'Ring of Fire' which girdles the Pacific. Of hundreds of fault lines across the state, the longest is the San Andreas fault, which runs for 600 miles and marks the meeting point of the Pacific and the North American plates.

Yosemite, shaped by glaciers

■ **Recent discoveries indicate that human habitation in the Americas may date much further back than previously believed, but it is still widely accepted in scientific circles that the earliest North Americans arrived by crossing by a land link over the Bering Strait, between Alaska and Siberia, around 12,000 years ago. .....■**

Estimates suggest that at the time of European discovery 300,000 native Americans lived in California (their forebears having settled around 6,000 years before), split into just over 100 groupings, each of which comprised several hundred people – communities too small to fit the usual definition of a tribe.

Culture and beliefs Across the land, a host of different skills and belief systems developed. In central California, for example, the Maidu, Pomo and Wintun Indians observed the Kukso cult, creating elaborate feathered costumes for use in dances and ceremonies, with the Pomo becoming renowned for their feathered basketry.
Further south, the Chumash demonstrated advanced artistic skills with the most intricate of rock art, and the Gabrieleño followed a one-

god religion and meted out severe punishment on any member who deviated from a strict moral code. Despite these differences, and with food abundant for all (except those groups inhabiting the desert regions), there were none of the tribal wars which occurred elsewhere in North America and trading between different groups was common.

<< Believed to be the last surviving Yaho Indian, 'Ishi' (as he was named) was discovered in California's far north in 1911, and spent the next five years living in the anthropology museum of the University of California in San Francisco, passing on details of his peoples' culture before dying of tuberculosis as a result of his first cold. >>

Preaching to native Americans

Arrival of the Europeans The talent which the native Americans displayed for living in harmony with each other, and with nature, were not traits shared by California's European settlers, who considered the Indians as barbarians, fit only for labouring tasks.
Although many of the first European settlers were guilty of mistreating the Indians, greater damage to the native population was caused by European-borne diseases, such as measles and smallpox, to which the indigenous people had no immunity, and by the enormous influx of land-hungry whites at the time of the gold rush, which resulted in most native Americans being forcibly resettled on reservations.

■ **An expedition in 1533 under the Spaniard, Hernando Cortés, is credited with making the first sighting of Baja (or Lower) California, a long peninsula which was mistakenly believed to be an island. This geographical error also applied to Alta (or Upper) California – what is now the state of California – for many years. .....■**

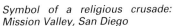

In 1542, the crew of Juan Rodríguez Cabrillo, a Portugese navigator in the employ of Spain, became the first to drop anchor off Alta California, pausing at what is now San Diego Bay and at the Channel Islands off Santa Barbara.

Not for another 25 years did a European set foot in California and it was not a Spaniard but a Briton, Francis Drake, who landed at a site near Point Reyes (the actual location is disputed) in 1579, claiming California – which he named Nova Albion – for Queen Elizabeth I of England.

Without fixed settlements it was impossible for any territorial claims to be made firm, however. After Sebástian Vizcaíno landed at what he called Monterey in 1602, he toured the coast bestowing many of the bays and headlands with their enduring Spanish names. Vizcaíno's claims for the area's topography were less successful, though, and his cartographer was hanged for producing a wildly inaccurate map of Monterey Bay.

With a Jesuit mission established in Baja California in 1690 and Alta California discovered to be part of the North American mainland in 1742, the Spanish king ordered the construction of a north-south string of Franciscan missions across California, with Monterey becoming the province's administrative centre. Ostensibly, this was a religious crusade to convert the native Americans to catholicism, but the building of the missions (fully described on pages 110 and 111), and four attendant presidios each housing several hundred troops, was also intended to bring a social

infrastructure to the region which it was (rather optimistically) hoped would deter any rival colonial power from intruding on California.

> << The first European sighting of California's greatest natural harbour, San Francisco Bay, was made from land in 1769 by a Spanish expedition heading north from San Diego hoping to find an overland route to Monterey. >>

Symbol of a religious crusade: Mission Valley, San Diego

■ **Despite 21 missions and the base at Monterey, California remained a large and sparsely inhabited territory, barely explored inland from El Camino Real, the route linking the missions from San Diego to Sonoma. Many of the missions – most of which were not completed until the early 1800s – became extremely prosperous, exploiting native American labour on vast tracts of farmland roamed by imported cattle. .....■**

The Russians During the mission period, a colony of Russian fur trappers had been making advances into California from Alaska (part of the then expanding Russian empire), seeking beaver and sea otter pelts. The Russians established Fort Ross, 60 miles north of San Francisco, in 1812. Through mutual necessity as much as anything else, the Russians and Spanish enjoyed friendly relations, neither side having the facilities to mount a serious challenge to the other.

The British They had been plotting routes across Canada from the late 1700s, in the hope of locating the Northwest Passage to speed trade between Europe and Asia. They failed to find the Northwest Passage but did succeed in developing British influence in the area through the Vancouver-based Hudson Bay Company, and were ever mindful of Drake's claim of California for the British crown as they mounted fur-trapping expeditions throughout the west coast.

The French Their interest in North America was growing and they made several expeditions to California during the 1820s. A few citizens of the US (whose ships were forbidden to land in California) also arrived.

The Californios As conflicts between the European powers became focused on issues closer to home (namely the rise of Napoleon), a change of control in California eventually came from those most directly affected by such a move: the *Californios*, the mostly California-born Mexicans, who took advantage of Mexico's independence from Spain to declare themselves under Mexican rule in 1822.

<< Total livestock holdings of the California missions in 1828: 252,000 cattle, 268,000 sheep, 3,500 mules, 34,000 horses, 8,300 goats, 3,400 pigs. >>

Russian stronghold: Fort Ross

In Mexico City, California was generally considered to be an unimportant outpost and the governing of the province was left to the *Californios* themselves. Through the distribution of enormous land grants, a handful of *Californio* families become prominent and organised life on the ranchos with themselves at the top of a feudal-type system.

fact, the *Californios* simply seized the land for themselves.

Through the early decades of the 1800s, many US citizens – some making the perilous overland journey, many more arriving after a three-month sea voyage around Cape Horn – arrived in California and acquired great influence by marrying into the leading families and displaying the entrepreneurial zeal

The Pala Mission, San Diego

Like their Spanish predecessors, the *Californios* exploited native American labour but, unlike the Spanish, they lacked agricultural skills. Rather than developing the land, the *Californios* were content to slaughter cattle and sell the hides to US traders – who turned the hides into leather goods and sold them back to the *Californios*.

>> I am afraid we shall see a great deal of trouble in California this year. There are 7 or 8,000 emigrants from the USA expected. >>
– W D M Howard, San Francisco merchant and landowner, 1846.

The influence of the missions had declined since the end of Spanish rule and their secularisation was ordered by the Mexican government in 1834. This act provided for mission land to be split equally between *Californios* and Indians. In

which the *Californios* lacked.

As the expansionist doctrine of Manifest Destiny came to hold sway over US foreign policy, California (and, indeed, much of the present southwest of the US) was increasingly seen as a desirable acquisition.

The US had made various illegal incursions into California and even attempted to buy the province from Mexico by the time the Mexican War broke out in 1846, following US actions in Texas. In June of that year, a group of US soldiers took over a barely defended presidio in Sonoma and declared California an independent republic – the short-lived Big Bear Republic. In July, there were unopposed US landings at Monterey and San Francisco, and very soon every major settlement in California had the stars and stripes flying over its Spanish plaza.

The conclusion of the Mexican War allowed the US to acquire California – along with Nevada, Utah, New Mexico and parts of Wyoming and Colorado – for $15 million, in a deal ratified in February 1848.

■ **On 24 January 1848, just nine days before California was formally handed over to the US, gold was discovered on the land of John Sutter, an European immigrant of the Mexican era, 50 miles east of his Sutter's Fort headquarters (the future site of Sacramento). Washed down from the Sierra Nevada mountains, flakes of gold had accumulated in California's rivers over countless centuries and, to all intents and purposes, were there for the taking. .....■**

The news of the gold strike was delayed, however, as Sam Brannan, owner of the *California Star* newspaper, waited until 12 May (and until he had equipped his supply shop at Sutter's Fort) before running down a San Francisco street waving aloft a vial of gold dust.

Lingering doubts Outside California, people continued to have doubts about the truth of the discovery until December, when President Polk not only verified the existence of

A 1905 prospector hits the trail

California gold but exhibited 230 ounces of it.

Gold fever Destined to be one of the greatest population movements in world history, the gold rush began in 1849, increasing the size of California from 7,000 non-native inhabitants in 1848 to 100,000 four years later.

These figures would certainly have been higher if were it not for the fact that reaching California still required a marathon sea trip or a high-risk overland trek across mountains or deserts.

Population boom A vast sea-borne influx of men and mining machinery caused San Francisco's population to increase from 500 to 25,000 within two years (at one point, San Francisco Bay became blocked by ships whose crews had absconded for the gold-laden rivers), and inland river ports such as Sacramento and Stockton became major population centres.

Other new towns were established on the bays and inlets of the north and central coasts, while scores of mining communities grew in the centre of the gold-producing area (what eventually became known as the Gold Country), on the western slopes of the Sierra Nevada mountains.

<< The biggest gold nugget found in California weighed 195lb. >>

The Wells Fargo Museum, LA

Finding gold was the stuff of dreams but more solid profits stemmed from feeding and housing the booming population: farming and lumber quickly became lucrative industries (this was the start of the decimation of the state's forests).

The Wild West Socially, the California of this time was the epitome of the fabled Wild West. The vast majority of its inhabitants were single males, and catering to their baser desires provided plenty of scope for unscrupulous entrepreneurs.

San Francisco's Barbary Coast area (demolished in the 1940s) became infamous the world over for its prostitution, gambling and drinking, yet it was only the largest and most notorious example of what was to be found in virtually every Californian community of the mid-1800s. What law there was tended to be upheld by vigilante groups and in many towns the gallows saw frequent use. Within three years, the gold rush was over. The river gold had quickly been picked clean and company-owned mines provided the only access to the gold-bearing quartz still embedded in the Sierra Nevada hillsides. Those who had arrived seeking their fortunes either returned to the east or settled in the new towns along the coast.

Though no longer promising instant riches for lucky individuals, gold mining continued to generate tremendous revenue – $81 million in the peak year of 1852 – and was to have a lasting effect on California's development.

With the wealth of the mines, California was able to bypass the usual transition period as a frontier

<< The great migration into California included many European vintners aware of the grape-producing potential of the Napa and Sonoma valleys north of San Francisco, where the the state's first winery was established in 1857. **>>**

territory and attained full statehood in 1850.

Geographically distanced from the core of the conflict and too busy getting rich to worry about it, California was barely affected by the Civil War which raged through the rest of the US from 1864. Attention focused instead on the construction of the State Capitol Building in Sacramento, which was completed in 1874 and which became a symbol of California's emergence as a self-reliant, economically powerful entity.

■ **The gold rush had made rich men of California's shop owners and merchants, but one group of Sacramento store keepers – Charles Crocker, Mark Hopkins, Collis P Huntington and Leland Stanford, later dubbed the Big Four – were set to become the wealthiest and most powerful men in the state by investing in what was to be the key component in California's rapid development: railways. .....■**

Armed with the plans of an established railway engineer, Theodore D Judah (who was later elbowed aside), the Big Four set about transforming the long-cherished dream of a coast-to-coast rail link into reality and formed the Central Pacific Railroad Company in 1861.

Big Money Playing on the US government's fear of losing California to the Confederate States as the Civil War loomed, the Big Four extracted enormous subsidies for their transcontinental railway project. For each mile of construction they received 12,800 acres of land and $18,000 in cash, with higher rates payable for building over difficult terrain.

Power and wealth Employing a host of scandalous schemes, the Big Four got the US government to meet the entire cost of the railway and bought themselves luxurious mansions in San Francisco's exclusive Nob Hill district in which to enjoy the profits.
After the transcontinental railway was completed in 1869, the Big Four absorbed the rival Union Pacific Railroad to create the Southern Pacific Railroad and hold a monopoly on trade routes across the state.

Resentment and racism Able to control the fate of entire communities, and with immense personal wealth, the Big Four wielded a level of political power unparalleled in California's history. There was much resentment of the

<< Of the Big Four, it was Charles Crocker who oversaw the actual construction of the transcontinental railway. Crocker, who weighed 250lb, allegedly stood on the freshly completed tracks 'bellowing like a bull' at the labourers. >>

rail barons, however, not least from the growing numbers of poor, who were feeling the effects of the post-gold rush depression.

Support The spread of poverty in northern California also spawned racism, directed in particular at the Chinese, who had provided the bulk of the railway labour force, and who were

Knotts Berry Farm, Buena Park

obliged to seek mutual support in the Chinatown areas taking root in San Francisco and in numerous other communities.

The boom spreads south As northern California had been enjoying the prosperity unleashed by the gold rush, southern California had remained an isolated and arid region inhabited only by a few thousand people, mostly divided between Los Angeles and San Diego, cities which the Big Four considered too remote to be worth joining to their rail network.

When a rival company, the Santa Fe Railroad (later to be taken over by the Big Four), began pushing westwards through Arizona in search of an outlet on the Pacific, the people of southern California saw their chance.

The rail race Tremendous competition developed between San Diego and Los Angeles to be first with a rail link. With its natural harbour, San Diego was the logical choice, but a subsidy (in effect a bribe) of $602,000 underwritten by the 5,000 citizens of Los Angeles swayed the balance, and the Angelenos were duly connected to the rest of the nation in 1886. San Diego acquired a spur line a year later.

There followed a vigorous advertising campaign promoting southern California as a Mediterranean paradise. This, together with absurdly cheap rail fares (bringing return tickets from

<< In 1899, the Los Angeles Police Department sought to improve their response time by forming their first bicycle squad. >>

Kansas City down to just $1), brought tens of thousands to the newly accessible region. In the property-selling frenzy that ensued, plots of southern California land increased their value tenfold within a year.

The railway also boosted the trade of southern California's harbours, making San Pedro (in Los Angeles), San Diego and Santa Barbara, outlets for the agricultural products of the Central Valley and for the sweet, seedless oranges that had recently been introduced to southern California.

Communities such as Pasadena, Venice and Hollywood (which was originally founded by two methodists as a temperance colony) took shape, oil was discovered beneath Los Angeles in 1892 and, through the early years of the 20th century, what were to evolve into gigantic aeronautical and automobile industries got started.

Looking south While all of California had its share of earthquakes, the San Francisco Earthquake of 1906, which razed the city, encouraged many in the depressed north to seek their share of the wealth which was now being generated in the state's booming southland.

THE EARTH—"I HOPE I SHALL NEVER HAVE ONE OF THOSE SPLITTING HEADACHES AGAIN."

The earth's 1906 headache

■ **The prosperity of the mid- and late 1800s did much to foster the myth of California as the American promised land, but it was Hollywood – a placid farming community on the outskirts of Los Angeles which transformed itself into the centre of the fledgling film industry – that was to present California as a latter-day Garden of Eden to the world at large. .....■**

Early days In the early days of cinema, a monopolistic patent company, the Film Trust, had sewn up film-making on the east coast, forcing aspiring directors to turn their attentions elsewhere. In 1907, William Selig's *The Count of Monte Cristo* became the first feature film to use a Los Angeles location and news of the area's suitability for film production quickly spread.

Besides being too distant for patent laws to be enforced, southern California promised daily sunshine at a time when technical limitations necessitated even indoor scenes being shot in outdoor sunlight. It also boasted a great stock of readily available natural backdrops which, with a few strategically placed props, could replicate almost any landscape in the world.

Nonetheless, once they had reached the West Coast, film-makers and their entourages were not welcomed with opened arms. In the small California towns where hardworking settlers were carving out new lives for themselves, film-shoots

Cecil B De Mille and Jesse Lasky, two greats from Paramount

disrupted business and the riotous behaviour of the crews outraged the God-fearing locals.

Several LA communities banned film-making altogether and, with rents in Downtown Los Angeles too high for impecunious movie makers, many camera-wielding arrivals travelled eight miles west to the farming town of Hollywood, quickly turning disused barns into production offices and filling the streets with standing sets.

<< One early Hollywood arrival was Cecil B De Mille, who in 1913 completed the first western feature to be shot in the district, *The Squaw Man*. In the make-do spirit of the times, De Mille shared his office with a horse. >>

Most early films were cheap one-reel Westerns, but by 1916 D W Griffith was employing 15,000 extras on *Intolerance* and had re-created the Hanging Gardens of Babylon on Hollywood and Sunset and boulevards.

The big time Five years later, 100,000 Los Angeles residents were making a living from the movies, which were now grossing a billion dollars annually, and the best-known faces in the country were the screen stars, such as Douglas Fairbanks and Mary Pickford, ensconced in the new mansions of Beverly Hills.

As the fame of Hollywood spread, so did its notoriety. Sensation-seeking scandal sheets fed an eager public, and found plenty to fill their pages in the bars, clubs and bedrooms of Tinseltown.

As one sordid revelation followed another, an initiative by top studios bosses to 'clean up' Hollywood resulted in the Hays Code of 1930 (in force until the 1960s when it was replaced by the ratings system), a form of self-censorship limiting what could be shown on the screen.

The studio system Formed as Hollywood's earliest producers banded together to create large companies such as Paramount, RKO and Warner Brothers, this also exerted a tight grip on what made it on to celluloid by signing staff – including actors and actresses – to exclusive, long-term contracts. The creative inertia inherent in this system was apparent by the 1950s, when a loosening of control enabled independent productions to thrive – particularly so during the 1960s and 1970s. Despite this, the major studios still carried considerable clout in deciding what reached the screen and by the 1980s there was a swing back towards carefully marketed big-budget blockbusters. Through diversification into TV and record production, the major film companies have retained a large slice of the world entertainment market and continue to be major southern Californian employers. This enables Los Angeles to justify its reputation as a stamping ground of budding actors, screenwriters and directors – and the home of the stars – regardless of the fact that Hollywood itself has become a slum and most of the studios have moved to the suburbs.

> Boris Karloff: **<<**It's not true I was born a monster. Hollywood made me one.**>>**

Sid Grauman's Chinese Theater

■ **Often to the amusement, and sometimes to the horror of Americans living elsewhere, there has been an undertow of radicalism in Californian life since the topsy-turvy days of the gold rush. While it was lampooned for many years as the place to which all of America's nuts eventually rolled, radical California really got into gear during the 1950s and the 1960s. .....■**

Birth of the beatnik Intent on breaking free from the conventions of American society, and variously inspired by bebop jazz, cheap wine and Zen Buddhism, a small band of unconventional writers and painters began colonising the Italian coffee bars and cheap rooming houses of San Francisco's North Beach during the mid-1950s. They called themselves 'Beats' but were derisively dubbed 'beatniks' by a local newspaper columnist mindful of the recent Soviet satellite, sputnik. The fame of the Beats was confirmed when Allen Ginsberg's epic poem *Howl* was banned for obscenity in 1956, and when Jack Kerouac's breathless novel, *On the Road*, became the literary sensation of 1957. Devoted to constant travel, the Beats were actually much less of a California-rooted phenomenon than the subculture which succeeded them, the hippies.

The genesis of hippiedom was a mind-altering drug called LSD (lysergic acid diethylamide, or 'Acid'), being tested on volunteers at Stanford University through the mid-1960s. Teaching a writing course at the university, Ken Kesey (author of *One Flew Over the Cuckoo's Nest*) brought a supply of the still-legal drug to San Francisco, where it was enthusiastically consumed at multi-media events.

LSD was soon outlawed but not before its ability to send the user on a quasi-mystical, psychedelic 'trip' had been widely recognised, and it was soon under production in illicit labs, more for the edification of mankind than for material gain.

Flower power The run-down but spacious Victorian homes of San Francisco's Haight-Ashbury made ideal communal hippie pads, and by 1967 it seemed every disaffected youth in the US had arrived there. Free concerts in Golden Gate Park were attended by tens of thousands of long-haired, painted-faced people, and the bands of the era, such as the Grateful Dead, Jefferson Airplane,

<< Women and men alike carried flowers and wore ribbons in their hair. There were more clean, long-haired males assembled in one place than at any time since the Crusades. **>>** – Journalist Ralph Gleason describing 1967's Human Be-In in Golden Gate Park.

Flower children announce the 'death of the hippie', 1967

and Country Joe and the Fish, were the first to turn rock music into a critically acclaimed (and mass marketable) art form.

As more addictive substances replaced LSD in popularity and Haight-Ashbury became squalid and overcrowded, hippiedom's slide from peace and love to horror was compounded by the activities of Charles Manson.

Recruiting his infamous 29-member 'family' in Haight-Ashbury, Manson moved with them to a desert base to launch a series of grisly killings in Los Angeles. Manson was subsequently convicted of seven murders and is currently making regular appeals for parole.

In their own ways, the Beats and the hippies both rejected the entire social order, but 1960s California also found the political establishment being challenged in (comparatively) more orthodox ways.

Political protest Formed on the campus at Berkeley in 1964, the Free Speech Movement (see pages 84 and 85) was the stimulus for a decade of nationwide campus revolts and anti-Vietnam War protests. Meanwhile, the increasingly diverse ethnic make-up of what was fast becoming the nation's most populous state was not reflected in the white-dominated corridors of power, and discontent simmered in various quarters.

Anger erupted most dramatically in Watts (a depressed black-populated section of Los Angeles) in 1965, when the National Guard were called upon to bring to quell a six-day battle which left 34 dead and caused $40 million of damage. During the following year the highly militant Black Panthers formed, pledging themselves to armed struggle .

State politics The turbulent 1960s had mellowed by the following decade, when there was (at least some) assimilation of ethnic minorities into policy-making bodies. Simultaneously, state governor (and future president) Ronald Reagan – who had always been willing to use force in response to protest – gave way to Jerry Brown, a fourth generation Californian who was viewed by many as the embodiment of Golden State wackiness.

<< The formation of the National Farm Workers' Union by Cesar Chavez in 1962 brought about improved conditions for California's vast army of undervalued agricultural workers through a series of strikes and public-supported boycotts. >>

Eschewing the governor's luxury mansion built by Reagan in favour of a simple apartment and conducting a much-publicised romance with fashionable rock-singer Linda Ronstadt, Brown imposed strict controls to reduce smog, decriminalised possession of marijuana, and set California on course to being the country's most environmentally-aware region by the time he left office with an eye on the White House in 1983.

33

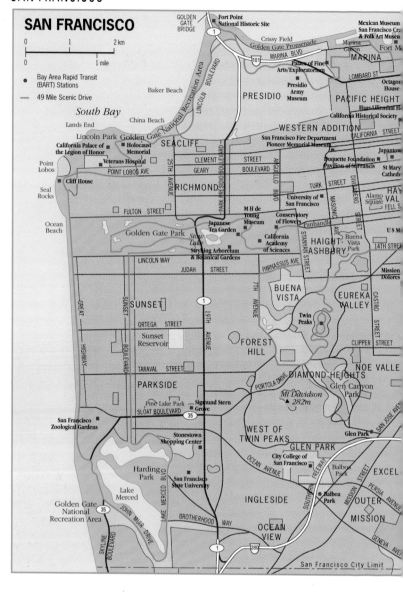

SAN FRANCISCO

0   1   2 km

0   1 mile

● Bay Area Rapid Transit (BART) Stations
— 49 Mile Scenic Drive

South Bay

Lands End
China Beach
Lincoln Park Golden Gate
California Palace of the Legion of Honor ■ Holocaust Memorial
Point Lobos
Seal Rocks
Cliff House
Ocean Beach

Baker Beach

Veterans Hospital □
POINT LOBOS AVE

Golden Gate Park
Stow Lake
Strybing Arboretum & Botanical Gardens

Great Highway
Sunset Boulevard

SUNSET
ORTEGA STREET
Sunset Reservoir
TARAVAL STREET

PARKSIDE
Pine Lake Park ■ Sigmund Stern Grove
SLOAT BOULEVARD

San Francisco Zoological Gardens

Harding Park
Lake Merced
Golden Gate National Recreation Area

Stonestown Shopping Center
San Francisco State University

GOLDEN GATE BRIDGE
Fort Point National Historic Site
Crissy Field
Golden Gate Promenade
MARINA BLVD
Palace of Fine Arts/Exploratorium

Mexican Museum
San Francisco Crafts & Folk Art Museum
Marina Green Fort M
MARINA
LOMBARD ST
Octagon House

PRESIDIO
Presidio Army Museum

PACIFIC HEIGHT
Haas-Lilienthal H
California Historical Society

SEACLIFF
WESTERN ADDITION
San Francisco Fire Department Pioneer Memorial Museum
CALIFORNIA STREET
Duquette Foundation ■ Pavilion of St Francis
St Mary's Cathedral
Japantown

CLEMENT STREET
GEARY BOULEVARD
RICHMOND
FULTON STREET

TURK STREET
University of San Francisco
Conservatory of Flowers
Panhandle
HAIGHT-ASHBURY
Buena Vista Park
14TH STREET

M H de Young Museum
Japanese Tea Garden
California Academy of Sciences
Alamo Square
HAY VAL
FELL S
US M

PARNASSUS AVE
LINCOLN WAY
JUDAH STREET

BUENA VISTA
7TH AVENUE
19TH AVENUE
1

FOREST HILL
Twin Peaks

EUREKA VALLEY
CLIPPER STREET
NOE VALLE

PORTOLA DRIVE
DIAMOND HEIGHTS
Glen Canyon Park
Mt Davidson ▲ 282m

WEST OF TWIN PEAKS
GLEN PARK
Glen Park
City College of San Francisco
OCEAN AVENUE
Balboa Park
EXCEL

INGLESIDE
Balboa Park
OUTER MISSION
PERSIA AVENUE

BROTHERHOOD WAY
OCEAN VIEW
San Francisco City Limit
GENEVA AVE

A beautiful city set on a small, hilly peninsula, San Francisco is an easy place to fall in love with. Since gold-rush times, settlers from the far corners of the globe have arrived here, their sheer diversity fostering a live-and-let-live attitude for which the city is renowned.

The compact city splits into a mosaic of tightly grouped neighbourhoods. The Financial District and the Civic Center mark either end of Downtown, linked by the city's main artery, Market Street. North of Downtown, Nob Hill, Russian Hill and Telegraph Hill are prime residential areas, yet they nestle close to the bustling streets and alleyways of Chinatown and the Italian-flavoured North Beach. Continuing northward,

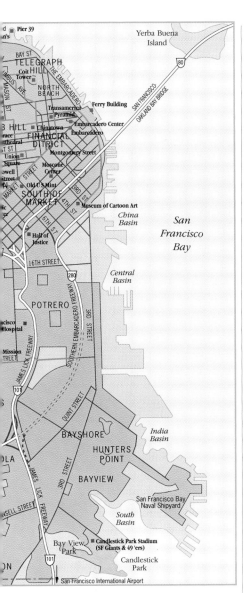

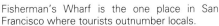

Fisherman's Wharf is the one place in San Francisco where tourists outnumber locals.

South of Market Street, the up-and-coming SoMa borders the mostly Spanish-speaking Mission District, just west of which the Castro is a predominantly gay-male area.

West of Downtown, Haight-Ashbury saw the rise and fall of flower power, and adjacent, the bucolic Golden Gate Park stretches almost to the ocean. North of Haight-Ashbury lies tiny Japantown and the broad streets of Pacific Heights, which lead on to the woodlands of the Presidio area, covering the city's northwest tip.

Districts

▶ ▷ ▷ The Castro

The largest and most famous of San Francisco's gay areas, the Castro is much changed from a decade ago when its streets were a wild celebration of gay-male life-styles. The city's raunchiest halloween parades continue to happen here, but the success of the Castro's many gay-run businesses – and the threat of AIDS – has instilled a sense of quieter respectability.

Regardless of their sexual persuasion, few people could be left unmoved after visiting the **Names Project** (2362 Market Street), where each grave-sized patch of a gigantic quilt represents one local victim of the AIDS virus – at present, the quilt has 6,000 patches.

▶ ▶ ▶ Chinatown

Squeezed into a few chaotic blocks between the Financial District and North Beach, Chinatown is a riot of exotic sights and smells, and the base of the banks, newspapers and schools that serve what is claimed to be the largest Chinese community outside Asia.

Dragon-tail entwined street-lights and pagoda- styled buildings overlook a ceaseless procession around the food stalls on Stockton Street and the herbalist shops, tea rooms, bakeries and gaily painted, century-old temples, that fill numerous alleyways.

▶ ▷ ▷ Civic Center

Rightly regarded as the best *beaux-arts* grouping in the US, the public buildings of the compact Civic Center are dominated by the dome of the elegant City Hall – raised in 1915 – and by hundreds of homeless people occupying their neat plazas.

▷ ▷ ▷ Downtown/Union Square

Downtown San Francisco encompasses the Civic Centre, Tenderloin, and the Financial District, and holds the bulk of the city's hotels, the top-name shops, and the well-known – though uninteresting – Union Square.

▶ ▷ ▷ Embarcadero

Many ambitious developments are changing the shape of the waterside Embarcadero, but so far only the views across the bay, and the shops and buskers of the Embarcadero Center, give the area any appeal.

▶ ▷ ▷ Financial District

Stride among the power-dressed power-brokers of the Financial District to find out why San Franciscans dread the 'Manhattanisation' of their city, a condition exemplified by the sterile glass and steel corporate towers built here during the 1970s and early 1980s.

▶ ▷ ▷ Fisherman's Wharf

The base of a substantial fishing fleet until the 1940s, today's Fisherman's Wharf is almost entirely devoted to serving the tourist trade. T-shirts and trinkets are flogged from every shop, street stands do a brisk trade in overpriced sourdough bread and seafood, and the best of among a glut of uninspired attractions are the San Francisco Experience (Pier 39), and the oddities of Ripley's Believe or Not (175 Jefferson Street).

Hardly a week passes without some kind of festival happening in San Francisco. The highlights are the Chinese New Year, usually in February, celebrated with firecrackers and a three-hour dragon-led parade through Chinatown; the St Patrick's Day parade in March; the Cherry Blossom parade in Japantown during April; the Bay-to-Breakers fun run across the peninsula in May; the Mission District Carnival in June; and the Halloween parade along Castro Street in October.

▶▶▷ Haight-Ashbury

Haight-Ashbury found itself at the forefront of the flower power revolution of the late 1960s, when thousands of long-haired youths poured into what had been a declining middle-class neighbourhood.

Some of hippiedom's leading figures now command respect in many walks of San Francisco life, and Haight Street, the area's main thoroughfare, still bears a pronounced counter-culture bias, with underground bookstores and kaftan-clad skateboarders. Lately it has also acquired wacky clothes stores and cafés.

▶▶▷ Japantown

Concealed behind Japantown's usually unexciting exteriors are the shops, temples and social centres serving the city's Japanese community, only a small percentage of whom actually live here. Between Post Street and the Geary Expressway, the large **Japan Center** contains numerous outlets for quality Japanese arts and crafts, and several temptingly priced eating places. Near by, Kabuki Hot Springs offers a traditional Japanese steambath and shiatsu massage.

▶▶▷ Mission District

A Spanish-speaking enclave whose population is chiefly drawn from Central and South America, the Mission district's earthiness – and its low rents – have also attracted some of the city's more poverty-stricken writers and artists. A number of left-wing political activists, including a strong feminist and lesbian contingent are based on Valencia Street.

Other than Mission Dolores (see page 54), the draws are well-preserved houses and vivid street murals.

The streets of San Francisco

Overall a remarkably safe city, the closest San Francisco gets to being seriously seedy is the 10-block strip between Union Square and the Civic Center known as the Tenderloin, where most of the city's homeless congregate and where prostitutes ply their trade from street corners. The Western Addition, a rough neighbourhood between Haight- Ashbury and Japantown, is also worth avoiding after dark.

The tastes of the middle classes, who swept into the city from the late 1800s, spanned Queen Anne, Italianate and Stick-Eastlake building styles. More than 14,000 of San Francisco's Victorian homes survived the great fire which followed the 1906 earthquake, and roughly half have been fully restored. The similarity of their fanciful wooden ornamentation should not be surprising: advances in mechanised carpentry enabled most of it to be mass-produced and sold by mail order.

▶▶▷   Nob Hill

In the late 1800s, California's first tycoons erected lavish homes on Nob Hill, overlooking the Financial District. Only one of the million-dollar mansions survived the 1906 earthquake – it is now the ultra-exclusive ivy-covered **Pacific Union Club** (1000 California Street) – though Nob Hill remains the city's priciest and most prestigious address, and holds a group of exclusive hotels and restaurants patronised by famous faces.

One place meriting a call is the reposeful **Grace Cathedral** (1051 Taylor Street), modelled on Paris's Notre-Dame. While ministering the spiritual needs of its ultra-rich congregation, the cathedral – controversially – shelters the city's homeless in its basement.

▶▶▶   North Beach

Italians were the first to give the North Beach a lasting style, arriving in force from the late 1800s and opening the first of the restaurants and cafés which make this the city's foremost place for pasta, pizzas, and for lingering over a cappuccino beside the seething Columbus Avenue.

During the mid-1950s, the North Beach's (then) cheap rents, wine and food, made it the home of the first beatniks – so dubbed by San Francisco newspaper columnist, Herb Caen – the most illustrious of whom are remembered by street names in their honour and by their still-standing haunts, such as the City Lights Bookstore and Vesuvio's Café. See the walk on page 50.

▶▷▷   Pacific Heights

A yuppie stronghold, Pacific Heights's Union Street – once known as Cow Hollow, and the location of several dairy farms – is packed with chic clothes shops and art-and-craft galleries. Close by are several landmark Victorian homes. See the stroll on page 50.

Artists are drawn to the low-rent Mission District

▶ ▷ ▷   Russian Hill

Most people stay in Russian Hill only long enough to photograph a section of **Lombard Street**, hailed as the crookedest street in San Francisco; its descent between Hyde and Leavenworth streets landscaped into a series of curves decorated by plants and bushes.

While in Russian Hill, find time for the **San Francisco Art Institute** (800 Chestnut Street), the oldest art school on the West Coast, with displays of student work, an outstanding mural by Diego Rivera, and a roof-top café with excellent views.

▶ ▷ ▷   SoMa

Until recently an uninteresting sector of warehouses, rail-freight yards and factories, SoMa ('South of Market Street') is changing its character faster than any other part of the city. Fashionable nightclubs and restaurants have made Folsom Street the playground of the city's hipsters, while new buildings, such as the Moscone Convention Center and the new home of the Museum of Modern Art (due to open in 1995), are appearing all over SoMa.

Many factory outlet stores here offer designer products at knock-down prices; see pages 60 and 61.

▶ ▷ ▷   Telegraph Hill

Telegraph Hill is a coveted address with some splendid modern residential architecture lining the steep streets that wind up to Coit Tower, a memorial to the city's volunteer fireman, erected in 1933.

The tower is notable less for the views from its summit (little better than those from its base) than for the outstanding Depression-era mural decorating its inner walls. Depicting scenes of Californian life of the time, the mural's militant symbols upset the authorities and delayed its unveiling for several years.

A view of Telegraph Hill

Anyone will tell you that Russian Hill's Lombard Street is the crookedest street in San Francisco. But nearly as crooked, and much less crowded, is Vermont Street in Pontrero, just east of the Mission District. Vermont Street also has the distinction of being the only city thoroughfare which fire-engine drivers refuse to navigate on account of its tortuous twists.

The master of hard-boiled detective fiction, Dashiell Hammett moved to San Francisco in 1920 to work for the Pinkerton Detective Agency. The booming but corrupt city made the ideal setting for his cynical investigator Sam Spade, and Hammett's writing reached a peak with *The Maltese Falcon* in 1930. Hammett's most productive years were spent at 1155 Leavenworth Street in Nob Hill. He departed to write film scripts in Hollywood, only to be imprisoned for refusing to testify during the anti-Communist witch-hunts of the 1950s.

Museums and Galleries

Invented by a Scot, Andrew Hallidie, the first cable car ran along Clay Street on 1 August 1873. A safer way of negotiating steep streets than horse-drawn wagons, the cable car also made possible the development of hitherto inaccessible high areas such as Nob Hill. By 1906, there were 600 cable cars in operation but that year's earthquake, and the subsequent rise of motorised transportation, conspired to render them obsolete. Preserved as a National Historic landmark, the system in use today – mostly for the enjoyment of tourists – was improved by a $60 million facelift in 1982.

The much-loved San Francisco cable car

▶ ▷ ▷ **African-American Historical and Cultural Society**

Building C, Fort Mason Center

African-American history and achievements in the San Francisco area and beyond chronicled through archival material and paintings, and the Howard Thurman Listening Room which has taped speeches by the liberal Baptist minister and author whose name it bears.

▶ ▶ ▷ **Cable Car Museum**

1201 Mason Street

Giving a potted pictorial record of the 120-year history of San Francisco's famous cable cars and showing off some early examples, the museum also reveals the simple but clever engineering principle that keeps the cable cars working: each car is pulled along the streets by an underground cable that never stops moving. The heavy whirring sounds, audible as you enter, are the steel cable being pulled over 14-foot wide winding wheels, visible in the museum's lower level.

▶ ▶ ▶ **California Academy of Sciences**

Golden Gate Park

Pitched at children and intended to stimulate an interest in the natural world, the California Academy of Sciences fares poorly with its static exhibits on California ecology and the native cultures of the world, but earns top marks for the wide-ranging selection of marine life in the Steinhart Aquarium – from bloated Amazon Basin predators to the mysterious splitfin flashlight fish.

Elsewhere, the safe-quake exhibit, inside in the Hohfeld Earth and Science Hall, vibrates the floor with the same magnitude that the earthquakes of 1865 and 1906 shook San Francisco's streets. Regain your balance by visiting the Far Side of Science gallery, lined with the hilarious cartoons of Gary Larson.

An additional fee brings admission to the adjoining Morrison Planetarium, humorously billed as 'California's largest indoor universe'.

▶ ▶ ▷ **Chinese Historical Society of America**

650 Commercial Street

An engrossing accompaniment to a walk through Chinatown, outlining the Chinese arrival in California, their labour on the region's first railways, and their banding together for mutual support in the face of 'Yellow Peril' racial hostility. Look, too, around the shows of the **Chinese Cultural Center,** on the third floor of the Chinatown Holiday Inn, 750 Kearny Street.

▶ ▶ ▷ **Esprit Quilt Collection**

900 Minnesota Street

Few people know that one of the best private collections of Amish quilts (the work of a long-established religious cult) decorates the open-plan offices of the Esprit company, intended to inspire the clothing company's own designers. Visitors can buy a catalogue of the quilts and make a self-guided walking tour of the best, masterpieces of inventive design mostly from the 1880s to the 1930s and all made with a deliberate mistake to show that only God is perfect.

The Balcutha, *one of Hyde Street's ships*

▶ ▷ ▷ Exploratorium
3601 Lyon Street
Working models and computers demonstrate the rudiments of sight, sound, light, gravity and electricity.

▶ ▷ ▷ Fort Point
Beneath Golden Gate Bridge
Finished in 1861 to protect the entrance to San Francisco Bay, Fort Point was never attacked despite becoming obsolete a year after its completion by advances in weaponry design. Some rooms within the three-storey granite fortress store historical artefacts, and enthusiasts in Civil War uniforms give tours.

▶ ▷ ▷ Hyde Street Pier Historic Ships
Hyde Street Pier, close to Fisherman's Wharf
Back when Fisherman's Wharf was filled by fishermen rather than tourists, ferries to Berkeley and Sausalito sailed from Hyde Street Pier, which now permanently moors several historic vessels. Among them are the 1890 ferry, *Eureka*, once the world's largest passenger ferry, and the *Balcutha*, a square-rigged sailing ship launched in Scotland in 1886, which rounded Cape Horn several times before ending its days transporting Alaskan salmon. Near by at Aquatic Park, the National Maritime Museum is a rather staid collection, mostly of models of sea-going vessels.

On chilly nights when the Golden Gate Bridge is eerily shrouded in fog, watch out for a phantom clipper, the *Tennessee*, gliding effortlessly through the waves. The two-masted vessel sank here 100 years ago but is regularly sighted – most famously in 1942 by several of the crew of a naval destroyer.

SAN FRANCISCO

▶ ▶ ▷   **Mexican Museum**

Building D, Fort Mason Center

Besides giving new Mexican-American artists a chance to break into the museum exhibition circuit, the Mexican Museum mounts outstanding shows on many aspects of Mexican arts and culture.

▶ ▶ ▷   **M H de Young Memorial Museum**

Golden Gate Park

There are few better places to observe how American art gradually turned away from European tastes and acquired a distinctive national identity. Many of the country's most influential names are on show here, though few individual pieces are as entertaining as the room of *trompe-l'oeil* paintings, notably William Harnett's *After the Hunt*, which turns a canvas into a door hung with freshly slaughtered rabbits and birds.

In contrast to the strong theme of the de Young collection, the breadth and diversity of the **Asian Art Museum**, in an adjoining building, is almost too vast to comprehend. In a large and glittering stock, it is the small pieces that stick in the mind: the 15th-century votive stele from China, Japanese Netsuke – wooden toggles for boxes and pouches, fashionable during the 18th and 19th centuries – and a human thigh-bone trumpet from Tibet.

▶ ▷ ▷   **Museum of Cartoon Art**

665 Third Street

Changing exhibitions taken from a vast permanent stock, tracing the development of a cartoon or comic strip from the hand of the artist to the finished product.

MH de Young Memorial Museum

▶ ▶ ▷ **Museum of Modern Art**

401 Van Ness Avenue

Already highly regarded for its collection of American abstract expressionism, German expressionism, its ground-breaking video installations, and the support it shows to Bay Area artists, even greater things are expected of the Museum of Modern Art once it moves to its spacious new SoMa home in 1995. Until then, a visit is worth while for the many top-rate travelling exhibitions, but displays of the permanent stock are subject to disruption.

▷ ▷ ▷ **Museum of Money of the American West**

400 California Street, Bank of California basement

Stable currency was not a feature of pioneer-era California, and here you will see a variety of bank notes issued by different states and even by the Mormon religion, before standardised laws were adopted.

▶ ▷ ▷ **North Beach Museum**

1435 Stockton Street, in the Eureka Savings Bank

Temporary shows, often borrowing the possessions of local people, illuminating the rise of one of San Francisco's most fascinating districts.

43

▶ ▷ ▷ **Old Mint**

Corner of Fifth and Mission streets

Raised in neo-classical style in 1874, the granite and sandstone Old Mint was one of the few San Francisco buildings to survive the devastating earthquake and fire of 1906. It won a place in local hearts by honouring the certificates issued by the city's destroyed banks, allowing cash to reach the stricken population.

Minting operations ceased in 1937, and government offices filled the elegant building until 1968. Restored to treasury ownership, the Mint's airy rooms and corridors contain items of numismatic interest – including $1 million in gold bullion – though none of them can match the imposing grandeur of the building itself.

Each week the *San Francisco Guardian* and *SF Weekly* provide excellent city-wide news, views and events listings. You will find them distributed in street bins and in many shops and restaurants. Also free, the monthly *North Beach Now* covers goings-on in the North Beach area and the weekly *San Francisco Bay Times* serves the city's gay and lesbian community.

▶ ▷ ▷ **Pacific Heritage Museum**

608 Commercial Street

Varied but rarely uninteresting exhibitions on the history and relationship of the countries of the Pacific Rim. On the lower level, the permanent displays recall the building's time as the city's original mint, established on the heels of the gold rush in 1854.

▶ ▶ ▶ **Palace of the Legion of Honour**

Lincoln Park

Modelled on its namesake in Paris and erected in memory to California's dead of World War I, the Palace of the Legion of Honour, on a bluff overlooking the ocean, makes an architecturally imposing showcase for San Francisco's major collection of fine art.

Amid a rich endowment of paintings and decorative arts spanning several centuries, and the Achenbach Foundation's excellent collection of graphic art, it is the superb collection of Rodin sculptures, ranging from early experiments such as *Man with a Broken Nose* to the accomplished *Victor Hugo*, that steals the show.

In the Tattoo Art Museum, at 30 Seventh Street, eye-boggling photos line the walls of a working tattoo parlour.

▷ ▷ ▷   Performing Arts Library and Museum

399 Grove Street

As a prelude to an evening of ballet or opera, take a peek at these changing exhibitions relating to San Francisco's performing arts heritage: displays include vintage costumes, photos and programmes galore.

▶ ▷ ▷   Presidio Army Museum

Corner of Lincoln Boulevard and Funston Avenue

Housed in a one-time military hospital in a verandaed building of 1863, the Presidio Army Museum charts the growth of San Francisco's military garrison, from its Spanish beginnings through its role in two world wars to the present. Alongside the massed uniforms and insignia, lies an excellent display on the city's 1906 earthquake, and outside are two of the 'refugee cottages', rented to homeless survivors of the catastrophe for $2 per month.

▶ ▷ ▷   San Francisco Art and Craft Museum

Building C, Fort Mason Center

Always worthwhile shows of curious arts and crafts: expect anything from decoy California ducks to mythical African figures.

▶ ▷ ▷   Society of California Pioneers

466 McAllister Street

Descendants of California's early arrivals run this small but interesting museum, displaying gold-mining tools, household objects, and assorted paraphernalia from the state's formative years.

▶ ▷ ▷   Wells Fargo History Museum

420 Montgomery Street

Founded in 1852, Wells Fargo ran the first stage-coaches between the eastern and western US, transporting people, gold and mail across thousands of inhospitable miles. An 1860s stagecoach suggests the discomfort of public transport, and much more in the museum represents the banking wing of the company, now one of the nation's biggest financial institutions.

Commandante's Quarters (1776), part of the Presidio

Gay Life

■ **In San Francisco you will quickly become aware that the city's fabled tolerance of unconventional life-styles has made it the base of the world's largest and most assertive gay and lesbian communities. .....■**

Many gay men landed in San Francisco towards the end of World War II after being discharged from the US military in disgrace for their homosexuality – or suspected homosexuality. Unable to face the stigma awaiting them at home, most stayed in the city, socialising in a network of discreet bars and clubs.

Gay rights The radicalism of the 1960s, and anger fuelled by continued police raids on gay-patronised establishments, brought many gays on to the streets to proclaim their sexuality and to demand their civil rights. Simultaneously the Castro district began changing from a working-class Catholic area to an almost totally gay neighbourhood.
As the Castro's fame spread far and wide, gays from all over the country moved into the district, their sheer force of numbers making the gay vote of crucial concern for aspiring city politicians. Many liberals running for public office adopted the gay rights agenda and in 1977, Harvey Milk (who ran a camera shop on Castro Street) became the country's first out-of-the-closet public official.

Homophobia was by no means eradicated, however. A year after his election, Harvey Milk – and the city's gay-supportive mayor, George Moscone – were assassinated. The light sentence of five years imprisonment passed on Dan White, the right-wing politician who committed the double murder, so incensed the gay – and large sections of the heterosexual – population, that 50,000 people took part in the protest which culminated in police cars being overturned and City Hall being attacked, in the 'White Night Riot'.

More than 20 years of standing up and being counted have left San Francisco's gays – and, to a lesser extent, lesbians – with a unique level of integration into mainstream city life.

AIDS Less happily, the impact of AIDS has perhaps been felt more powerfully here than anywhere else in the western world. Yet the crisis has revealed hitherto unknown reserves of community solidarity and, with the US government failing to treat the issue with urgency, has provided a new focus for political activity.

Gay culture is an established part of the San Francisco community

Walk Looking around Chinatown

See map on pages 48–9.

Begin at the Chinatown Gates at the junction of Bush Street and Grant Avenue.
Since 1970, the **Chinatown Gate** has made a less than imposing entrance to Chinatown's main street.

Walk north along Grant Avenue, pausing at the corner with California Street.
At 600 California Street, the **Old St Mary's Church** was the first Catholic cathedral on the West Coast, blessed in 1854.

Turn east off Grant Avenue into Commercial Street for the Chinese Historical Society of America.
At 650 Commercial Street is the **Chinese Historical Society of America** (see page 40).

Turn left into Kearny Street, turning left again after one block into Clay Street and cross into Waverly Place.
Many definitive Chinatown buildings line **Waverly Place**, in particular the 1852 **Tien Hou Temple**, on the top

Chinatown's distinct style

floor of Nos 123–9.
Exit Waverly Place turning left on to Washington Street and shortly turning left on to Stockton Street.
Crowded **Stockton Street** is where the city's Chinese community buys its fresh meat, fish and vegetables.

From Stockton Street, take any street to Grant Avenue, a block east, and return to the Chinatown Gate.

• **Stroll** *Entering Golden Gate Park (see page 57) on John Kennedy Drive takes you past the ivy-covered McLaren Lodge, now the park headquarters and formerly the home of John McLaren, a Scot who spent 50 years cultivating the park, and on to the colourful blooms and luscious palms surrounding the Conservatory. Just ahead, Hagiwara Teagarden Drive branches left, running between the California Academy of Sciences and the M H de Young Museum (see pages 40 and 42 respectively), and the wistful Japanese Tea Garden with its statue of Buddha, cast in 1790. A short way on, two bridges cross Stow Lake to the foot of Strawberry Hill, the highest point in the park.*

Walk The Financial District

See map on pages 48–9.

Begin at the Federal Reserve Bank at 101 Market Street.
Using computer simulations in the lobby of the **Federal Reserve Bank**, you can rearrange the country's finances.

Cross Market Street and walk west along Pine Street to the junction with Montgomery Street for the Bank of America building.
At the foot of the Bank of America building, a severe red carnelian granite sculpture has earned the nickname, 'Banker's Heart'.

Continue north along Montgomery Street for the Wells Fargo Museum.
At 420 Montgomery Street, the Wells Fargo Museum documents the rise of the Wells Fargo company (see page 44).

Continue three blocks north along Montgomery Street for the Transamerica Pyramid.
The city's tallest structure, the 853-foot tall Transamerica Pyramid, at 600 Montgomery Street, offers disappointingly restricted views from its 27th-floor observation level.
Continue north along Montgomery Street, turning right into Jackson Street for Jackson Square.
Around Jackson Square, many buildings which pre-date the Financial District's high-rises by a century or more have been restored.

From Jackson Square, walk west along Washington Street and return to Montgomery Street.
Throughout the year, the City Guides conduct hour-long walking tours around particular places of interest, including City Hall, Coit Tower, Nob Hill, Japantown, and the Mission District murals. For more details, call (415) 557 4266.

• **Stroll** *From Mission Dolores walk south along Dolores Street to Liberty Street, turning left for the heart of the Liberty Hill Historic District, filled by late 1800s buildings. From the end of Liberty Street, walk north along Valencia Street and turn right on to Twentieth Street. At the junction with South Van Ness Avenue, Tribute to Carlos Santana is among the biggest and boldest of the Mission district's many murals.*

Walk Golden Gate Promenade

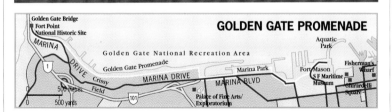

Begin at Aquatic Park, just west of Fisherman's Wharf.
Nearly four miles of breezy but enjoyable waterside walking, the Golden Gate Promenade covers a tiny section of the Golden Gate National Recreation Area, leading over the hills of Fort Mason (see page 53) and past the flashy yachts which are tethered alongside the Marina, finally concluding your walk close to Fort Point (see page 40) at the foot of Golden Gate Bridge (see page 54).

SAN FRANCISCO

TELEGRAPH HILL

LOMBARD

North Beach Playground

Coit Tower

GREENWICH

St Peter and St Paul Church

FILBERT

Washington Square

UNION

NOR

JONES

UNION

RUSSIAN

Club Fugazi

GREEN

Powell - Mason Line

HILL

Ina Coolbrith Park

GREEN

VALLEJO

VALLEJO

BROADWAY

JACK KEROUAC STREET

TAYLOR STREET

Tunnel

California Historical Society of America

48

BROADWAY

STREET

Chin Cult Cen

PACIFIC AVENUE

Powell - Hyde Line

JACKSON

Cable Car Barn

Kwan Yin Temple

WAVERLY PLACE

Portsmouth Square

LEAVENWORTH

WASHINGTON

Kong Chow Temple

Tien Hou Temple

Chinese Historical Society of America

NOB

Tien Hou Temple

COMMERCI

HILL

CHINATOWN

Old St Mary's Church

SACRAMENTO STREET

Wax Museum

Grace Cathedral

Huntingdon Park

California

Street Line

St Mary's Square

MASON STREET

Powell - Hyde Line

Powell - Mason Line

Chinatown Gateway

Masonic Auditorium

CALIFORNIA

PINE

JONES STREET

STOCKTON

BUSH

STREET

SUTTER

Marines Memorial Theater

STREET

POST

Showcase Theater

Union Square

STREET

0   200 metres
0   200 yards

GEARY

Curran Theater

American Conservatory Theater

O'FARRELL STREET

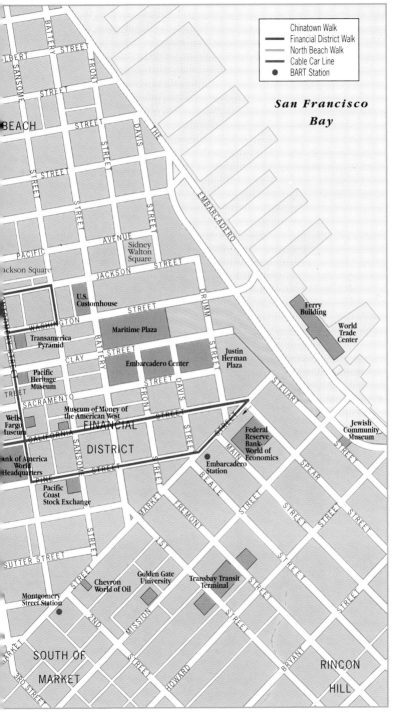

Chinatown Walk
Financial District Walk
North Beach Walk
Cable Car Line
● BART Station

San Francisco Bay

Ferry Building

World Trade Center

Sidney Walton Square

Jackson Square

U.S. Customhouse

Maritime Plaza

Transamerica Pyramid

Embarcadero Center

Justin Herman Plaza

Pacific Heritage Museum

Clay

Museum of Money of the American West

FINANCIAL

Wells Fargo Museum

DISTRICT

Federal Reserve Bank-World of Economics

Jewish Community Museum

Bank of America World Headquarters

● Embarcadero Station

Pacific Coast Stock Exchange

Sutter Street

Montgomery Street Station ●

Chevron World of Oil

Golden Gate University

Transbay Transit Terminal

SOUTH OF

MARKET

RINCON

HILL

BEACH

PACIFIC

AVENUE

JACKSON STREET

WASHINGTON

SACRAMENTO

CALIFORNIA

PINE

BATTERY

SANSOME

DAVIS

FRONT

THE EMBARCADERO

DRUMM

STEUART

SPEAR

MAIN

BEALE

FREMONT

1ST

2ND

MISSION

HOWARD

BRYANT

3RD STREET

See map on pages 48–9.

Begin at Jack Kerouac Street, on the 1,000 block of Grant Avenue.
Named after one of the beat generation's brightest lights, **Jack Kerouac Street** marks the transition from Chinatown to the North Beach.

Take a few strides north to the junction of Columbus Avenue and Broadway.
With strip joints nestling alongside heavy-metal rock clubs, the area around the **junction of Broadway and Columbus Avenue** is the scene of some of the city's lewdest and loudest nightlife – as it has been for decades.

Walk north along Columbus Avenue for the City Lights Bookstore.
At 261 Columbia Avenue, the **City Lights Bookstore** became the first paperback bookshop in the US when it opened in 1953; its owner, poet and painter Lawrence Ferlinghetti, published many works of the best of the Beat writers, beginning with Allen Ginsberg's controversial poem, *Howl*, in 1956. Facing City Lights across Adler Place, **Vesuvio's Café** is another beatnik-era survivor.

Continue north along Columbus Avenue for Washington Square.
Overlooked by the twin spires of the Romanesque Church of St Peter and St Paul, **Washington Square** has amateur art exhibitions each weekend, and elderly Chinese practising the slow, artful exercises of Tai Chi every morning.

Cross Washington Square and walk south along Grant Avenue.
From here to Broadway, **Grant Avenue** holds some of the area's best-value restaurants, many oddball shops, and some crusty R&B venues.

Continue south along Grant Avenue and return to Jack Kerouac Street.

The Octagon House, in the Union Street area of Pacific Heights

Given a week or a weekend in San Francisco, there are endless permutations of where to go and what to see. The following itineraries are designed to give a balanced impression of the city.....

Week's itinerary

Day one Explore the Financial District and Chinatown on foot (see pages 46 and 47). Lunch in the North Beach. Take a cable car north to explore Fisherman's Wharf and Fort Mason, or take a journey by bus to Golden Gate Bridge.

Day two Take a cable car to Nob Hill, explore the area and adjoining Russian Hill. Lunch on Union Street (see page 50). Walk south through Pacific Heights to Japantown.

Day three Travel by BART to Berkeley and explore the town and university campus. Lunch on Telegraph Avenue. Take BART to Lake Merritt for the Oakland Museum. Return by BART to the city.

Day four Visit Alamo Square, and continue to the Haight-Ashbury area. Lunch on Haight Street and spend the rest of the day exploring Golden Gate Park.

Day five Tour Alcatraz in the morning (see page 80). Have lunch in North Beach. During the afternoon, explore Telegraph Hill and walk along the Embarcadero to the Embarcadero Center.

Day six Sail across the bay and spend the day at Sausalito or Tiburon.

Day seven Tour the Civic Center and walk south into SoMa for lunch on Folsom Street. Visit the small museums and factory outlet shops in SoMa or take a journey by bus into the Mission District.

Weekend's itinerary

Day one Spend a day following the blue and white seagull signs marking the 49-mile Scenic Drive. The route is designed to take in all the major areas and points of interest in San Francisco. A map of the drive is available free from most hotels and tourist information offices.

Day two On the second day, walk around Chinatown (see page 47), and take a bus to Golden Gate Park for a picnic lunch by Stow Lake and visits to the Academy of Sciences (ideal for children) or the M H de Young Museum and Asian Museum. Or simply walk around the park.

You will know you are talking to a Bay Area resident if they refer to San Francisco as 'the city'. You will know you are talking to a tourist if they call the city 'Frisco'.

Visit Washington Square or Huntington Park on any morning and you will see dozens of Chinese engaged in slow-motion movements. Tai Chi is based on co-ordinated, carefully balanced rhythmic movements which use all the body's joints, ligaments and muscles, and help to regulate blood flow.

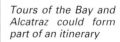

Tours of the Bay and Alcatraz could form part of an itinerary

Prussian-born Adolph Sutro devised a tunnel that improved ventilation and drainage in the mines. The idea earned him a fortune. Mayor of the city from 1894 to 1896, Sutro also founded the Sutro Library.

The plain exterior of the Buddhist Church of San Francisco, at 1881 Pine Street, conceals a richly furbished interior, complete with screens of painted peacocks flanking the altar and carvings from Kyoto gracing the ceiling's timber beams.

▶ ▷ ▷ Buddha's Universal Church
720 Washington Street
Built by donations from its congregation, Buddha's Universal Church welcomes the public every Sunday to its free lectures and tours of the church, whose symbolic design culminates in a roof-top lotus pool.

▶ ▷ ▷ The Cliff House
1066–90 Point Lobos Avenue
The seven-storey 'French-château-on-a-rock' erected by wealthy one-time Populist city mayor Adolph Sutro in 1896, remains the most famous of several Cliff Houses which have occupied the headland site since 1853. A limp collection of souvenir fare and a tourist-aimed restaurant fill the present Cliff House, although you can pick up information here on the Golden Gate National Recreation Area (of which this area is a part), and enjoy a clear view of sea lions and marine birds.
Just to the north, ruins are all that remain of the 1896 Sutro Baths, where up to 24,000 people at a time could swim in a lavish three-acre complex of salt-water tanks beneath a massive glass dome – for just 10¢ a day.

▶ ▶ ▷ City Hall
Civic Center, Van Ness Avenue
Easily the city's most opulent building and the centrepiece of the Civic Center's grouping of often exquisite public buildings, San Francisco's 1915 City Hall was conceived by the young architectural firm of Brown and Bakewell, who decided they had nothing to lose by submitting the boldest, grandest scheme they could think of. Marble, granite, gold-inlays and sumptuous arches, are the building's characteristics, and the main staircase is a sight to behold.

The jewel in the crown: San Francisco's City Hall

Moonlight over city lights: Columbus Tower

▶ ▷ ▷ **Columbus Tower**
Corner of Kearny Street and Pacific Avenue
Bought and restored by locally based film director Francis Ford Coppola in the 1970s, the flat-iron Columbus Tower dates from 1905. With the towering Transamerica Pyramid nearby, Columbus Tower adds to the view from the North Beach towards Chinatown.

▶ ▶ ▷ **Ferry Building**
Eastern end of Market Street
Until the construction of the city's bridges, the turn-of-the-century Ferry Building was the emblem of San Francisco – also its tallest structure – and the landing point for tens of thousands of commuters who made the daily voyage across the bay. A greatly reduced number of sailings still depart from the rear terminal, but the building itself is filled with uninteresting offices.

▶ ▶ ▷ **Fort Mason**
West of Fisherman's Wharf, across Van Ness Avenue
In 1796, the Spanish garrison based at the Presidio (see page 55) built a battery on this bluff overlooking the bay. It became a US Army command post from the 1860s, and 80 years later was the embarkation point for over a million soldiers headed for war in the Pacific.
Some Victorian buildings on the hilltop are still used by the military, while the former hospital serves as the headquarters of the Golden Gate National Recreation Area (of which Fort Mason is a part, see page 56).
At the foot of the bluff, several converted warehouses hold the museums of the **Fort Mason Center** – or 'Fort Culture' as it is called locally – and, a short walk away, the *Jeremiah O'Brien*, a World War II supply ship, can be boarded and toured.

On 18 April 1906, an earthquake measuring 8.3 on the Richter scale, and a three-day fire which followed it, destroyed much of the city, leaving 3,000 dead and 300,000 homeless. Increased earthquake awareness and strict building codes helped prevent a similar catastrophe when a 7.1 earthquake struck the city on 17 October 1989. Eleven were killed and 1,800 lost their homes.

The simple elegance of Golden Gate Bridge

▶▶▶ Golden Gate Bridge

Named for the bay it crosses rather than its colour (a reddish orange, the colour most visible in fog), the Golden Gate Bridge is a remarkable artistic as well as engineering feat, its construction defying the currents and depth of the bay and the simplistic design looking entirely at home in a stunning natural landscape.

Designed by Joseph B Strauss, the bridge was completed in 1937 at cost of $35 million (a sum paid off in tolls by 1971). Almost two miles long with towers as high as a 48-storey building, it is still among the world's largest suspension bridges. The bridge can be crossed by car or by foot (and often is, by joggers), though the steady rumble of traffic tends to upset contemplation of the views – as do the often ferocious winds.

▶▶▶ Mission Dolores

320 Dolores Street

The sixth of the 21 Spanish missions which spread the length of California, Mission Dolores (originally titled Mission San Francisco de Asís to honour the patron of the Franciscan order), was completed in 1791.

Thick adobe walls have enabled the mission to withstand earthquakes and years of neglect, and to become the oldest building in San Francisco – even the original bells and various other artefacts which arrived from Mexico by mule remain – and an evocative reminder of the California of two centuries ago.

Behind the atmospheric chapel, with frescos on its walls, a museum stocks a small collection of early mission items and a courtyard leads to the cemetery, burial place of over 5,000 Castonoan Indians – many of whom succumbed to European diseases – in unmarked communal graves. Several Spanish, and later Anglo-American, bigwigs lie in marked tombs.

The mastermind of the Golden Gate Bridge and several hundred other gigantic suspension bridges around the world, Joseph B Strauss, who died in 1938 aged 68, stood barely five feet tall.

▶▶▶ Palace of Fine Arts

Baker and Beach streets

A collection of dreamy *beaux-arts* structures grouped around an immense rotunda, Bernard Maybeck's Palace of Fine Arts was intended as a temporary contribution to the city's Panama-Pacific Exposition of 1915. At the Expo's conclusion, public feeling staved off the planned demolition and a well-heeled local resident funded a total restoration during the 1960s.

▶▷▷ Presidio

Main Gate on Lombard Street, junction with Lyon Street

Across the 1,500 acres of hills and woodlands that cover the northwest corner of the city, a Spanish Presidio (or garrison) was founded in 1776. The area is currently (closure is imminent) the base of the US Sixth Army, but is freely accessible to the public and a couple of its buildings are noteworthy. The Officers' Club (on Moraga Avenue) is still partly walled by Spanish-era adobe; across Pershing Square, the 1857 Old Station Hospital, which holds the Presidio Army Museum (see page 44), is the oldest complete building on the base. In the nearby National Military Cemetery, some tombs date back to the Civil War.

You will often find yourself thinking that San Francisco's steepest street must be the one you are on. You will be correct if you are climbing the section of Filbert Street between Hyde and Leavenworth streets, which rises at an angle of 31.5 degrees.

▶▶▷ Rincon Center

101 Spear Street

Enter the spacious indoor plaza of the Rincon Center at lunchtime and you will find snack-munching office-workers being entertained by a dinner-suited pianist and the gentle patter of a fountain. This modern building has enclosed the delectable art deco form of the 1940 Rincon Annexe Post Office Building. A series of controversial murals by Anton Refregier, grittily portraying several murky moments in San Franciscan history surround the new building's 85-foot high atrium.

▶▷▷ St Mary's Cathedral

Corner of Geary and Gough streets

In a city better known for its Victorian architecture, St Mary's Cathedral is a forceful piece of modern design completed in 1971. During services, an organ rises dramatically on a concrete pedestal.

Uncompromisingly modern: St Mary's Cathedral

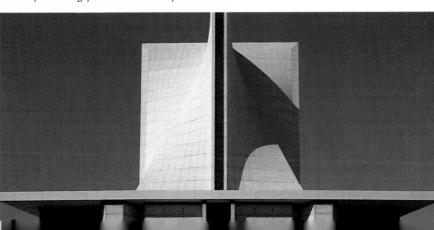

The 'Painted Ladies' on parade

San Francisco is twinned with 11 cities: Abidjen, Assisi, Caracas, Cork, Haifa, Manila, Osaka, Seoul, Shangai, Sydney and Taipei.

Created in 1972 to limit commercial development, the Golden Gate National Recreation Area safeguards nearly 70 square miles of mostly coastal terrain, embracing much of the city's northern and western edges and extending across the bay to the rugged Marin County Headlands. There are several museums, as well as the blustery Coastal Trail, between Lincoln Park and the Golden Gate Park.

▶▶▷ Alamo Square

A pretty, rolling park on the crest of a hill between the Western Addition and Pacific Heights, Alamo Square's eastern side is faced by six 'Painted Ladies', well-maintained Victorian homes with the modern city skyline for a backdrop – a regular stop for photo-hungry visitors.

▶▷▷ Aquatic Park

A grassy area with a concrete bandstand close to Fisherman's Wharf and the historic ships of Hyde Street Pier, Aquatic Park is mostly used by walkers and joggers following the Golden Gate Promenade (see page 47).

▷▷▷ Baker Beach

Accessed from Lincoln Boulevard

If you can brave the stiff breezes, the mile-long Baker Beach makes a pleasant place to pass half a day; keen anglers spend considerably longer here.

▶▷▷ Buena Vista Park

Blocks 1100 and 1200 of Haight Street

The name means 'good view' and that is precisely the reward for scrambling through the twisted mass of Monterey pine and California redwoods filling this very steep park, ringed by graceful Victorian mansions.

▶▷▷ China Beach

Near Seacliff Avenue

A small and marvellously secluded beach hemmed in by bluffs, Calm waters make China Beach ideal for swimming (rare for San Francisco). Its name comes from the Chinese fishermen who once camped here.

▶▷▷ Dolores Park

Blocks 500 and 600 of Dolores Street

Often bathed in sunshine when the rest of the city is shrouded in fog, Dolores Park is a few blocks from the Dolores Mission and makes a fine picnic-lunch stop when exploring the Mission District.

▶ ▶ ▶ Golden Gate Park

City parks rarely come any better or bigger than Golden Gate Park, extending for more than three miles between Haight-Ashbury and the ocean.

Large enough to hold a polo field, soccer pitches, a golf course, 10 separate lakes and a couple of major museums, several busy roads also slice through the park but pedestrian crosswalks make life safe for walkers.

A **Dutch windmill**, a **Japanese tea garden**, and a tiny turn-of-the-century **railway station**, are just three of the park's unexpected features.

▶ ▶ ▷ San Francisco Zoo

Sloat Boulevard

Founded in 1889, San Francisco Zoo is enjoying a major renovation, swapping its cages for detailed re-creations of its inmates' natural habitats. Another welcome recent addition is the excellent Primate Center, which explains more than you will ever need to know about such creatures – many of whom belie their endangered status by swinging merrily from the branches of the zoo's artificial rain forest. Koalas, penguins, pygmy hippos and leopards are among the zoo's other popular residents, while the tarantulas, black widows and scorpions of the insect zoo are, in every sense, the creepiest inhabitants.

▷ ▷ ▷ Sutro Heights Park

Sutro Heights Park covers the former estate of Adolph Sutro, one of the leading and most benevolent figures of late 1800s San Francisco life (see page 52). On a bluff above the Cliff House, the park is a great venue for sunset watching and for raking around the ruined pieces of statuary which remain from Sutro's time.

There is no beach in the North Beach, no statue of George Washington in Washington Square, and no square in Jackson Square

The nearly 1,00ft-high dual summits of Twin Peaks give unmatched views of San Francisco and beyond. The first Spanish arrivals named these humps of high ground *Los Pechos de la Chola* – Breasts of the Indian Girl – and they're easy to locate by looking for the Sutro TV Tower, which is close by on Mount Sutro.

57

Golden Gate Park's Japanese tea garden

From hiking in untamed hills to an in-depth study of the state's renowned wines, day-long excursions from San Francisco are many and varied. Most can be undertaken using public transport or by driving, but if you really want a stress-free day, use one of the tour operators listed across the page; the list also includes several tours of specialist interest within the city.

Suggested Routes

Coast Seaside towns seldom come more picturesque than **Sausalito**, an eight-mile ferry ride north of San Francisco, where scores of expensive hillside homes rise steeply above a waterfront lined by enjoyable cafés, galleries and shops.

Many high points in San Francisco give views of the strikingly barren headlands of **Marin County**, directly north across the bay and forming part of the **Golden Gate National Recreation Area (GGNRA)**. A network of hiking trails winds over them, passing through sheltered valleys to isolated beaches, and there are other routes leading to the shady redwood groves of **Muir Woods**.

Travelling by BART east from the city brings you to **Berkeley**, and its famous university, and the more industrialised **Oakland**, noted for the souvenir shops along its waterfront and the outstanding Oakland museum. Both of these make a pleasurable day's break. Further descriptions are on pages 76, 77 and 83.

Scenery Ninety-four miles to the south, California's one-time capital **Monterey** (see page 96) and the mission town of **Carmel** (see page 92) stand on either side of

Golden Gate National Recreation Area

the scenic Monterey Peninsula, and within easy reach of Big Sur (see page 92), rightly acclaimed as the most photogenic portion of the entire central coast.

Wineries are found all over California but the major centre of production is the so-called Wine Country (see pages 244-55), occupying the verdant valleys of **Sonoma** and **Napa**, beginning 50 miles north of San Francisco. Many wineries are open for tastings, and balloon rides above the valleys are offered at many sites. A more unabashed tourist attraction is the combined **Africa USA/Marine World**, 25 miles northeast of the city close to Vallejo, where many exotic animal species fill a 160-acre park, and where tigers, lions, sea lions and dolphins are among the creatures expertly trained to entertain the public.

Tour Operators and Specialist Tours

A Day in Nature (tel: (415) 673 0458). Half-day naturalist-led tours of the Marin Headlands and Muir Woods, and full-day tours to the Napa Valley; price includes a gourmet picnic.

Artistic Tours (tel: (510) 525 2142). Visits to the studios of some of the Bay Area's internationally known painters, sculptors, ceramists and glass-blowers.

Blue and Gold Fleet (tel: (415) 781 7877). Eight crossings daily to Oakland from Pier 39 in Fisherman's Wharf.

Golden Gate Ferries (tel: (415) 332 6600). Ten crossings daily to Sausalito from the Old Ferry Building.

Golden Gate National Recreation Area Any GGNRA visitor centre will supply maps and general information. For detailed hiking information, contact the Marin Headlands office (tel: (415) 331 1540).

Gray Line (tel: (415) 958 9500). Excursions by coach to Monterey and Carmel, Muir Woods and Sausalito, and the Wine Country.

Great Pacific Tour Co (tel: (415) 626 4499). Excursions by coach to Monterey and Carmel, Muir Woods and Sausalito, and the Wine Country.

Martha Johnson Shopping Tours (tel: (415) 388 3319). Tours individually tailored to suit the consuming interests of visiting shoppers in search of bargains.

Napa Valley Self-Guided Tours (tel: (707) 253 2929). A package which includes a cassette tape, booklet and map, to aid unaccompanied exploration of the Napa Valley wineries.

Red & White Fleet (tel: (1-800) BAY CRUISE). Ferries to Sausalito and catamaran trips to Africa USA/Marine World, from Pier 41 in Fisherman's Wharf.

San Francisco Helicopter Tours (tel: (510) 635 4500). A bird's-eye view of the city and points beyond.

Shopping

Unlike many Americans, the shoppers of San Francisco value personal contact and so the vast shopping malls, common in other cities, have not made much impression on the city. Shopping is undertaken enthusiastically, however, and every neighbourhood has a street worth browsing in.

Predictably, it is mostly tacky tourist fare that fills **Fisherman's Wharf** although the shops and galleries filling two converted factories – the **Cannery** (2801 Leavenworth Street) and **Ghirardelli Square** (9800 N Point Street) – are entertaining places to wander around and can turn up unexpected finds, such as the fine craftworks sold by Folk Art International.

If you are simply shopping for souvenirs, more fruitful territory might be the Chinatown section of Grant Street, where **Canton Bazaar** (No 616) is just one of dozens of places liable to unearth unusual items, from carved jade figures to kitsch toys.

For more mainstream buying The classy department stores of Macy's, I Magnin, Neiman-Marcus and Saks Fifth Avenue stand within a credit card's throw of one another beside Union Square. If you only have time to visit one such emporium, though, make it Nordstrom's (865 Market Street), where spiral escalators whisk you between the fashionably stocked floors.

For those with eyes bigger than their bank accounts, the windows to watch are along Maiden Lane. Among this street's stylish boutiques, **Chanel** (No 155), has three floors laden with the French company's finest products, and **Orientations** (No 34) stocks exquisite Far Eastern furnishings and ornaments.

Take a peek also at the nearby Gump's (250 Post Street), an institution among the city's swells for its fine crystal and world-class jade and pearls – all at world-class prices.

Worth a wander: Ghirardelli Square

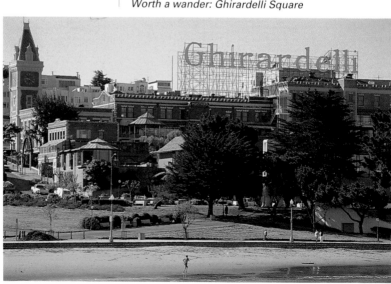

Union Street is a good place to pick up antiques

The toughest antique hunt This could well end with a tour around the 21 varied shops comprising the **Jackson Square Art & Antique Dealers Association** (455 Jackson Square); if it does not, try Telegraph Hill Antiques (580 Union Street), which has good deals in porcelain and glassware, or Old & New Estates (2181A Union Street), specialising in art nouveau jewellery.

There is more that is old among the wild and wacky stores springing up in the Haight-Ashbury area. Much of the clothing here is salvaged from decades past or imported: The Ritz (1157 Masonic Avenue), carries some great gear of yesteryear; more of the same fills Held Over Too (1537 Haight Street); Spellbound (1670 Haight Street) has finer clothing from the 1890s to the 1920s; while Dharma (1600 Haight Street) has some intriguing apparel from Third World countries.

In the same neighbourhood, Revival of the Fittest (1701 Haight Street) recycles and re-creates crazy American household knick-knacks of the 1940s and 1950s, Bones of Our Ancestors (624 Shrader Street) turns crystals and semiprecious stones into pricey talismans, and the giant-sized rolling papers and waterpipes of Pipe Dreams (1376 Haight Street) have delighted discerning smokers since Haight-Ashbury's hippie times.

In a city of bookworms, you will discover plenty of bookshops in which to browse and buy. Widely found chain stores such as Crown and Doubleday are well-stocked with the latest titles, often at reduced prices.

However, it is with specialist book stores that San Francisco excels. These include: Forever After (1475 Haight Street), with a tremendous stock of used volumes on all subjects; City Lights (261 Columbus Avenue), carrying the definitive stock of writings by and about the Beat generation, plus a wide range of political and general titles; Lighthouse Books (2162 Union Street), with the city's biggest selection of books on metaphysical and New Age subjects; and A Different Light (489 Castro Street) stocking a huge amount of gay and lesbian literature.

Well within the range of the average pocket are the numerous factory outlet stores occupying former warehouses in the SoMa area. Many top companies discount their damaged or discontinued lines here and the bargains can be tempting. Esprit (499 Illinois Street) is one of the major names for California casualwear, or you might cruise the multi-store complexes of the Six Sixty Center (660 Third Street) and Yerba Buena Square (899 Howard Street).

Food and Drink

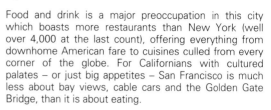

Food and drink is a major preoccupation in this city which boasts more restaurants than New York (well over 4,000 at the last count), offering everything from downhome American fare to cuisines culled from every corner of the globe. For Californians with cultured palates – or just big appetites – San Francisco is much less about bay views, cable cars and the Golden Gate Bridge, than it is about eating.

Prices Fierce competition helps keep prices low, and all but the most exclusive restaurants are well within the range of the majority of travellers. Even the tourist-packed eateries of Fisherman's Wharf are not the gastronomic damp squibs that they could be. Despite claims to the contrary, though, comparatively little of what is offered in the area's seafood restaurants comes from local waters.

Italian Just south of Fisherman's Wharf, the streets of the North Beach are jammed with Italian restaurants offering authentic regional cuisine from every inch of the Mediterranean country and providing excellent value for money.

North Beach dining is no secret, however, and for evening meals you should plan to dine early (before 19.00hrs) to avoid the crowds. Earlier in the day, you will have no problems finding a cosy niche inside of the neighbourhood's many atmospheric cafés, where you can linger over a cappuccino, and a wide choice of light Italian lunches and dessert delicacies, to your heart's (and your stomach's) content.

Crab speciality During its mid-November to June season, look out for Dungeness crab, which many Italian restaurants serve as the centrepiece of a seafood dish called cioppino. The same creature turns up in Chinese restaurants, deliciously prepared in ginger and garlic.

A taste of Italy on Washington Square

While visiting Fisherman's Wharf it is wise to limit your eating to snacks from the seafood stalls on the street – clam chowder in a bowl of sourdough bread (a chewy, slightly bitter bread otherwise best eaten toasted) being one tasty option – and preserve your appetite for more inspiring surrounds.

The Empress of China – a San Francisco favourite

Chinese This type of food has long been a feature of San Francisco and Chinatown is its culinary hot-spot, despite the fact that many of the top Chinese chefs have departed for other areas – notably the Richmond district, just west of Pacific Heights, where Clement Street in particular holds many Asian restaurants of merit.

Diversity Within Chinatown, cooking styles have been expanded by the diverse ethnic backgrounds of recent immigrants: besides Cantonese (and variations on it such as Hakka and Choazhou), Hunan and Szechuan fare, unusual Vietnamese-Chinese and Peruvian-Chinese dishes enliven many menus.
The best way to sample Chinatown's food is inside one of the large and lively Dim Sum restaurants, catering mostly to a local Chinese clientele and usually open between 11.00 and 15.00hrs. Only in Hong Kong are you likely to encounter a bigger variety than here of Dim Sum – pastries and dumplings filled with seafood, meat and/or rice and noodles.

Expressing preferences Shouting and pointing is the surest way to get what you want as the dishes are wheeled on trolleys in front of diners. If, as is likely, you are not sure what you are looking at, simply select whatever looks interesting. When you have finished, the bill is determined by the number of empty dishes on your table.

Gourmet American Elsewhere around town, particularly on Union and Fillmore streets in Pacific Heights, some of the city's more innovative restaurants are blazing a trail with 'contemporary American' cuisine – gourmet variations on regional American dishes that bear the nutritional and aesthetic imprint of California cuisine (see pages 78–9), which itself has largely faded from fashion.

French The city's more traditionally inclined, and the longer established power-brokers don dinner suits and head for the upper-crust restaurants of Nob Hill, noted for their classic French food.

Popular Dim Sum dishes in Chinese restaurants include *Jow Ha Gok* – shrimp turnovers; *Siu Mai* – steamed meat dumplings; *Cha Siu Bow* – barbecued pork inside buns; and *Gee Cheung Fun* – rolls of rice and noodles.

San Francisco is well stocked with bakeries

Mexican Much more down to earth – and much more filling – are the innumerable low-priced Mexican food outlets crammed into the Mission District. These range from dirt cheap hole-in-the-wall takeaways to restaurants where the food is tasty and well priced and the service is swift and cheerful.

Asian and Far Eastern Japanese food is substantially less expensive in the US than in Europe and is far more widely available. Aim for Japantown's Japan Center and you will come across several dozen restaurants and sushi bars providing a treat for the taste-buds at a good price.

There is even cheaper food of Asian origin secreted among the grotty fast-food joints of the Tenderloin (not the safest area in the city, see page 36), where dozens of small Vietnamese, Laotian and Cambodian cafés have recently appeared. Yet to be discovered by the city's food fashion-leaders, they all provide exotic, spicy food at giveaway prices.

Bohemian For a meal in the company of the city's artists, writers, lesser media celebrities and full-time nightclubbers, try any of the restaurants and cafés that drift in and out of style along Haight-Ashbury's Haight Street or SoMa's Folsom Street. Many of these serve no more than basic, filling American food – such as massive omelettes and huge sandwiches – but do so surrounded by bizarre décor and a carefully cultivated bohemian atmosphere.

Tea and coffee drinking When it comes to washing the food down, devoted tea drinkers are generally in for a rough ride in the US. In this coffee-drinking country, tea usually means iced-tea or a weak tea-bag being briefly dipped in lukewarm water.

In San Francisco, however, a growing band of hotels has taken up the practice of serving afternoon tea, which usually features a good range of real teas and snacks such as scones (an American version which is more like a rock cake than the softer British variety) and various pastries.

NEECHA
THAI CUISINE

(415) 922-9419
2100 SUTTER STREET
(Near Steiner)
SAN FRANCISCO, CA 94117
LUNCH 11 a.m. - 3 p.m.
DINNER 5 p.m. - 10 p.m.

The exceptional freshness of coffee, particularly in the North Beach where the rich aroma of roasting coffee beans regularly drifts across the streets, might persuade tea devotees to break their habit. Certainly, there is no better place than a North Beach *caffè* to down an invigorating espresso.

Alcohol Irish coffee – with whiskey, sugar and whipped cream – turns up in many of the city's bars, cafés and restaurants, and a glassful will undoubtedly help you face the city's sea breezes.

Many but not all restaurants are licensed; in those that are, a glass or two of **California wine** makes a nice accompaniment for a meal of any quality, particularly if you are not making the journey north to tour the Wine Country (see pages 244-55). To imbibe with a view, sample one of the roof-top hotel cocktail lounges (see page 66).

It is more in keeping with the mellow mood of the city, though, to drink the night away in a street-level bar – of which there are many, and most are much safer than their somewhat scruffy appearance might at first suggest.

American brew Beer-lovers whose idea of **American beer** begins and ends with Budweiser are in for a treat. Alongside the usual wines and spirits, most bars stock the products of the area's many micro-breweries: beers whose body and flavour – and strength – are well worth sampling.

Anchor Steam Beer is among the most widely found of the local brews in San Francisco but there are many more, their names often chalked up on a board above the counter.

Bars are not just places for refreshment in San Francisco: they're a way of life

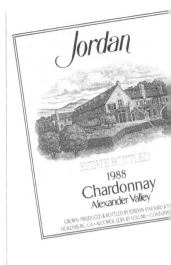

Irish coffee (allegedly) made its first US appearance in San Francisco, at the Buena Vista Café in Fisherman's Wharf (2765 Hyde Street).

Nightlife

For a major city, San Francisco's nightlife is on a surprisingly small and friendly scale, with little evidence of the social snobbery and price-hiking that goes on down the coast in Los Angeles.

What's on The free weekly papers, the *San Francisco Bay Guardian* and *SF Weekly* (see page 43), are the best sources of nightlife listings.

The main ticket agency is BASS/TM (for bookings, tel: (415) 762 2277; for recorded information, tel: TELETIX), with outlets all over the city. STBS, on the Stockton Street side of Union Square (open Tuesday to Saturday, 12.00-19.30hrs; tel: (415) 433 STBS), offers half-price, day-of-performance tickets for selected performing arts shows.

Watering holes Affable and socially very diverse, cafés and bars are found all over the city with the greatest concentration in the North Beach. You should also plan to spend a few daylight hours at one of the roof-top cocktail lounges, which provide views along with the (usually expensive) drinks. Top of the tops is the Carnelian Room, on the 52nd floor of the Bank of America Building at 55 California Street.

Classical music, opera and ballet San Francisco enjoys a deservedly strong reputation for its classical music, opera and ballet. Major performances by the **San Francisco Symphony Orchestra**, based at the Louise M Davies Symphony Hall, 201 Van Ness Avenue (tel: (415) 431 5400), take place from September to May, with many special shows filling the summer months.

The **San Francisco Opera** has a star-studded September to December season at the Civic Auditorium, 99 Grove Street (tel: (415) 864 3330). During the summer, the **Pocket Opera** (tel: (415) 346 2780) mounts lesser-known operas at the Florence Gould Theater, at the California Palace of the Legion of Honour.

Rated among the world's best, the San Francisco Ballet performs from February to May at the Opera House, 301 Van Ness Avenue (tel: (415) 864 3330), returning for special Christmas performances.

Theatre Between October and May, there is high-standard drama at the Geary Theater, 415 Geary Street (tel: (415) 749 2200), from the respected **American Conservatory Theater**, and throughout the year at the tiny Magic Theater, Building D, Fort Mason Center (tel: (415) 441 8822). More in the mainstream, Broadway hits prevail at the Curran Theater, 445 Geary Street (tel: (415) 474 3800).

The longest running theatrical show in San Francisco, however, is *Beach Blanket Babylon*, a witty and raucous revue that has been packing them in throughout its 17-year run; see it at Club Fugazi, 678 Green Street (tel: (415) 421 4222).

Comedy Cutting-edge comic Lenny Bruce got arrested in San Francisco in the early 1960s. The gags of today are unlikely to get bring police raids, but the city still has a fair number of lively comedy clubs. The pick are Holy

Cult films show at the Castro Theater

City Zoo, 408 Clement Street (tel: (415) 386 4242), and the Punch Line, 444 Battery Street (tel: (415) 397 7573).

Cinema Each May, the popularity of the San Francisco Film Festival confirms the city's liking for good movies. Besides many first-run complexes, such as the eight-screen Kabuki Center, corner of Post and Geary streets (tel: (415) 931 9800), rarely seen cult and arthouse films play at the Castro Theater, 429 Castro Street (tel: (415) 612 6120), the Roxie, 317 16th Street (tel: (415) 863 1087), and the Red Vic, 1727 Haight Street (tel: (415) 668 3994).

Jazz, rock and R&B With many of the top US and international bands including the city on their US tours, rock music fans are well catered for. The major venues for contemporary sounds are I-Beam, 1748 Haight Street (tel: (415) 668 6006), and the DNA Lounge, 375 Eleventh Street (tel: (415) 626 1409).
On the local live music circuit, it is R&B which predominates and sounds best at spit-and-sawdust venues like The Saloon, 1232 Grant Street (tel: (415) 989 7666). For the novelty value alone, show up at one of the early evening shows at Brainwash, 1122 Folsom Street (tel: (415) 861 FOOD) – a combined bar and laundrette.
Jazz fans will be disappointed with the city's dearth of good venues, but will find some solace at Roland's, 2513 Van Ness Avenue (tel: (415) 567 1063), or Slim's, 333 Eleventh Street (tel: (415) 621 3330).

Discos The discos of SoMa are where the city's fashion slaves show themselves, although it is a fairly tame scene for the discerning international clubber, with only Club DV8, 540 Howard Street (tel: (415) 777 1419), likely to please.

There's no shortage of accommodation in the city; some hotels, like the Marriott, are hard to miss

Places to stay in San Francisco are as abundant as the hills and views, with options to suit all budgets and all tastes. In fact, this is one of the best places in California to find affordable and atmospheric alternatives to the uniformity of chain hotels and motels.

Making an advance booking is always a good idea, but only during the busiest period – summer and early autumn, when prices will be around $10–20 higher than during the rest of the year – is it essential.

The **San Francisco Visitors and Convention Bureau** (see page 71) publish a free guide to lodgings, with copious listings and room rates, and their office stocks many leaflets detailing individual properties.

Hotels In a city which is small and easy to get around, precisely where you stay is of minor consequence. Most large hotels are close to Union Square and there is a group of newer chain hotels close to Fisherman's Wharf. But it is a smart move to avoid these congested areas in favour of the more characterful residential areas.

The luxurious 'grand hotels' of Nob Hill pride themselves on in pampering their guests, though the price (starting at around $130 and rising swiftly) will deter all but the most wealthy visitor.

A better bet are the so-called 'boutique hotels' ($75–140), several of which are situated between Nob Hill and Downtown. These are small hotels with attentive staff and a limited number of rooms in what used to be an affluent family home. The fittings and fixtures are carefully chosen to add period charm, breakfast is inclusive, and often complimentary wine or sherry will be served in the afternoon. Their relaxing mood makes boutique hotels popular with business travellers and advance booking is advised.

Broadly similar to the boutique hotels, many rambling Victorian homes throughout the city have been refurbished and converted into bed and breakfast inns. Widely fluctuating prices ($40–120) reflect the fact that both the individual properties and the rooms within them vary greatly: some rooms may be small with a shared bathroom; others might be large and equipped with a

Be warned that quoted prices for accommodation rarely include the city's 11 per cent 'transient occupancy' tax, which guests have to pay.

jacuzzi and CD player.

It is the very lack of hotel-like standardisation which is part of the appeal of B&Bs, however, and describing one's room is a favourite topic at breakfast, usually a hearty affair served around a communal table.

The enormous popularity of B&Bs means that you should make a reservation early, especially if arriving during the summer or staying over a weekend. Use one of the specialist agencies such as Bed & Breakfast International, 1181-B Solano Avenue, Albany CA 94706 (tel: (415) 525 4569), or San Francisco Reservations, fourth floor, 22 Second Street San Francisco, CA 94105 (tel: (415) 227 1500).

Budget accomodation While accommodation prices are generally above what you will pay elsewhere in the state, and campsites are non-existent, San Francisco is good news for travellers on tight budgets, with dozens of official AYH and privately run hostels, plus two YMCA's, offering dormitory beds, single rooms and double rooms from around $12 to $40.

The hostels include the 170-room San Francisco International Hostel at Fort Mason, one of the largest youth hostels in the US; others are found all across the city, giving a wide range of options. Many impose a three-night maximum stay during the busy summer season, and some may operate an evening curfew.

Listings of recommended San Francisco accommodation begin on page 266.

Wherever they stay in this tolerant city, gay and lesbian travellers are unlikely to encounter discrimination. Indeed, a number of hotels and bed and breakfast inns, particularly in the Castro area, are staffed by, and cater specifically for gays and lesbians.

A Nob Hill landmark: Mark Hopkins Hotel

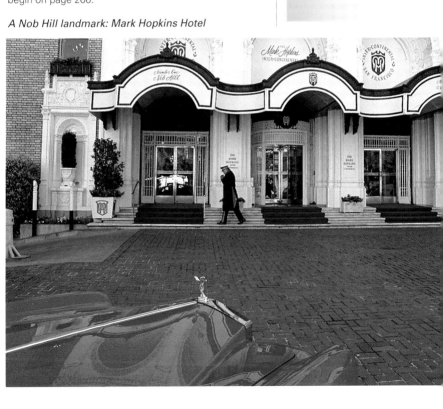

Practical Points

Arriving by air San Francisco's airport (tel: (415) 761 0800) is 13 miles south of the city. Transport links into the city are generally quick and reliable.

A number of companies, such as Express Airport Shuttle (tel: (800) 675 1115) and Super Shuttle (tel: (415) 558 8500), run minivans from the traffic island directly outside the terminal's upper (departures) level. The information desk on the airport's lower (arrivals) level can supply a full list of operators and prices, usually $9-14 to any city address.

Alternatively, the SFO Airporter (tel: (415) 673 2433) coach runs every 20 minutes (06.00–23.10hrs) between the airport – departing from the blue column outside the lower level – and the main hotels around Union Square.

Routes 7F and 7B of the local SamTrans bus service (tel: (800) 660 4BUS) are a cheaper but slower alternative, and baggage is limited to one small item. The buses depart from marked stops outside the airport's upper level.

Only for three of four people sharing the cost are taxis from the airport to the city financially worthwhile. Fares are likely to range from $28 to about $35.

Airline phone numbers America West (800) 247 5692; American (800) 433 7300; British Airways (800) 247 9297; Delta (800) 221 1212; TWA (800) 221 2000; United (415) 397 2100; US Air (800) 428 4322.

Arriving by train Trains (tel: (800) 872 7245) to San Francisco terminate across the bay in Oakland, where free shuttle buses continue to the city's Transbay Terminal, 425 Mission Street.

Arriving by bus Greyhound buses (tel: (415) 558 6789) to San Francisco also stop at the Transbay Terminal.

Car hire In a city which is so easy to walk around and served by an excellent public transport system, you will not need a car to see San Francisco. If you are travelling further afield, however, and have not arranged car hire from the UK, you will find that all the main firms have desks at the airport and offices around the city. Contact

Buses are a good option for reaching the city

them on the following numbers:
Alamo (tel: (800) 327 9633);
Avis (tel: (800) 331 1212);
Budget (tel: (800) 527 0700);
Hertz (tel: (800) 654 3131);
Thrifty (tel: (800) 367 2277).

Car parking Local law requires a car's front wheels to be turned towards the kerb when parked, to prevent the vehicle rolling down the street.

Climate San Francisco enjoys year-round mild weather, the temperatures seldom above 70°F (21°C) or below 40°F (4°C). Stiff breezes often whip in off the bay, however, and fogs are a regular feature, liable to make the city feel cooler than it actually is. Play safe by bringing a warm jumper or jacket even in the summer, and be prepared for very chilly winter evenings when a coat is essential.

Consulates Most foreign embassies are based in Washington DC. For passport emergencies and other needs, you should contact the relevant consular office in San Francisco:
UK, 1 Sansome Street, Suite 850 (tel: (415) 981 3030);
Ireland, 655 Montgomery Street, Suite 930 (tel: (415) 392 4214);
Germany, 1960 Jackson Street (tel: (415) 775 1061);
Netherlands, 601 California Street (tel: (415) 981 6454);
Norway, Two Embarcadero Center (tel: (415) 986 0766);
Sweden, 235 Montgomery Street (tel: (415) 788 2272).

71

Disabled visitors For the disabled, San Francisco is a welcoming city. All public buildings are wheelchair accessible and have disabled toilets; most buses can 'kneel' to the curb, and all BART stations have lifts between street and platform levels.
Published annually, the free publication *A Guide to San Francisco for the Person Who is Disabled* is a useful source of information; call (415) 554 6141 to request a copy.

Foreign exchange Foreign currency and foreign currency travellers' cheques can be changed at the airport and at the following locations:
American Foreign Exchange, 315 Sutter Street (tel: (415) 391 9913);
Bank of America, 345 Montgomery Street (tel: (415) 622 2451); and
Thomas Cook, 100 Grant Avenue (tel: (415) 362 3452). These offices all open during regular business hours, and all except Thomas Cook also open on Saturday morning.

Emergency numbers:
Dial 911 for fire, police or ambulance. San Francisco's Women against Rape serive operates a 24-hour crisis hotline: call (415) 647 7273.

Information For free maps, brochures and general information, call into the Visitor Information Center, on the lower level of Hallidie Plaza by the junction of Market and Powell streets.
Open: Monday to Friday 09.00–17.30hrs; Saturday 09.00–15.00hrs; Sunday 10.00–14.00hrs. Tel: (415) 391 2000).

One of the city's most popular sports: jogging

Newspapers Both the city's daily newspapers, the morning *San Francisco Chronicle* and the evening *San Francisco Examiner* (combined on Sundays), are of a poor standard. Owned by the same company, there is a strong possibility that one or the other will soon close.

For hard news, the *LA Times* and *New York Times* make a better read, and for city features and events listings, the free papers detailed on page 43 are the prime source.

Also worth flicking through are the tourist-aimed free magazines such as *San Francisco Key* and the *Bay City Guide*, found in most hotels.

TV and radio Affiliated to national networks, the main San Francisco TV channels are 4 KTVU (NBC); 5 KPIX (CBS); 7 KGO (ABC); and 9 KQED (PBS). Many hotels also offer selected cable TV channels. A multitude of radio stations cover the AM and FM frequencies, mostly devoted to musical nostalgia.

Participant sports Like most Californians, San Franciscans are enthusiastic participants in outdoor activities, and visitors will find a whole range of physical pursuits on offer; the following are just a few suggestions.

Cycling – the city has two excellent signposted bike routes, one through Golden Gate Park, the other crossing the city to the Golden Gate Bridge. Bike hire costs from $2 an hour and rental outlets are plentiful along Stanyan Street.

Golf – there are public 18-hole courses at Lincoln Park (tel: (415) 221 9911) and Harding Park (tel: (415) 664 4690), a nine-hole course at McLaren Park (tel: (415) 587 2425), and a pitch-and-putt nine-hole course in Golden Gate Park (tel: (415) 751 8987). Rates range from $5 to $17 per person.

Hang-gliding – constant breezes make San Francisco a popular place for hang-gliding, the 200-foot high cliff at Fort Funstan, near Lake Merced, being the main venue.

Sailing and parasailing – you will get the best views of the city by bobbing about on the bay. Numerous companies operate yachts and other small craft from Pier 39 in Fisherman's Wharf. If you want a rush of adrenalin with the views, contact Golden Gate Parasailing and Power Boat Rides (tel: (415) 399 1139), with whom you can parasail above the bay or skim across it in a powerboat.

Spectator sports Tickets for major sporting events are available through Ticketron (tel: (415) 392 7469), and the outlets mentioned below.

Baseball – during the April to September baseball season, the San Francisco Giants draw crowds to Candlestick Park, eight miles south of the city. Match tickets are available at the stadium or from Giant's Dugout, 170 Grant Avenue (tel: (415) 762 BASS). On match days, the 'Ballpark Express' bus runs between Downtown and Candlestick Park.

Football – the city's football team, the San Francisco 49ers (tel: (415) 468 2249), also play at Candlestick Park. Their season runs from August to November.

Baseball and basketball – further professional sporting action takes place across the bay, with the Oakland A's baseball team and the Golden State Warriors basketball side, who both appear at the Oakland Coliseum (tel: (510) 638 0500).

Public transport San Francisco's famous **cable cars** are tourist attractions rather than a practical means of getting about. They operate on two routes between Downtown and Fisherman's Wharf, and another between Nob Hill and the Financial District. Tickets can be bought from self-service machines.

More useful are the **buses** and **streetcars** run by MUNI (tel: (415) 673 MUNI). Exact change is necessary on buses, and a single-journey ticket with free transfers is valid for two changes of route within 90 minutes. If you are using public transport a lot, a MUNI Passport will save money; these are valid on all MUNI services for one- or three-days. MUNI routes are shown in the phone book, and at most bus stops.

The state-of-the-art **Bay Area Rapid Transit (BART)** system is chiefly of use for crossing the bay to Berkeley and Oakland. Fares range from 80¢ to $3 according to distance travelled; tickets can be bought from machines at BART stations.

Taxis can be ordered by phone but are usually easy to hail in the street. Average charges are approximately $2 for the first mile and $1.50 for each additional mile. Scores of cab companies are listed in the phone book.

Transport for tourists

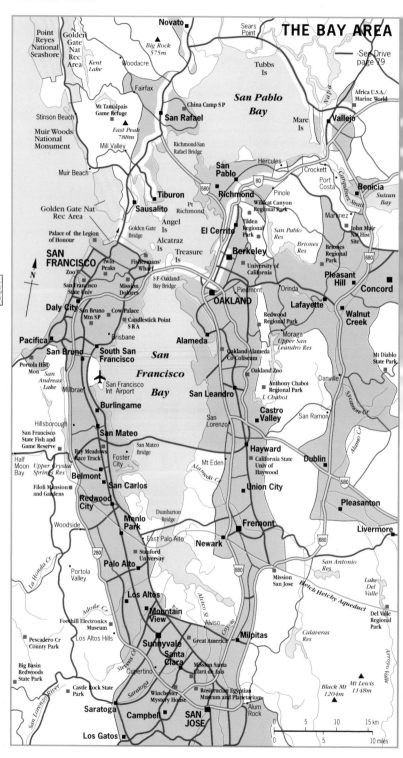

74

From the wild hills of Marin to the high-tech suburbia of Silicon Valley, the Bay Area encompasses a host of contrasting communities with only their proximity to San Francisco Bay in common. The area is by no means dull, but there is no single spot justifying a long-term stay and its is ideally examined on day trips from San Francisco.

In the East Bay, backed by steep hills holding rustic homes and covered by a great number of parks, life in Berkeley (for all but devoted gastronomes, who know it as the birthplace of California cuisine) revolves around a world-famous university campus, noted as much for its student politics as for its breakthroughs in nuclear physics. Neighbouring Oakland is enjoying a revival of its fortunes, and tempts passers-by with one of the state's best museums and an immense tidal lake.

Main routes Along the 55-mile-long peninsula stretching south from San Francisco, Highway-1 charts the coast (see pages 90-101) while Highway-101 keeps to the bayside of the peninsula's central mountains, passing tree-shrouded foothill communities before hitting the dense suburbia filling Santa Clara Valley, now better known as Silicon Valley, home of high-tech industries and San José – the fastest growing US city.

Stanford University is the outstanding sight here, although Silicon Valley's towns are at pains to polish up whatever historical remnants and natural areas they possess to make themselves attractive to visitors whose interests extend beyond micro-circuitry.

North from San Francisco, the green spaces of Marin County were partly colonised two decades ago by San Francisco's original hippies, whose inner-self explorations developed into the New Age pursuits of Marin's more recent, much better bankrolled, arrivals.

Other than a couple of pretty bayside towns, there is not a lot to Marin and it is best tasted as part of a loop around San Pablo Bay, on the inland side of which lie several small towns of historical interest on the scenically appealing Carquinez Straights.

Fireworks over Oakland Bay Bridge

THE BAY AREA

Arguably the greatest, and certainly one of the most influential architects of the 20th century, Frank Lloyd Wright erected 25 buildings in California, none of them more instantly striking than the 1957 Marin County Civic Center, a buff- and blue-coloured concrete and steel creation linking three hilltops just east of Highway– 101 on the northern edge of San Rafael. The architect's first government commission, it was also the last job undertaken before his death in 1959.

▶▷▷ Angel Island

Native Americans hunted seal and otter from the banks of Angel Island long before its discovery by the Spanish in 1775. The island – the largest in San Francisco Bay – was used in various ways by the US government, including as an arrival point for Asian immigrants, as a quarantine centre, and as a prisoner-of-war camp, before becoming a state park. Walking trails cross the tree- and scrub-covered island, and the wind-sheltered beaches at Ayola Cove (landing point for Fisherman's Wharf ferries) and Quarry Point are perfect for picnics.

▶▷▷ Benicia

In the frenzy of the gold-rush years, a deep-water harbour enabled the town of Benicia to keep pace with San Francisco in the race to become California's number one port. It even enjoyed 13 months as state capital from 1853, and the **Benicia State Capitol Park** preserves the handsome Greek Revival building in which state business was carried out. The **Fischer-Hanlon House**, a renovated gold-rush hotel beside the park, is also open for tours, and in the nearby **Benicia Arsenal** building, local artisans have studios and shops.

▶▶▷ Berkeley

Beginning with the Free Speech Movement of the early 1960s, student activity on the campus of the **University of California at Berkeley** has brought one of the country's top educational establishments a reputation for radicalism and caused the town of Berkeley to be nicknamed 'Berserkely'.

Stalls dispensing literature and views on any number of controversial topics are still a common campus sight,

Berkeley, known as a centre of radical thought

and Berkeley has one of the most left-leaning local governments in the country. But these days revolt against authority seems the last thing on the minds of the 30,000 students, most of whom earnestly pursue their studies with an eye on the ever-shrinking graduate job market.

Berkeley is easy to reach by BART from San Francisco and the campus is within easy walking distance, directly east of the station. Devote most of the your time to the campus, as only the well-stocked bookshops and lively restaurants along **Telegraph Avenue** are of interest elsewhere.

For more on Berkeley's militant past, see pages 84-5.

Once the scene of anti-Vietnam War protests, **Sproul Plaza**, close to Berkeley's Bancroft Plaza, is jammed by milling students and makeshift stalls manned by ecological and political activists. The 200-foot high **Campanile** (to the right), modelled on the bell-tower of St Mark's in Venice, has been a landmark since 1914.

Immediately north, safeguarding the university's rare books, the **Bancroft Library** also has a small museum of Californian history. The adjoining **Le Conte Hall** is where physicist Robert Oppenheimer laboured over plans for the first atomic bomb.

Further north, across University Drive, is the 1907 **Hearst Mining Building**. Beneath its impressive rotunda the building displays mineral collections and exhibits on mining in California. The **Lowrie Museum**, on Bancroft Way (to the south), holds an intriguing anthropological stash, including much from native American cultures; and across Bancroft Way is an architectural *tour de force* – the imposingly modern **University Art Museum**, which has an impressive permanent stock and regularly stages important temporary exhibitions.

▷▷▷ Fremont

If you are passing through Fremont, you might be tempted by the 1797 Mission **Jose de Guadalope** (43300 Mission Boulevard), although a $5 million rebuilding has left the mission looking far grander than it ought to.

A better stop is the **Ardenwood** Historic Farm (on State Road 84), whose animals, gardens and shops re-create local rural life over the turn of the century. Between August and April, thousands of migratory birds also pass through Fremont, some of them using the **San Francisco Bay National Wildlife Refuge** (on Marsh Land Road) as a food stop.

▷▷▷ Hayward

Eight miles south of Oakland, Hayward's Historical Society Museum (22701 Main Street) charts the growth of this sizeable residential community from its origins as a supply stop on the gold-mine route. A peek into the spacious rooms of the **McConaghy House** (18701 Hesperian Boulevard) shows how the town's wealthy enjoyed life during the late 1800s, and a leisurely hour can be passed strolling among the native Californian vegetation artfully arranged in the Japanese Garden (22372 N Third Street).

The Birdman of Alcatraz, murderer Robert Stroud, had his last taste of freedom in 1909, aged 19. It was at Leavenworth jail in Kansas that Stroud began keeping and studying birds, and wrote the highly regarded *Stroud's Digest of the Diseases of Birds*. The 'Bird Doctor of Leavenworth' was transferred to Alcatraz in 1942, leaving his birds behind. A biography of Stroud, published in 1955, first coined the phrase 'Birdman of Alcatraz', which was later used as the title of a 1962 film about Stroud, starring Burt Lancaster.

77

Eight miles south of San Francisco, the laboratories of Acres of Orchids (1450 El Camino Real) experiment with the gene pool of the much-loved plant. Free tours pass through the labs, the greenhouses, and around a lush garden filled with more types of orchid than you ever imagined possible.

■ **In no part of California is eating taken more seriously than it is in and around San Francisco, and it was in the upmarket restaurants on Berkeley's Shattuck Avenue – an area known as the 'gourmet ghetto' – that the strange concoctions of California cuisine were first served to the Bay Area's salivating foodies. .....■**

It has been with the gourmet approach to pizza that California cuisine has really hit the high streets: California Pizza Kitchen outlets bake pizzas in traditional brick ovens and serve them with exotic toppings such as goat's cheese, duck or lobster.

78

All the ingredients In retrospect, the most surprising thing about California cuisine was that it took so long to happen. The state is spoiled for natural produce: the vast farms of the Central Valley raise cattle and grow all manner of vegetables; the waters of the Pacific yield seafood in abundance; and a warm and sunny climate make fresh fruit available all year round. For decades, the ethnic diversity of the state's inhabitants have made international and regional American cuisines widely available and well known.

A unique blend In the late 1970s, Berkeley's top chefs began crossing the borders of international cuisine, juxtaposing tradition methods of preparation, flavouring and styling, and using whatever local produce was in season. In some cases, animals were reared and vegetables grown to the exact specifications of a particular restaurant, and chefs bought seafood directly from individual fishermen.

A matter of taste Coming to the fore just as healthy eating was becoming a national preoccupation, the masterminds of California cuisine selected ingredients for their nutritional balance, appealing to the digestive tract as much as the tastebuds. And to satisfy the true gourmet's aesthetic sense, colour co-ordination was also important, aiding the artful presentation of food on the plate.

Although the fame, and some of the techniques of California cuisine spread far and wide, the highly valued individuality of each chef prevented any single dish – which might be anything from grilled pigeon breasts to red snapper in peanut sauce – becoming uniquely associated with California cuisine.

California benefits from a wealth of home-grown produce: Farmers' Market, Marin County

Drive Marin County, the North Bay and the East Bay

See map on page 74.

Leave San Francisco on the Golden Gate Bridge, entering Marin County on Highway-101 and shortly exiting for Sausalito.
A picturesque and very upmarket 'artist's colony', **Sausalito** is a pleasant bayside town of steep, narrow streets and a strollable – though very commercialised – waterfront area.

Return to Highway-101 and drive north for two miles, exiting for Tiburon.
Another affluent bayside community, placid **Tiburon** boasts the **Richardson Bay Audubon Center and Sanctuary**, which offers birdwatching from an effortless but rewarding nature trail.

Return to Highway-101 and drive north for six miles to San Rafael.
The seat of Marin County, **San Rafael** holds a 1949 replica of an 1817 mission chapel and the architecturally significant **Marin County Civic Center**.

Continue north on Highway-101, after nine miles reaching Novato.
In **Novato**, a dairy-farming town named after a Hookooeko Indian chief, the **Marin Museum of the American Indian** details local native American prehistory and culture.

Leave Highway-101 and drive 20 miles east on State Road 37 to Vallejo.
The large ship-building town of **Vallejo** is mostly visited for the Africa USA/Marine World theme park on its outskirts (see page 87), although the **Naval and Historical Museum** merits a quick look.

Drive south from Vallejo, crossing the Carquinez Strait on Highway- 80 and landing at Crockett. Turn left to follow the Carquinez Strait Scenic Drive as far as Port Costa.

In the pretty riverside hamlet of **Port Costa**, a look inside **Muriel's Old Doll House Museum** reveals an astonishing doll collection.

Return to Crockett and head south along Highway-80 for Berkeley.
The university town of **Berkeley** is described on pages 76 and 77.
Take any road south from Berkeley for Oakland.
A major East Bay community with an outstanding museum, **Oakland** is described on page 83.

Return to San Francisco on Interstate-80, crossing the Bay Bridge.

Sausalito's waterfront district

Alcatraz

■ **Angel Island (see page 76) might be the largest, Treasure Island (see page 88) may have the best views, but the lump of granite known as Alcatraz is by far the most famous – or most infamous – of San Francisco Bay's islands. .....■**

High security A mile and a half north of Fisherman's Wharf, Alcatraz (whose Spanish name means 'Pelican') became the most feared place of incarceration in the US from 1934, when 'incorrigible' criminals – those deemed beyond salvation and considered too dangerous to be held in conventional jails – were moved to this top-security, strict-discipline penitentiary.

At Alcatraz, even work was regarded as a privilege and had to be earned by a prisoner through good behaviour. There was one guard for every three inmates, and any prisoners who did escape from their cells were faced with the prospect of crossing the freezing, swiftly moving waters of the bay to freedom. Although stays at Alcatraz averaged nearly 10 years, inmates were denied access to newspapers, radios and TVs, and 80 per cent of them never received a visitor. Only 36 of the 1,576 convicts (Al Capone, Machine Gun Kelly and Robert Stroud – the so-called 'Birdman of Alcatraz' – see panel on page 77 – being the most notorious) imprisoned here ever attempted escape: all but five were recaptured within an hour; of the five, nothing has been heard.

Change of use The costs and difficulties of running an island prison, and the severity of the regime, led to Alcatraz's closure in 1963. After a period of native American occupation, Alcatraz became part of the Golden Gate National Recreation Area, in 1972 throwing open its once tightly guarded doors to the curious public. Most of the semi-ruined prison buildings – the cellblock, the mess hall with its tear-gas cylinders fixed to the ceiling, and the prison hospital

– can be toured, and there is a small museum and a short documentary film. It is also worthwhile taking the audio-cassette tour, which carries a terse commentary by former Alcatraz guards and inmates.

Frequent crossings between Pier 41 on Fisherman's Wharf and Alcatraz are operated by the Red & White Fleet (tel: (1-800) BAY CRUISE), though you should book a day in advance during the summer.

An Alcatraz prison cell

The John Muir National Historic Site, Martinez

▷ ▷ ▷ Los Altos Hills

When Silicon Valley boffins get bored with their microchips, they head for Los Altos Hills and wallow in nostalgia at the **Foothill Electronics Museum**, where dozens of valve-driven radios, TVs, and other vintage electrical devices are lovingly maintained.

▶ ▷ ▷ Los Gatos

Sumptuous homes fill the hillsides and lanes of Los Gatos, 16 miles west of San José, their owners sometimes emerging to scour the pricey shops and boutiques of the Old Town (on University Avenue) for antiques. Other pastimes include visiting the science and nature displays of Los Gatos Museum (corner of Main and Tait streets), and riding the mildly entertaining Billy Jones Wildcat Railroad in Oak Meadow Park.

▷ ▷ ▷ Martinez

When he wasn't blazing a hiking trail through California's backcountry, Scottish-born naturalist John Muir lived in comfort in Martinez, inside a 17-room house built by his father-in-law in 1882. A former Spanish rancho, Martinez itself is filled with oil refineries and fish canneries. The Muir house, known as the **John Muir National Historic Site** (4202 Alhambra Avenue) and kept as it was on Muir's death in 1914, is well worth a visit. Be sure first to catch the free film show, which reveals Muir's crucial role in the creation of national parks and forests.

The Martinez Adobe, built in 1849, shares the site and carries displays on Mexican life in early California.

▶ ▷ ▷ Menlo Park

Few Californians fail to bury their noses once a month inside *Sunset*, a magazine devoted to the stylish upkeep of gardens, homes and life-styles in the Western US, and whose own experimental gardens, kitchens and offices, can be visited in Menlo Park, north of Palo Alto.

Also in the town, a grouping of elegant Spanish-style buildings set across a 3-acre garden hold the **Allied Arts Guild**, where several craft studios are open to the public.

81

Top-secret weapon research is one of the main sources of employment in the Livermore Valley, 48 miles east of San Francisco. A more sociable local occupation is turning the verdant valley's grapes into wine. Several valley wineries are open for tours and tastings and at one of them, the Wente Brothers Sparkling Wine Cellars, 5050 Arroyo Road (tel: (415) 447 3023), you might bump into the Oakland Symphony Orchestra giving a summer performance.

■ **It may lack the majestic peaks of Yosemite or the mysterious landscapes of Death Valley but, as natural regions go, San Francisco Bay is one of the most ecologically important – and most threatened – places in California. .....■**

Delicate balance The bay forms a huge estuary with much of its 100-mile shoreline lined by cordgrass, an important oxygen- and nutrient-producing plant. In the bay's marshes, microscopic marine creatures thrive and provide food both for migratory birds – beneath whose flight path the bay stands – and, once the tiny organisms are swept out to sea, for large sea dwellers, including the celebrated (and enthusiastically watched) California gray whales who pass by the bay on their annual journey between the frozen Arctic Ocean and the warmer waters off Baja California.

Damage There are two main causes for the damage to the bay's subtle ecology: increased urbanisation, which has led to 75 per cent of the marshland disappearing beneath new housing districts and industrial sites; and the diverting of the Sacramento and San Joaquin rivers to the farms of the Central Valley which has severely reduced the amount of fresh water tempering the salty environment of the bay.

Conservation measures In the mid-1960s, continued lobbying by concerned citizens forced the state government to create the San Francisco Bay Conservation and Development Corporation, which first stopped the pumping of raw sewage into the bay, and then introduced new laws in order to restrict landfill practices.
None the less, the decline of the bay has been slowed rather than halted, despite marshland reclamation projects and the requirement for any new landfill project to be matched by an equal-sized area being returned to the water.

Audubon Canyon Ranch, in Marin County

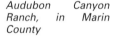

Further information More about the bay and its ecology can be gleaned at San Mateo's Coyote Point Museum (see page 88), Palo Alto's Baylands Nature Interpretive Center (2775 Embarcadero Road), the Environmental Education Center of the San Francisco Bay National Wildlife Refuge (at Alviso, on the northern edge of San Jose), and at Hayward Regional Shoreline (eastern end of San Mateo Bridge, close to Hayward), a major marshland reclamation project.

Canoes For a closer look, take a canoe trip on the bay. These are run by several companies, including the following:
the Marin County-based Canoe Trips West (tel: (415) 461 1750);
the Palo Alto-based Nature Expeditions International (tel: (415) 328 6572).

Jack London Square, Oakland

▶ ▷ ▷   Mount Diablo

The highest point in the Bay Area, moody Mount Diablo is well named as Devil's Mountain. Spanish soldiers reported seeing a mysterious figure taking the side of the Indians during battles around its slopes, and another group believed they had encountered Satan himself when a native American shaman appeared. From the 3,849ft summit you will see (fogs permitting) out to the Pacific and 200 miles to the Sierra Nevada mountains.

▶ ▶ ▷   Oakland

Most tourists see no more of Oakland than the waterfront shops of **Jack London Square**, reached with a free shuttle bus from the 12th Street BART stop, but this is far less interesting than Oakland's **Chinatown**, or the **Oakland Museum** (corner of 10th and Oak streets), with its candid account of California's history.

▶ ▶ ▷   Palo Alto

Affluent Palo Alto is the site of **Stanford University**, founded by railway magnate Leland Stanford in 1885. Long viewed as the conservative counterpart to radical Berkeley, Stanford reputedly earns $5 million a year in royalties on its inventions. Romanesque sandstone buildings sit at the heart of the campus, the nicest of them being the mural-decorated **Memorial Church** on the Main Quad. The Quad is also a pick-up point for free shuttle buses across the 9,000-acre campus, best appreciated from the observation level of the **Hoover Tower**. 'Must sees' include the Asian and Egyptian collections of the **Stanford Museum of Art** (due to reopen following earthquake-damage repairs), the **Cantor Sculpture Garden**, where an eight-ton *Gates of Hell* is the most imposing of several pieces by Rodin, and the **Stanford Linear Accelerator Center**, tours of which (appointment only; tel: (415) 854 3300) are conducted by students.

A pale shadow of the goings-on in San Francisco, the Bay Area's festivals tend to be very small, localised affairs. Among them, the enjoyable Marin and San Mateo county fairs (based in San Rafael and San Mateo respectively) are held each July; the Sand Sculpture and Sandcastle competition takes place on Alameda Island, off Oakland, in June; and September is enlivened by Redwood City's Great Milk Carton Boat Race, when local lunatics race boats made from milk cartoons.

■ **While California's reputation as a safe haven for strange cults and oddball behaviour is well founded, the state is much less the hotbed of revolution that the world at large often seems to think it is. The only time complete social upheaval was seriously on the Californian political agenda was during the nationally turbulent years of the 1960s, and it was the Bay Area that saw the bulk of the action. .....■**

Organised student revolt This began in Berkeley during the autumn of 1964, when the university authorities attempted to halt fund-raising activities and the distribution of political leaflets on the edge of campus by citing a clause in the state constitution requiring the university to be free of religious or sectarian influence.

Fronted by Mario Savio, the resultant Free Speech Movement (FSM) arranged student sit-ins and protest rallies, and an occupation of Sproul Hall which led to the largest mass arrest in California's history as police dragged 750 students from the building.

Eventually the university powers-that-be softened their attitudes, forced to take heed of student demands for participation in the running of the university.

The success of the FSM in encouraging student activism across the country laid the foundations for the massive anti-Vietnam War demonstrations of later years, when Berkeley was again the state's focal point of dissent. The civility of the FSM actions had became a very distant memory by 1968 though, when several days of rioting took place after the police blocked off a student march along Telegraph Avenue.

More violence Berkeley saw more violence in 1969 when a pocket of university ground earmarked for development was turned – by the spades of a disparate bunch of radicals – into People's Park, an open space intended for community use. To take possession of the park (which still survives, mostly occupied by the homeless), the county sheriff and the National Guard fired teargas and buckshot, causing the death of one bystander and blinding another.

The Black Panthers While Berkeley was a centre for student activity, Oakland was the birthplace in 1966 of the Black Panthers, who advocated self-determination for America's blacks by any means necessary. Founded by Bobby Seale and Huey Newton, the Black Panthers' best-known figure was their Minister for Information, Eldridge Cleaver.

Influenced to varying degrees by Malcolm X, Karl Marx, Che Guevara and Mao Tse-tung (one way the panthers raised money was through buying 20¢-copies of Mao's *Little Red Book* in San Francisco's Chinatown and reselling them to Berkeley's students for $1 a time) the Black Panthers dressed in black jackets, black berets, dark glasses and brandished automatic weapons.

Described by the FBI as 'the gravest threat to domestic peace' as their message spread across the country, the Black Panthers were far smaller in number than their publicity suggested. Following shoot-outs with police and the imprisonment of many of its members (including Cleaver, who, while on parole, stood as a US Presidential candidate for the Peace and Freedom Party), the Oakland Panthers grew increasingly less militant, devoting their time to local community projects and canvassing black support for the Democratic Party.

The SLA The demise of the Black Panthers did not mean the end of armed insurrection in the Bay Area, however. By killing, with arsenic-coated bullets, an Oakland schools superintendent for his plans to instigate surveillance of high-school students, the Symbionese Liberation Army (SLA), an underground revolutionary group, announced their presence in 1973.

The following year, the SLA kidnapped the heir to the Hearst publishing fortunes, Patti Hearst, from her Berkeley home. The ransom for her return involved a programme of food distribution to California's poor; following which, Hearst announced that she had decided to join the organisation.

After a bank raid, six SLA members were killed in Los Angeles and in 1975 Hearst herself was arrested in San Francisco and sentenced to seven years imprisonment.

Since then, the emphasis of Bay Area politics has largely switched towards community and ecological issues. The Berkeley campus has been quiet – perhaps a mark of the lasting achievements of the FSM – while, as in San Francisco, the clearest gains have been made by the Bay Area's gay and lesbian communities.

Black Panther Bobby Seale addresses students, 1968

Atop Mount Hamilton, 19 miles east of San José and reached by a twisting road, the 36-inch telescope of the Lick Observatory has been scanning the heavens since 1888 – less efficiently since urbanisation filled the sky with smog. The observatory was created with the money of James Lick, whose body lies here, an eccentric gold-rush-era millionaire who believed there was life on the moon. Open daily, the observatory conducts an informative interpretive programme each Friday evening (tel: (408) 274 5061 for details).

▷ ▷ ▷ **Redwood City**

Everything from cement to chrysanthemums passes through the port at Redwood City, a few miles north of Palo Alto, but the sole attraction for visitors is the Gothic Revival **Lathrop House** (627 Hamilton Drive).

▶ ▶ ▷ **San José**

San José, is loaded with unlikely sights. Within the sphinx- and hieroglyph-decorated Rosicrucian Park (1342 Naglee Avenue), run by the mystical order, a re-creation of an avenue from ancient Thebes leads to the **Egyptian Museum**, whose collection includes an explorable replica of a 2000BC pyramid. Close to Interstate-280, the **Winchester Mystery House** (525 Winchester Boulevard) is an extraordinary building – 160 rooms, with stairways leading to ceilings, corridors leading nowhere, and doors opening on to walls. Its construction was financed by Sarah Winchester, heir to the weaponry fortunes, to appease the spirits of those killed by Winchester rifles. Sarah believed she would die if the house was completed, and work continued for 38 years until her death in 1921.

Other local discoveries include the **Chinese Culture Garden**, inside Overfelt Gardens (Educational Park Drive); the Japanese Friendship Garden and the **San José Memorial Museum** in Kelley Park (635 Phelan Avenue); and the American Museum of Quilts and Textiles (776 S Second Street).

▷ ▷ ▷ **San Leandro**

Just south of Oakland, San Leandro once had a large Portugese farming community but is now a residential and manufacturing base, of note for **Casa Peralta**, a tourable 1897 home.

A strange legacy: Winchester Mystery House

Theme Parks

■ **The pick of California's theme parks are in the south of the state, close to Los Angeles (see pages 160–2), although enthusiasts can sample a couple of major parks in the Bay Area and also find several places to don swimsuits and splash about when the temperature soars. As you would expect, the parks are excellent places to visit with children, but even unaccompanied adults can have a good time. .....■**

Great America Close to Santa Clara, Great America (on Great America Parkway) tugs at the patriotic sentiments of Americans, offering wholesome family fun around several themed re-creations of important places and moments in US history – New England during the Revolutionary War, and Klondike at the time of the gold rush, for example.

Besides countless minor amusements, more than a hundred major rides fill the 100-acre park, ranging from stomach-churning roller-coasters to white-knuckle cascades through white-water rapids.

The park is rarely overcrowded,and a day is ample time to see and do everything in Great America.

Africa USA/Marine World Near Vallejo (on Marine Parkway, off Interstate-80), this one is more about watching than participating. In the Marine World aquatic section, killer whales, dolphins and sea lions demonstrate their trick-learning skills to the crowds, while in Africa USA, it is lions, tigers, orang-utans and elephants who put on the shows. Not to be outshone in the intelligence stakes, a group of specially trained humans entertains audiences with a water-skiing performance.

Lesser attractions include a tropical bird aviary, a walk-through greenhouse of dazzlingly colourful butterflies, and a children's playground equipped with nets, ropes and tunnels.

Raging Waters If you are in San José when the sun beats down, cool off at Raging Waters (in Lake Cunningham Regional Park, off the Capitol Expressway), a 14-acre park where everything involves getting wet.

Much the same applies if you are in the Livermore Valley, where four twisting flumes make up the Rapids Waterslide, part of the **Shadow Cliffs Regional Recreation Center** (two miles east of Pleasanton on Stanley Boulevard), or at Milpitas, which holds the Splashdown Waterslide (1200 S Dempsey Road).

Dolphins on show in Marine World

Of several rambling mansions secreted in the foothills and forests of the Bay Area, only the Filoli Estate, a 43-room dwelling with exquisitely landscaped gardens, is likely to be familiar: it starred as the Carrington estate in the top TV soap, *Dynasty*. You will find it on Canada Road in Woodside (tel: (415) 368 2880 to reserve a place on a guided tour).

A man-made island in San Francisco Bay, created for the 1939 Golden Gate Exposition, Treasure Island was taken over by the US Navy after the Expo. The Treasure Island Museum details the history of the sea services, though a stronger reason for making the ferry crossing from Fisherman's Wharf might be the fantastic views of the Golden Gate and Bay bridges, and of San Francisco itself.

▶ ▷ ▷   **San Mateo**

With computers, diaramas and films, San Mateo's four-storey **Coyote Point Museum** (Coyote Point Drive) presents an exceptionally informative account of the intricacies of – and the threats faced by – the natural life of San Francisco Bay. The museum, designed to blend in with its wooded surrounds, also exhibits a functioning beehive and an industrious colony of termites, while the tranquillity of the bayside setting – interrupted only by the jets in and out of nearby San Francisco airport – makes its grounds a likely picnic stop. San Mateo itself is the seat of San Mateo County, the past of which can be traced at the **San Mateo County Historical Museum** (1700 W Hillsdale Boulevard).

▷ ▷ ▷   **Santa Clara**

A fast-growing but largely uninteresting community just north of San José, Santa Clara evolved around Mission Santa Clara de Asís, founded in 1777 but survived only by a replica of its third (1825) church within the grounds of Santa Clara University. The university's **de Saisset Museum** has objects from the original mission, alongside temporary art exhibitions. Most visitors pass right through the town, however, headed for the Great America theme park (see page 87).

▶ ▷ ▷   **Saratoga**

One of many to live comfortably in Saratoga, nestling in the lower slopes of the Santa Cruz foothills west of San José, was James D Phelan, one-time US senator and three times mayor of San Francisco. Since 1930, Phelan's 19-room **Villa Montalvo** (15400 Montalvo Road), complete with terraced gardens, arboretum and bird sanctuary, has been a retreat for writers and painters, with numerous cultural events taking place in the theatre occupying the villa's converted carriage house.

If Saratoga's wealth becomes overwhelming, focus your mind on higher things at the reposeful 15-acre Hakone Gardens (21000 Big Basin Way), landscaped along formal Japanese lines.

The Bay Bridge, seen from Treasure Island

Recreational Parks

■ **Large tracts may be densely populated residential land, but an impressive amount of the Bay Area is wide open countryside, where hiking trails, sedate lakes and threatened wildlife all exist within a hour's drive of suburbia. .....■**

Bubble-juggling, Golden Gate Park

Big is beautiful On the hills above Berkeley and Oakland, the second-largest park system in the US consumes 63,000 acres and divides into 43 separate parks. The largest and most popular section of the network is **Tilden Regional Park** (off Grizzly Peak Boulevard), where weekend crowds enjoy swimming in and sunbathing around Lake Anza, doing sporting battle on the golf course and tennis courts, and strolling in the botanical garden as their children amuse themselves riding a miniature steam train and going dizzy on a vintage merry-go-round.

Peacefully pastoral Nice though it is, the recreational development of Tilden is at odds with the purely pastoral landscapes of the East Bay's other parks. Wildcat Canyon Regional Park, for example, borders Tilden but its appeal is thoroughly rustic with quiet hiking trails winding around a creek and across wooded hillsides.

From Wildcat Canyon, ambitious hikers can pick up the **Skyline National Trail** and thread their way south over 30 view-laden miles to the Anthony Chabot Regional Park, well-known to local anglers for the bass and trout in its Lake Chabot and to wildlife watchers for the deer, racoons and bobcats resident in the neighbouring **Redwood Regional Park**.

Landscapes are generally less dramatic directly south of San Francisco, although part-time lepidopterists should make a stop at San Bruno Mountain Regional Park (take the Brisbane exit off Highway-101), the last remaining habitat of the mission blue and a couple of other waning butterfly species. The Friends of Endangered Species lead free guided walks to see the butterflies, and to the sites of native American significance within the park.

Elsewhere, earthquake enthusiasts might fancy a close inspection of the San Andreas fault, the geological hiccup behind many of California's earthquakes, a section of which runs through the **Los Trancos Open Space Preserve** (seven miles southwest of Palo Alto, on Page Mill Road) and which is flanked by a walking trail.

89

<< Oakland's Lake Merritt is the world's largest saltwater tidal lagoon. Canoes and a variety of boats can be hired for $4 to $10 per hour from the Sailboat House (tel: (510) 444 3807). >>

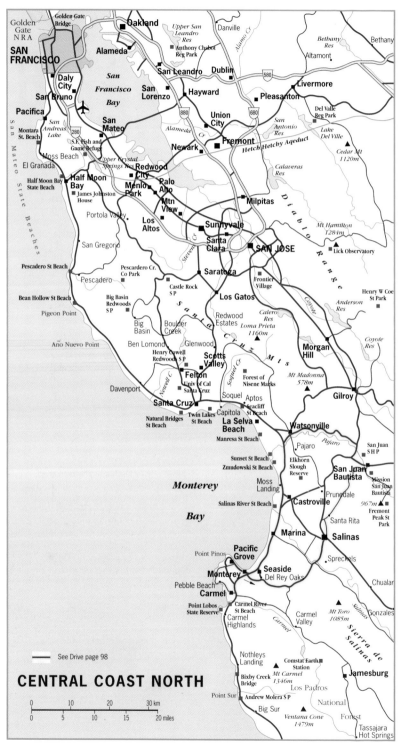

See Drive page 98

CENTRAL COAST NORTH

| 0 | 10 | 20 | 30 km |
| 0 | 5 | 10 | 15 | 20 miles |

California pumpkins

Much of California's Central Coast, covering almost 400 miles between San Francisco and Los Angeles, has not changed a great deal since it was sighted by seafaring Spaniards in the 16th century.

Pacific breakers continue to smash against the granite headlands, groves of towering redwood trees still smother many of the coastal valleys, and the colonies of honking sea lions and seals emphasise the fact that, even today, it is nature that holds the upper hand.

Completing the sense of remoteness from the state's developed portions, the sole coastal road (Highway-1, also called the Coastal Highway) makes hair-raising crossings of deep canyons as it charts a winding two-lane course linking the region's scattered towns.

The first settlement of appreciable size is Santa Cruz, an affable university community noted for its eccentrics, left-wing politics, and the massed surfers who perform off its attractive beaches.

Fifty miles south, Monterey was California's capital for a period from 1770 and proves the fact by keeping plenty of its historic buildings intact. The town also marks the edge of the Monterey Peninsula, a fist of forested granite jutting into the ocean, on whose southern edge sits the pretty – if over-visited – village of Carmel.

A few miles inland from the coast, state parks cover many of the hikeable hillsides, and out-of-the-way farming towns form the heart of what is sometimes called Steinbeck country, after the Salinas-born writer, John Steinbeck, one of many literary figures associated with the Central Coast.

Beyond the Monterey Peninsula Big Sur comprises more than 70 miles of dramatic, wide open country populated by barely a thousand souls, and brings the northern section of the Central Coast to an end on the outskirts of San Simeon.

Big Basin Redwoods State Park

▶▶▶ Big Basin

The first of California's state parks, Big Basin Redwoods State Park was created in 1902 to protect groves of 2,000-year old redwood trees covering the ocean-facing slopes of the Santa Cruz Mountains, 25 miles south of Half Moon Bay. A simple self-guided walking trail leads around the biggest and best of the park's majestic redwoods, and 100 miles of hiking trails descend from the inland hills, passing waterfalls, fern glades and meadows, on the way to secluded sandy beaches.There is hiking and horse-riding amid the 4,000 pristine acres of the Henry Cowell Redwoods State Park, close to Big Basin, and also an excellent self-guided walking trail through the Redwood Grove, home to some of the Central Coast's most handsome trees.

▶▶▶ Big Sur

Coastal California reaches its scenic climax with Big Sur, a barely populated stretch between Carmel and San Simeon, where the scrub-covered slopes and forested river canyons of the Santa Lucia Mountains meet the ocean in a captivating spectacle of granite and sandstone bluffs being pounded by crashing surf.

Obscure tracks lead to hidden-away beaches but even from the winding and dipping Highway-1, Big Sur cannot fail to impress. The **Henry Miller Memorial Library** recalls just one of numerous writers and artists who have found inspiration here, and the Esalen Institute further attests to Big Sur's mood-enhancing qualities.

▷▷▷ Bixby Creek Bridge

The largest of a series of tall, narrow bridges carrying Highway-1 across the canyons of Big Sur is the Bixby Creek Bridge, some 10 miles south of Point Lobos State Reserve, completed in 1932 and claimed to be the world's largest single-arch bridge.

▶▶▷ Carmel

Founded by the Spanish and turned into a unconventional leafy retreat by turn-of-the- century San Franciscan bohemians, Carmel is a self-consciously quaint seaside town with about 5,000 wealthy residents (including ex-mayor, Clint Eastwood) fiercely protective of their cottage homes and narrow streets, who have banned neon signs, traffic-lights and hot-dog stands.

Carmel's lanes and courtyards merit a brief browse, although most hold only souvenir shops, pricey restaurants and art galleries touting undistinguished depictions of coastal landscapes. More deserving of time are the town's beach, the granite **Tor House** (on Ocean View Avenue) built by poet Robinson Jeffers, and the **Carmel Mission** (3080 Rio Road), where Junípero Serra, founder of the California Missions, died in 1784 .

▶▶▷ Castle Rock

Rising high above coastal fogs and city smogs, the 3,600 acres of Castle Rock State Park offer rich pickings for backcountry enthusiasts. The mountain ridges, waterfalls, giant boulders and fantastic views cannot be fully appreciated without the requisite equipment and stamina for at least a day's heavy-duty hiking.

A flag-bearer of the human potential movement, the Esalen Institute took its name from the local native Americans and grew up around the natural hot springs at Big Sur in 1962. With yoga, meditation, holistic medicine, Gestalt therapy and much more, Esalen's workshops and seminars attract the wealthiest of California's New Agers. Expect little change from $300 for an introductory weekend, though if your head is already screwed on right, you might treat the rest of your body to a massage (for details, tel: (408) 667 3000).

 **Felton**

A handy accommodation base when exploring the parks which lie around it, Felton, a mountain town five miles north of Santa Cruz, also boasts the century-old **Covered Bridge** spanning the San Lorenzo River valley, and two scenic railways: the Roaring Camp Big Trees Narrow Gauge Railroad, which navigates redwood groves on the way to Bear Mountain; and the Santa Cruz Big Trees & Pacific Railroad, which descends to Santa Cruz.

 **Forest of Nisene Marks**

By 1923, 40 years of commercial logging had decimated 10,000 acres of forest inland from Santa Cruz. When logging finished, the land was purchased by a Danish immigrant family, who later put it under state protection. Hiking trails reveal young redwoods – proof of the forest's regenerative powers – and pass many remnants of the lumber industry.

▶ ▷ ▷ **Half Moon Bay**

Increasingly populated by rich refugees from Silicon

Men were men in frontier-era California, and at least one woman was too. Born in New Hampshire in 1812, one-eyed Charley Parkhurst chewed tobacco with the best of them and piloted stagecoaches over a rough route through the Santa Cruz Mountains. Only on Parkhurst's death in 1879 was 'he' discovered to be a 'she'.

93

Valley suburbia, the small oceanside town of Half Moon Bay maintains a picturesque main street, where Victorian buildings house various cosy restaurants and bakeries.

Several miles of quiet, scenic beaches add to the town's appeal, and if you are passing through in October, you are sure to find the local Art and Pumpkin Festival in full swing.

Just south of Half Moon Bay, the **Higgins Purisma Road** branches from Highway-1 to wind for eight miles through tiny, time-locked farming settlements, before rejoining the main highway.

The Carmel Mission

■ From turn-of-the-century bohemians to 1950s beatniks, writers and poets have long been a feature of the Central Coast. Inspired by fleeting visits or besotted enough to take up permanent residence, they have put the area's powerful landscapes to use as potent backdrops, or simply waxed lyrical about the region's natural splendour. .....■

94

Steinbeck's house and library in Salinas

Steinbeck No writer has had stronger links to the area than Salinas-born John Steinbeck, much of whose work focused on California's forgotten people, such as the migrant farming communities around his home town and the fish-cannery workers of nearby Monterey.

Of a prolific output during his peak years of the 1930s and early 1940s, Steinbeck's best-known book, *The Grapes of Wrath*, dealt with the plight of a Depression-era family arriving in California in search of the promised land but finding only an exploitative system of agricultural labour. It won the Pulitzer Prize but enraged the state's land barons who branded Steinbeck a communist, and in Salinas he was widely condemned as a traitor to his native town. Even today, some local libraries refuse to stock his titles.

Other famous names Long before Steinbeck was born, Robert Louis Stevenson arrived flat-broke in Monterey in pursuit of Fanny Osbourne, a married woman from Oakland whom he had met in France; he married her the following year. Although he was only in the town for a few months during 1879, Stevenson penned *The Old and New Pacific Capitols* – a perceptive contrasting of Monterey's decline with San Francisco's rise – and tramped the local coastline gaining inspiration for the landscapes which were later to appear in his famed *Treasure Island*.

Anti-Steinbeck feeling in Salinas has subsided sufficiently for the town to mount a Steinbeck Festival in early August, with tours, films, lectures and discussions relating to the author. Among the region's many other festivals, none are stranger than Half Moon Bay's Pumpkin Festival throughout October, or the Brussels Sprout Festival held during the same month in Santa Cruz, celebrating the town's major farm crop with dozens of bizarre, sprout-themed events.

From 1906, Carmel gained an infamous, if comparatively short-lived, bohemian community led by romantic poet George Sterling. Many influential writers of the day – including Upton Sinclair, Mary Austin and Jack London – joined him in what was then an idyllic, unheard-of coastal town. In 1926, Sterling published a biography of a longer-lasting Carmel resident, Robinson Jeffers. Born in Pittsburg, Jeffers was a graduate in forestry and medicine, who published his first volume of poetry in 1912 and moved to Carmel two years later.

It was not the Carmel bohemians that had attracted Jeffers but the natural beauty of the town and its surrounds, and what he saw as the earthy purity of the local people. These things convinced Jeffers to abandon conventional poetry and devote himself to lengthy verses, likened to Greek epics, which used a wild, coastal setting in their explorations of human dilemmas. Not content with constructing epic poems, Jeffers also constructed an epic dwelling, Tor House, using granite stones hauled up from Carmel Beach.

Henry Miller Given the salacious content of his 1930s novels, *Tropic of Cancer* and *Tropic of Capricorn* (which were denied publication in the US until the 1960s), Henry Miller's 17-year presence in Big Sur, from 1944, caused much local speculation as to what debauched scenes were taking place in his secluded house.

In fact, other than an awful lot of writing, not much was taking place, although Miller's intensely personal narrative style had drawn the fledgling authors of the Beat generation to him, who in turn became obsessed with Big Sur's landscapes. Miller wrote about the area in 1958's *Big Sur* and the *Oranges of Hieronymus Bosch*, while Beat-author Jack Kerouac (who liked its fictional potential but hated Big Sur's isolation) loosely used Miller as the inspiration for his 1962 novel, *Big Sur*, a tale of a retired Beat idol seeking peace and seclusion.

In the self-styled 'artichoke capital of the world' town of Castroville, just north of Monterey, Marilyn Monroe was crowned California Artichoke Queen in 1947.

95

Tor House, built by Robinson Jeffers

Pacific Grove

▶ ▶ ▷   Pacific Grove

A band of tent-carrying Methodists moved to the northern tip of the Monterey Peninsula 1875, and the resultant town of Pacific Grove evolved into a fenced-in enclave of religious devotions and high moral virtue, with laws restricting the sale of alcohol only being lifted in 1969.

An abundance of shingle cottages gives the quiet seaside town a homely appeal. Monarch butterflies certainly find Pacific Grove to their liking – tens of thousands of them migrate here each November to hang from the pine trees (especially plentiful on Ridge Road), forming vast rippling flags of orange and black.

The **Museum of Natural History** (165 Forest Avenue) has a good display on the butterflies, and the **John Steinbeck Memorial Museum** (222 Central Avenue) fills a small Victorian home with knick-knacks belonging to the writer who once endured poverty inside it. On a weekend, round off a tour of the town with a call to the 1855 Point Pinos Lighthouse (on Lighthouse Avenue).

▶ ▷ ▷   Salinas

Author John Steinbeck was born in 1902 in Salinas (at 132 Central Avenue, now an uninteresting restaurant and gift shop), a down-to-earth town dominated by the agricultural industry and off the beaten tourist track despite being just 15 miles from Monterey. A room of the **John Steinbeck Public Library** (110 W San Luis Street) displays photographs and manuscripts relating to the prize-winning writer, who featured the town and its problems in many of his books.

You will get a broader sense of Salinas's unglamourous past inside the 1840s Jose Eusebio Boronda Adobe (333 Boronda Road), packed with period furnishings and local historical items, although local energies are less concerned with preserving the past than looking forward to the annual California Rodeo, four days of cowboy-style activities each July. The rodeo is amusingly commemorated by *Hat in Three Stages of Landing*, a Claes Oldenburg sculpture in the gardens of the Community Center (940 N Main Street).

A sailor from Boston who jumped ship in the then Mexican-owned California in 1816, Thomas Doak became the first US citizen to settle in the region. Before marrying into the wealthy Castro family, Doak painted the reredos of Mission San Juan Bautista in return for board and lodging.

Inland Parks

■ **Tear yourself away from the scintillating coastal scenery for even half a day and you will discover natural sights of no less beauty just a few miles inland, in the foothills of the Santa Cruz Mountains and in the untamed territory above Big Sur. ...■**

It is here, too, that you will encounter the southernmost strands of the coastal redwood trees; though slightly smaller than their counterparts further north, they are still wide enough and tall enough to be the highlight of any backcountry ramble.

Wet and wild Before setting out on any foot-powered exploration, however, give due respect to the region's notoriously changeable weather and remember that chilly fogs are a regular occurrence. It rains a lot, too, and if you get caught in a downpour, some solace might be found in the knowledge that the redwoods cannot grow without at least 40 inches of rainfall a year.

The region's major parks are described elsewhere, but many smaller state- and locally-run tracts make the wilderness accessible. There is a particularly strong grouping close to the hamlet of La Honda, on State Road 84, between Half Moon Bay and Santa Cruz. The best of the bunch here is **Portola State Park**, a deep, rugged canyon lined by redwoods and firs, with trails leading up to the chaparral-covered higher slopes, and others winding through the thicker vegetation carpeting the forest floor.

Camping and hiking Thirty miles south of Monterey, Highway-1 passes through part of the redwood forest making up a large section of Pfeiffer Big Sur State Park. There is an excellent programme of ranger-led walks and hikes here, and views of the surf-pounded coast which are better than those from the coastal highway.

The main base for camping in the Big Sur area, the park is rarely short of customers but the crowds can be left far behind on any number of lengthy hiking trails, some of which cross into the Ventana Wilderness, a region of oak-cloaked gorges, scrublands and even a few bristle-coned pines, which in turn feeds into the immense Los Padres National Forest.

The pick-your-own produce of the rich farmlands around Santa Cruz will improve the quality of the best-stocked picnic basket. Depending on season, large and juicy apples, strawberries or raspberries will be among the crops that can be stuffed into your bag for a very modest sum. Look for the roadside signs, or drop into the Santa Cruz Visitor Bureau (105 Cooper Street) for the free Country Crossroads brochure.

A ranger shows the attractions of a Monterey beach

Drive The Monterey area

See map on page 90.

From Monterey, drive 18 miles east on State Road 68 to Salinas.
Birthplace of writer John Steinbeck and the home of the California Rodeo, the farming town of **Salinas** is described on page 96.

Drive 15 miles north from Salinas on State Road 68 to San Juan Bautista.
With a fine collection of 19th-century adobe buildings, **San Juan Bautista** gives a taste of a bygone California (see page 100).

Drive west from San Juan Bautista on State Road 156, shortly turning north on to Highway-101, and after three miles turn west on State Road 129 for Watsonville.
Famed for its apples, strawberries and mushrooms, the small town of **Watsonville** has several streets of well-preserved Victorian homes.

Drive south from Watsonville, joining Highway-1 to reach Moss Landing.
A weather-beaten fishing village dwarfed by a gigantic power station, **Moss Landing** gives access to the **Elkhorn Slough Reserve**, where a four-mile boardwalk crosses wildlife-rich mudflats and salt marshes.

From Moss Landing, continue south on Highway-1 for 10 miles to Marina.
The sand dunes of **Marina** hold hardy shrubs and wild flowers, and hang-gliders soar overhead.

From Marina, continue south on Highway-1, turning west at Monterey for Pacific Grove to join the 17-Mile Scenic Drive toll road.
The **17-Mile Scenic Drive** loops through the **Monterey Peninsula**, passing the hilly peninsula's most photogenic sections.

Leave the 17-Mile Scenic Drive following signs for Carmel.
The pretty and affluent town of **Carmel** is described on page 92.
From Carmel, drive three miles north on Highway-1 to return to Monterey.

The 17-mile Scenic Drive

■ In his 1945 novel, *Cannery Row*, John Steinbeck described the mean streets of Monterey at a time when the town – set on an impressive bay – was the world's busiest sardine processing centre, annually canning 250,000 tons of the greasy creatures until stocks were fished to exhaustion. .....■

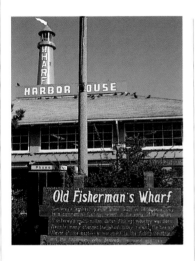

Fisherman's Wharf, Monterey

99

The former fish factories of Cannery Row are now occupied by lacklustre trinket shops aimed at the town's 3 million yearly visitors. Close by, Fisherman's Wharf, where ocean-going schooners once berthed, now sports seafood restaurants and snack bars, and is chiefly of appeal for the noisy sea lions basking around it.

History Make a short walk inland from these obvious tourist traps, however, and you will discover well-preserved evidence of Monterey's crucial role in California's past. Settled by the Spanish from 1770, Monterey became capital of Mexican California in 1822, and gave birth to California's first state government in 1849.
New England seafarers who settled in Monterey adapted much of the town's Spanish Colonial architecture to what became the 'Monterey-

style', typified by the 1835 **Larkin House** (corner of Jefferson Street and Calle Principal), a redwood-framed, porched adobe with an added second storey supporting a balcony. The antique-stuffed Larkin House, and many other landmark buildings, comprise **Monterey State Historic Park**, a seven-acre area spreading outwards from Custom House Plaza, near Fisherman's Wharf.
The **Monterey Path of History** is a two-mile walk covering more of historic Monterey, including the Royal Presidio Chapel (555 Church Street), in continuous use since 1795 and decorated with native American and Mexican folk art.

<< The three-day Monterey Pop Festival in 1967 was the first large outdoor rock festival. It starred Jimi Hendrix, Janis Joplin, and local psychedelic stalwarts, The Grateful Dead and Jefferson Airplane. >>

Anyone lured to Monterey by its links with John Steinbeck will find further literary links at the **Robert Louis Stevenson House** (530 Houston St), where the Scottish writer lived during the autumn of 1879 and is remembered by a roomful of mementoes.
One place that definitely should not be missed, despite having no historical significance, is the $40-million **Monterey Bay Aquarium** (886 Cannery Row), a state-of-the-art facility cogently displaying and describing the ecology and the creatures of the ocean – from anchovies to octopuses.

The creature washed up on a Santa Cruz beach in 1925 was nearly 50 feet long, with its body tapering to a fin-like appendage and with what looked like an elephant's foot sticking from its neck. One expert claimed the foul-smelling beast to be a plesiosaurus – a marine species believed to have become extinct 65 million years ago – and suggested it had been preserved by glacial ice. However, an official explanation held that the creature was a rare type of North Pacific whale, but this is still disputed.

▶ ▶ ▷ San Juan Bautista

Being an important stagecoach stop promised a rosy future for San Juan Bautista in the mid-1800s, but missing out on the railway a few years later condemned the town to stagnation – and enabled many of its earliest buildings to survive intact into the present.

The town, three miles east of Highway-101, began in 1797 with the largest of California's missions, **Mission San Juan Bautista**, in use ever since.

San Juan Bautista State Historic Park holds several 19th-century adobe structures, including the 1840 Castro House, the two-storey Plaza Hotel (opened as a one-storey bar in 1858 with an extra deck for travellers), and the Plaza Stables' stagecoach memorabilia.

▶ ▶ ▶ Santa Cruz

Scores of congenial bars and restaurants, 30 miles of beaches and a population spanning all income levels, age groups and political persuasions, make Santa

Cruz one of California's most instantly likeable towns.

When conservation got the upper hand over logging, Santa Cruz switched from being a timber-shifting centre to being a holiday resort, and from 1904 its major landmark has been the Boardwalk, a beachside amusement strip with a vintage carousel and a 1924 big dipper, but whose tacky charm barely warrants the steep entry fee. More interesting points of call are the Surfing Museum (in the lighthouse on W Cliff Drive); the Santa Cruz City Museum (1305 E Cliff Drive); and the work of the town's many artists on show at the Art Museum of Santa Cruz County (224 Church Street).

Do not expect to tour the Santa Cruz Mission: founded in 1791, it succumbed to disuse and earthquakes, and only a dull half-size model of it can be seen (at 126 High Street). And do not expect real mystery at the Mystery Spot, a patch of redwood forest on the town's northern edge with manipulated distortions of perspectives.

Coastal Parks

■ **Anyone drawn to the Central Coast by the stereotypical picture-postcard view of sundrenched Californian beachlife are in for a surprise. They will find more sea lions than surfers, an ocean that is usually too cold and too treacherous to swim in, and a shoreline that has more coves and tidal pools than tanning torsos. .....■**

Natural beauty Few of the protected parks and beaches strung almost the whole length of Highway- 1 will disappoint; and those mentioned below will reveal the Central Coast – whether with wildlife, geology or classic coastal views – at its natural best.

Eighteen miles north of Santa Cruz, **Ano Nuevo State Reserve** was set up in 1958 to protect the elephant seal, a sea mammal weighing up to three tons which had been hunted almost to extinction for its oil-rich blubber. Between December and March, thousands of the creatures waddle ashore here, the males to indulge in macho shows of strength prior to mating with 50 or so females. To join the large crowds of humans observing the noisy mating rituals, reserve a place on the three-hour ranger-led tour (tel: (415) 879 0227).

Just south of Carmel, surf crashes against six miles of oddly shaped granite bluffs protruding from **Point Lobos State Reserve**. Sharp eyesight might reveal sea otters feeding from the offshore kelp forest, while you are unlikely to miss the honking of sea lions from Sea Lion Rocks. Spare a thought for the Monterey cypress tree, a species unique to the area which sprouts on granite peaks only to spend its life tormented by ocean winds.

In Big Sur, turn off Highway-1 about two miles south of Julia Pfeiffer Burns State Park (not to be confused with the inland Pfeiffer Big Sur State Park), for **Pfeiffer Beach**, whose sands are sheltered by an extraordinary multi-coloured rock formation a short way off shore.

Follow Pfeiffer Beach south and you cross into **Andrew Molera State Park**, set around the lagoon marking the mouth of the Big Sur River. Sixteen miles of hiking trails run through the sycamores and maples lining the bank.

101

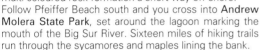

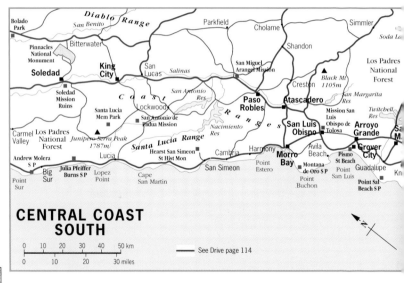

Oil platform off the California coast

Passing from the northern into the southern section of the Central Coast does not bring any immediate changes: crashing waves and jagged bluffs, and occasional quiet, secluded beaches, continue to dominate the view from Highway-1. As a man-made curtain-raiser to the region, however, it is hard to better Hearst Castle, a monument to incredible wealth – and incredible architectural aspirations – which sits dreamily on a mountain slope above the village of San Simeon, just beyond Big Sur.

San Luis Obispo grew up around one of the area's several Spanish missions and now draws most of its energy from a student population.

For picturesque settings, though, it is smaller towns like Cambria which rule the day, even if the numerous artists and artisans who have populated them are locked in permanent battle with the souvenir shops which are steadily encroaching into their serene, wooded valleys.

One of the richest and also one of the nicest looking towns in California, Santa Barbara's Mission-style architecture enhances what is already an enviable setting beside a palm-fringed beach, where the hedonistic traits of typical southern California beachlife announce themselves for the first time on the Central Coast.

Thirty miles along the coast, the region's southernmost town, Ventura (which is only just spared the sprawl of Los Angeles), sports another fine set of sands and an enjoyable historic quarter. It also provides an embarkation point for the Channel Islands National Park, volcanic islands free of human settlement which share this section of the ocean with oil rigs: a symbol of the Central Coast's struggle between commercial and ecological interests.

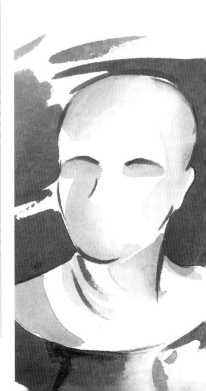

Forty-seven miles east of San Luis Obispo, at the junction of State roads 41 and 46 close to the village of Cholame, 24- year old teen idol James Dean was killed when his Porsche collided with another car on 30 September 1955. The actual site of the junction has changed since Dean's last journey, but a memorial to the actor and enduring symbol of disaffected youth, stands outside the Cholame post office.

Gifts, letters, jelly beans and other miscellanea accumulated during Ronald Reagan's eight-year stint as the world's most powerful man fill the spacious galleries of the Ronald Reagan Memorial Library, east of Ventura in the Simi Valley. If the library's hagiographic tone becomes overwhelming, try banging your head against the three-ton chunk of Berlin Wall which sits on the patio, beside Ronald and Nancy Reagan's intended grave site.

Old Worlde charm and rural calm: Cambria

▶ ▷ ▷ Cambria

Great fun to explore despite its contrived Olde Worlde atmosphere and preponderance of half-timbered gift shops, Cambria lies about nine miles south of Hearst Castle and splits its time between pandering to tourists and providing the rural serenity that has inspired a community of artists, whose work can be seen in a dozen browse-worthy galleries.

Friendly and affordable restaurants are also a feature of the pine-shrouded town, and culinary overindulgence can be remedied by a lengthy stroll along the town's magnificent beaches: a scene of picturesque coves, broad sands, a large sea otter refuge, and seals sharing waves with surfers.

Just outside Cambria, Nit Wit Ridge (on Hillcrest Drive) provides an anarchic counterpoint to Hearst Castle. Beginning life in 1928 as a one-room shack, generous applications of cement, sea shells, glass, old car parts and other rubbish, turned the dwelling into a wild and unwieldy mansion which, at the time of writing, was still lived in by its 90-year old creator.

▷ ▷ ▷ Carpinteria

Named by Spanish arrivals impressed with the woodworking skills of the local Chumash Indians, Carpinteria is a quiet coastal town between Ventura and Santa Barbara worth a pause for **Carpinteria State Beach**, beckoning sands and – thanks to an offshore reef – some of the safest swimming waters to be found along the entire coast.

▷ ▷ ▷ Harmony

Blink and you will miss Harmony, a minuscule privately owned town just inland from Cambria. Most of its 20-strong population are glass-blowers, potters or jewellery-makers, who sell their wares from roadside shops. In the fields around Harmony, Arabian horses are bred and trained on ranches owned by the Hearst family.

▷▷▷ King City

There is a very worthwhile detour to be made from Highway-1 along the Nacimiento-Fergusson Road, which cuts dramatically across Plaskett Ridge in the Santa Lucia Mountains towards King City, a dot-on-the-map community on Highway-101.

Twenty miles southwest of King City stands **Mission San Antonia de Padua**, one of the most isolated and most evocative of the Californian missions. Authentic restoration of the buildings aids appreciation of the mission life-style, but it is the secluded setting, in a quiet river valley, that really makes the place special. Oddly, although the mission sits miles from any built-up area, it is inside the Fort Hunter-Liggett military base and visitors have to go through a security check at the gates.

▶▷▷ Morro Bay

Some agreeable seafood restaurants cook up the daily catch of the fishing fleet in Morro Bay, a moderately interesting coastal town whose best feature is the volcanic hunk of Morro Rock, a near-vertical slab rising to 576 feet little more than a pebble's throw off shore, the last visible link in a chain of nine volcanic rocks between here and San Luis Obispo, nine miles south.

Morro Rock is a protected nesting ground for peregrine falcons and climbing it – once a popular local pastime – is prohibited. You can, however, climb the dunes of **Morro Sand Spit**, which wraps a sheltering arm around the bay and is reached by the 'Clam Taxi' ferry.

Just south of the town, Morro Bay State Park stretches over the inland hills and around the dead-flat coastal marshlands, which are one of the country's foremost birdwatching spots, home to an abundance of great blue herons. The ecological significance of the area is described in detail at the **Museum of Natural History**, opposite the park's entrance.

The imposing, volcanic Morro Rock

On more than one occasion, guards at the Fort Hunter-Ligget military base have drawn their weapons only to see the suspected intruder vanish before their eyes. The apparition is thought to be the ghost of a headless Indian woman who roams the grounds of Mission San Antonia de Padua on horseback searching for her head, which her furious husband tore from her body as a punishment for her infidelity.

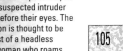

105

■ **Whether you are looking for palm-fringed beaches covered with bronzing flesh or want to seek out secluded coves and spend hours discovering the secret life of the tidal pool, the southern section of the Central Coast has something to suit your needs. .....■**

Albacore, salmon and rock cod are among the species that make the Central Coast a happy hunting ground for anglers. Fishing piers are plentiful and rare is the coastal town that does not also offer guided fishing trips or run specialist sportsfishing excursions to do battle with marlin. Prices for guided trips start at around $25 per day.

North–south split Note that the coast here splits into two distinct halves. North of Point Conception (between San Luis Obispo and Santa Barbara) the predominantly rocky coast faces west, and fogs are prone to roll in off the ocean and fill the inland valleys. South of Point Conception, the coast faces south, and the beaches are generally better suited to sunbathing and surfing.

After sampling the opulence of the multi-millionaire's castle (see page 109), the William Randolph Hearst Memorial State Beach, close to San Simeon, is the ideal spot to rediscover life's simpler pleasures: a rustic fishing pier juts out from the quiet sands, which are fringed by eucalyptus trees and shaded picnic tables.

To the north The 1874 Piedras Blancas Lighthouse marks the edge of Big Sur (see page 92) and the start of the northern section of the Central Coast. A few miles in the other direction, the sands of San Simeon State Beach are broad but busy, especially so during the summer when the campsite is usually fully occupied.

Heading south Six miles beyond Morro Bay (see page 105), the Estero Bay area has a trio of rewarding stops. Swimming is feasible at peaceful Morro Strand State Beach (though there are no lifeguards), and the Los

Tranquil beaches lie near Morro Bay

Osas Oaks State Reserve protects one of the longest surviving strands of handsome coastal oaks.

The biggest natural draw around Estero Bay, however, is Montano de Oro State Park, whose Spanish name means 'Mountain of Gold', and derives from a springtime bloom of wild flowers which turn the park's hillsides into a bright carpet of yellows and oranges.

The park's 8,000 acres encompass sandy beaches, tidal pools and surf-pounded cliffs – around which seals, sea lions and sea otters are commonly sighted – and reach inland to racoon-infested river canyons, through which deer descend to spend the evening grazing on the coastal plain. Several trails snake through the most scenic sections of the park, and a four-mile loop trail climbs Valencia Point, a trek repaid by a stirring view of the coast – fogs permitting.

With a livelier time in mind Head for Avila Beach, 10 miles west of San Luis Obispo, whose beachside boardwalk is lined with bars and snackstands, where the waves are challenged by scores of surfers and where you will find the rowdiest nightlife for miles.

A lot of the revellers in Avila Beach are holiday-making teenagers who leave their parents in Pismo, a fairly dull coastal town a few miles south along Highway-101. Pismo State Beach is worth a look though, and is a place well known to Californians for its Pismo clams, a succulent crustacean now almost hunted out of existence.

Magnificent sand dunes These are another feature of Pismo State Beach and they reach southwards, almost obliterating the diminutive community of Oceano, into the 10-mile long **Nipomo Dunes Preserve**. Propelled by wind and wave action, the dunes are ever moving and belie their forlorn appearance by performing an important ecological service, allowing numerous species of coarse vegetation to thrive, and providing a habitat for brown pelicans and California least terns among other creatures. The tallest dune reaches almost 500 feet high, but the most famous dune is the one where movie-maker Cecil B de Mille buried the set of his 1923 film, *The Ten Commandments*, four-ton plaster sphinxes and all. Since 1990, excavation has been underway in an attempt to salvage the evidence of one of Hollywood's greatest cinematic excesses.

The southern edge of the preserve is marked by Point Sal, an imposing headland best admired by scrambling down the cliff wall of the usually empty Point Sal State Beach.

A set of state beaches occupies the approaches to Santa Barbara. Thirty miles north of the town, Gaviota State Beach spreads across either side of Highway-101 and is enticing less for its sands than its trail inland, winding to Gaviota Hot Springs. Palm-lined Refugio State Beach, 12 miles ahead, is a nicer place to catch some rays, and is linked by foot and bike paths to El Capitan State Beach, where seals and sea lions bask offshore alongside surfers.

Five islands off the coast between Ventura and Santa Barbara comprise the Channel Islands National Park, whose unique plant- and bird-life is staging a comeback after being devastated by California's first white settlers, who trampled over the islands hunting sea lions and seals. The islands have no tourist facilities and can be explored only on marked hiking trails. Trips are run by the Nature Conservancy, based on Stearn's Wharf in Santa Barbara (tel: (805) 962 9111), and from Spinnaker Drive in Ventura (see page 115).

▶ ▷ ▷ Ojai

With its tennis courts, golf courses and luxury hillside homes, Ojai (pronounced 'O-hi') has all the trappings of a rich country retreat but enjoys a more enduring reputation as a place where the mystically minded seek enlightenment.

The idyllic crescent-shaped valley which the town occupies has long promised a spiritual Shangri-La (and did indeed provide the setting for Shangri La in the 1937 film, *Lost Horizon*). The well-stocked library of the Krishnamurti Foundation (1130 MacAndrew Road)

Comfort and wealth are features of life in Ojai

remembers an Indian mystic who lectured here in the 1920s, while the similarly Eastern-influenced **Krotona Institute of Theosophy** (on Krotona Hill), also has a library packed with esoteric tomes and landscaped grounds affording exquisite views of the valley's orange and avocado groves, and the mountains which enclose the town.

Less ethereal matters are dealt with by the Ojai Valley Historical Museum (109 S Montgomery Street), filling a former fire station with an entertaining clutter.

▶ ▶ ▷ San Luis Obispo

The 1772 Mission **San Luis Obispo de Tolosa** sits at the heart of likeable San Luis Obispo, 12 miles from the coast but within easy striking distance of Hearst Castle. If you are only passing through, try to do so on a Thursday evening, when the **Farmer's Market** brings the whole town to Higuera Street to feast on barbecued offerings.

The mission is not the most striking in California, but the historic plaza on which it stands – split by a river creek and filled with lunchtime picnickers – also holds the **County Historical Museum** (969 Monterey Street), where the community's past is put on show, and the Art Center (1020 Broad Street), determined to raise the profile of local artists.

Dominated today by the agricultural students of nearby Cal Poly, often gathered around the art deco Fremont Theater (on Santa Rosa Street), the San Luis Obispo of the late 1800s housed a large Chinese community employed in railway construction: the Ah Louis Store (800 Palm Street) is a rare reminder of their presence.

In 1925, a San Luis Obispo hotel owner renamed his property, at 2223 Monterey Street, the 'Milestone Motel', thereby creating the world's first motel. As the affordable, mass-produced automobile changed the travel habits of millions, motels sprang up beside every busy road junction and along the main approach routes to towns, becoming the most popular form of budget accommodation for Americans on the move.

Impossible to miss, beside Highway-101, San Luis Obispo's shocking pink Madonna Inn offers food and lodging to anyone keen to put their tolerance of kitsch excesses to the test: the waterfall flushing the Coffee Shop's gents' urinal is just the appetiser for 100 individually themed rooms.

Hearst Castle

■   **In California, only Disneyland attracts more visitors than Hearst Castle, the former part-time home of publishing mogul William Randolph Hearst. Set on a hilltop above the village of San Simeon, Hearst Castle was built (but never officially completed) at an estimated cost, at today's prices, of $400 million. ....■**

Given the *San Francisco Examiner* by his rich father in 1887, Hearst went on to head a media empire that spanned newspapers, magazines, radio stations and film studios. Aside from becoming phenomenally wealthy, with one in four Americans reading his newspapers, Hearst also had incredible power to influence: most notoriously, he fanned the nationalistic fervour which led to the Spanish-American War in 1898.

After work began on Hearst Castle in 1919, architect Julia Morgan spent the next 28 years struggling with Hearst's constantly changing ideas and the five-ton wagonloads of Flemish tapestries, French fireplaces, Italian ceilings, Persian carpets, candelabras and coats-of-arms, which Hearst collected from the great homes of Europe. Visiting the castle, it is impossible not to be struck by the incongruity of a would-be medieval palace sprouting on the rugged slopes of a Californian coastal mountain, or be less than awed by the sheer scale and extravagance of the place.

It is also easy to imagine the likes of Charlie Chaplin, Greta Garbo and Clark Gable (friends of Hearst's long-time companion, actress Marion Davies) lurking amid the million-dollar classical statuary or admiring the lions and cheetahs which once roamed the grounds, enclosed in the world's largest privately owned zoo.

109

Luxury and eclectic style at Hearst Castle

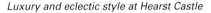

Plagued in his later years by debts and astronomic tax bills, Hearst died in 1951 (10 years after his life had been the subject of Orson Welles' film Citizen Kane), and six years later the Hearst family donated the castle to the state in return for a $50 million tax write-off.

Three separate 90-minute guided tours visit different sections of the castle, while a fourth tour concentrates on the lavish gardens. All tours begin from the visitors centre beside Highway-1. Reservations are recommended, especially in summer: call (800 444 PARKS).

■ **Anticipating monumental buildings stuffed with historic and religious treasures, many visiting Europeans are underwhelmed by California's Spanish missions, 21 of which (plus five smaller branch missions, or *asistencia*) were established between 1769 and 1823. ....■**

Historical significance Beginning at San Diego in the south and finishing with Sonoma in the north, the missions (each one a day's horse-ride from the next) played a crucial role in the development of the state – but cathedrals they are not, and you should be selective about which ones you visit if you want to discover more than a few dusty ruins beside the highway.

The southern portion of the Central Coast has some of the better examples: Mission Santa Barbara maintains a majestic presence in the town which grew around it; Mission San Antonio de Padua, near King City, survives in moody isolation; and Mission La Purisma Concepcion, near Lompoc, is so comprehensively re-created that you cannot fail to leave it without gaining some insights into the trials and tribulations of the mission times.

Origins The missions began when Spanish possession of what was then undeveloped Alta (or Upper) California was perceived as being under threat from Russia, active to the north, and the European settlers becoming established on North America's east coast.

The Spanish king despatched a missionary party – the Sacred Expedition, led by Father Junípero Serra – to establish a series of missions across the territory. Their intention was to convert the indigenous population to Christianity while gaining their loyalty in any future colonial conflict; several missions were constructed side by side with a presidio – or fort – into which Spanish troops were barracked.

Effects on the native people Besides learning the rudiments of Spanish, the Indians were supposedly taught skills such as farming, building, blacksmithery, weaving and wine-making, but in reality their labour was exploited to further the wealth and self-sufficiency of the missions, many of which had vast land holdings and many heads of cattle.

Few solid facts of mission life have been recorded, although reports of torture and other abuses of the neophytes (as the mission Indians were known) have greatly tarnished the benevolent façade which the Spanish sought to maintain.

It is certainly true that many native Americans resisted the lure of beads and brightly coloured clothes, used to tempt them into the missions, and in some cases they attacked the mission buildings.

Eventually, the mission system all but destroyed California's native cultures and caused the death of many thousands (thought to be half the indigenous

The first in line: San Diego Mission

Mission Santa Barbara is one of the best examples of surviving missions in California

population) through contact with European diseases, such as measles, to which native Americans lacked immunity.

Some 88,000 Indians had been baptised by the time ownership of California switched to Mexico and the missions underwent secularisation at the behest of the *Californios* (California-born people of Spanish or Mexican descent).

In theory, the neophytes were then allowed to live free, independent lives but in fact many became the servants of the *Californios*, who grew rich by buying and cultivating the former mission land.

Although the mission churches were usually maintained to serve as parish churches, other mission buildings – such as the workshops, priests' living quarters, and the outhouses where the neophytes slept – were put to general public use, and during the early years of US rule in California, some were functioning as saloons and hotels.

The mission buildings Always simple structures of tiled roofs and stuccoed adobe lightly decorated with Moorish designs, the missions endured earthquakes as well as decades of neglect, and not until 1903 was there any concerted effort to protect and restore their buildings.

All the missions are open to the public and each has a museum storing at least a few original objects, some still being used by the Franciscan order of monks. Comparatively few original features still remain, but the small mission chapels, often bathed in candlelight and decorated by Indian-painted frescos, are charged with atmosphere.

Strolling the grounds can be rewarding, too, both for the well-kept gardens and for the sombre feelings evoked by the cemeteries, where thousands of neophytes lie in unmarked graves beside ostentatious markers to their Spanish masters.

Walk A tour around Santa Barbara

Begin at the County Courthouse, 1100 Anacapa Street.
The architecturally magnificent **County Courthouse** is described on page 113.

Walk southeast from the County Courthouse along Santa Barbara Street, turning right into Cañon Perdido for El Presidio State Historic Park.
Several buildings form the **El Presidio State Historic Park**: on the north side of Cañon Perdido, **the El Presidio Chapel** is a detailed re–creation of a mission-era Spanish chapel; and across the street, the 1788 **El Cuartel** adobe is the second-oldest surviving building in California.

Return to Santa Barbara Street, walking one block southeast to De La Guerra Street for the Historical Museum.
The displays of the **Historical Museum** fill the gap between Santa Barbara's Spanish origins and its emergence as an affluent US town.

Walk southwest along De La Guerra Street, turning right into State Street and continuing to the Museum of Art.
On the corner with Anapamu Street, the **Museum of Art** spreads over three floors and features many major American and European names.

Santa Barbara County Courthouse

From the Art Museum, walk two blocks northeast on Anapamu street to return to the County Courthouse.

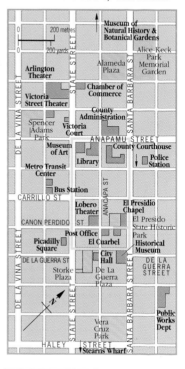

<< Heritage celebrations make the largest and most enjoyable festivals along the southern section of the Central Coast. The biggest bash is Santa Barbara's week-long Old Spanish Days held in August; the following month, Solvang remembers its Scandinavian founders with the traditional events of Danish Days; while the strangest annual spectacle takes place 16 miles north of San Luis Obispo in the otherwise unexciting Atascadero, where September Mud Olympics honour the town's Spanish name – which means 'muddy place'. >>

▶ ▶ ▶ Santa Barbara

A wealthy and conservative but appealingly sybaritic community, Santa Barbara's low-lying red roofs poke through thickly wooded green hillsides, the town having rebuilt itself in the image of California's missions after being flattened by an earthquake in 1925.

Ironically, **Mission Santa Barbara** (2201 Laguna Street), overlooking the town, is architecturally far grander than the average mission, acquiring classically influenced twin towers and columns in 1820. Restored rooms and a museum record the missions's heyday, and there is an atmospheric cemetery holding the unmarked remains of 4,000 Chumash Indians.

Near by, the **Museum of Natural History** (2599 Puesta del Sol Road) provides a thorough background on the Chumash tribe, and five miles of walking trails weave around diverse native Californian vegetation at the **Botanical Gardens** (1212 Mission Canyon Road).

Other than the mission, Santa Barbara's historical sights are concentrated in the downtown area. The jewel among them is the 1929 **County Courthouse** (1100 Anacapa Street), whose exaggerated Mission-style architecture confirms the look Santa Barbara adopted after the 1925 earthquake. Fine Tunisian tilework and

Founded by Danes in 1911, Solvang's thatched roofs, wooden storks and pseudo-windmills are intended to convince tourists that a piece of Denmark has been transported to California. Any Dane visiting today would struggle to hold back the laughter, but the village does make an enjoyable interlude between Santa Barbara and San Luis Obispo, if only to discover that Danish pastries prepared to traditional recipes are much nicer than the sugar-saturated imitations sold elsewhere in the US.

Getting together on Steams Wharf

some outstanding murals are among the courthouse's decorative features; take the elevator to the top of the **El Mirador bell-tower** for a view over the town. Within a few strides stand a couple of 18th-century adobe buildings and the State Historic Park (123 E Cañon Perdido Street), where several Spanish military buildings are being renovated; the **Historical Museum** (136 East De La Guerra) is, at present, a more rewarding call.

A mile west of Downtown, joggers and skaters are a constant sight beside the broad and inviting Santa Barbara beaches, which centre on the 19th-century Stearns Wharf, where gift shops and seafood eateries are joined by the Nature Conservancy, dispensing literature on the Channel Islands National Park.

Twelve miles east of Ventura, Santa Paula's Unocal Museum of Oil explains Californian oil production with the aid of computer simulations and a working model of an oil rig. There is little, though to explain why offshore drilling is among the state's most sensitive topics, not least in Santa Barbara, where an offshore spill in 1969 devastated local wildlife.

Drive The Santa Ynez Valley

The reconstructed version of Mission La Purisma Concepcion

See map on pages 102–3.

From Santa Barbara, drive 10 miles north on State Road 154, turning right along the twisting Painted Cave Road for the Chumash Painted Cave.
Brilliantly-coloured abstract designs, dating from ad1000 and used in rituals by the Chumash Indians, can be glimpsed through the screen covering the entrance to the **Chumash Painted Cave**.

Return to State Road 154 and continue north, crossing the San Marcos Pass and descending into the Santa Ynez Valley; after 26 miles turn left on to State Road 256 for Santa Ynez.
In Santa Ynez, the **Valley Historical Society Museum** and the **Parks-Jane Carriageway House** record the 19th-century settlement of the valley. On the town's periphery, the **Gainey Vineyard** and the **Santa Ynez Winery** offer a chance to sample the wines which have made the valley famous among California's discerning wine drinkers.

From Santa Ynez, continue for three miles on State Road 256 to Solvang.
The Danish features of **Solvang** are described on page 113.

From Solvang, drive 10 miles north on Ballard Canyon Road, passing the hamlet of Ballard, for Los Olivos.

In 1975, the **Firestone Vineyard** in Los Olivos was the first to use local grapes in the wine-making process; sitting amid 275 acres of vines, the winery is open for tours.

From Los Olivos, drive three miles north on State Road 154 and turn south on to Highway- 101, continuing for six miles to Buellton.
Surrounded by thoroughbred- horse farms, Buellton's **Vega Vineyards** offer wine tastings and picnics.

Leave Buellton on State Road 256, driving west for 17 miles to Mission La Purisima Concepcion.
Founded in 1787, **Mission La Purisma Concepcion's** original buildings have long been destroyed, but detailed reconstructions make this the most authentic looking mission site in the state.

From the mission, join Highway-1 and drive 26 miles east to the junction with Highway-101, then taking the side road to Las Cruces Hot Springs.
Comprising two geothermal springs at the end of a short foot-trail, **Las Cruces Hot Springs** are described on page 115.

Continue east on Highway-101, passing Refugio and El Capitan state beaches (see page 107), on the 35-mile drive back to Santa Barbara.

▶ ▶ ▶ Ventura

Mainly concerned with farming and industry, and blighted by a large oil refinery, Ventura, 30 miles south of Santa Barbara, does not at first seem to have a lot in its favour. The outlook is immeasurably improved once you locate the town's two-mile long beach.

There is more to enjoy on foot in the historic area of Old San Buenaventura, which surrounds the Spanish mission from which the town adapted its name. Founded in 1782 and completed in 1809, the small church of **Mission San Buenaventura** (211 E Main Street) is all that survives of the mission's buildings, described in a small museum, while the once famous 17-acre gardens now stand buried beneath gift shops.

Close to the mission, a productive archaeological dig has yielded valuable finds from the time of Spanish settlement, and also unearthed native American relics dated to 1600BC, some of which are in the **Albinger Archaeological Museum** (113 E Main Street).

A few doors along, the **Ventura County Museum of History and Art** (100 E Main Street), documents the diverse nationalities who settled the region in the late 19th century, and charts the discovery of oil deposits.

Elsewhere in Ventura, **Olivas Adobe Historical Park** (4200 Olivas Park Drive) holds a two-storey adobe house, a prime example of the Monterey-style prevalent in California during the mid-1800s and packed with furnishings typical of the period, while the grandiose columns of the **Ventura County Courthouse** (501 Poli Street) highlight a later period's obsession with neo-classical architecture.

The Spanish Mission, San Buenaventura

Mineral-rich hot springs crop up fairly often throughout the Central Coast, some of which have been adopted by commercial spa resorts. One place to see springs as nature intended them is at Las Cruces Hot Springs, close to the junction of Highway-101 and Highway-1, four miles north of Gaviota. From the car-park, a trail leads to two pools of water fresh from the bowels of the earth: the first is fairly cool, while the second is warm and ideal for a dip.

115

A good reason to be in Ventura is for the opportunity to visit the Channel Islands National Park, 15 miles offshore. The Visitors Center (1901 Spinnaker Drive) provides background on the islands, and Island Packers (1867 Spinnaker Drive) run boat trips to them.

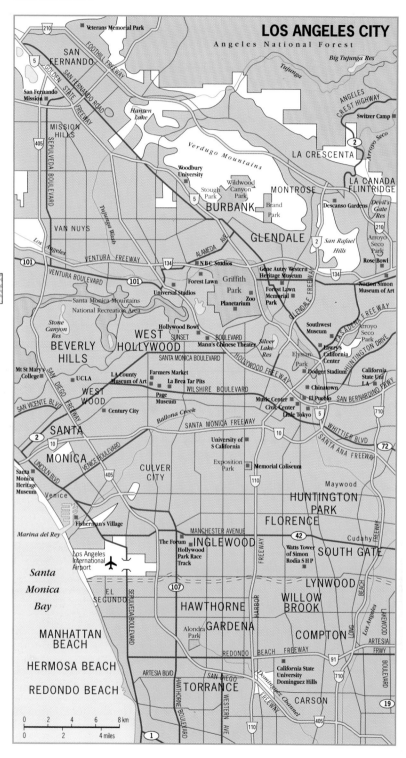

LOS ANGELES CITY

Simultaneously one of the most privileged and one of the most dangerous cities in America, Los Angeles is a mad metropolis of contradictions and extremes.

In LA, the finest of fine art collections are surrounded by garish billboards; image-conscious trendies pose in nightclubs within spitting distance of Skid Row's homeless; and celebrity-filled movie premières vie with gang wars and inter-ethnic feuding for TV attention.

The show goes on The entertainment industry, which has brought LA more wealth than it knows what to do with and a population packed with household names, has also bred a self-absorbed, façade-obsessed city that frequently strives to turn itself into a make-believe fantasy land at odds with the reality around it.

For every fat cat living it up in the Hollywood Hills, there are thousands enduring grinding poverty in LA's less salubrious areas, and discontent among the city's dispossessed recently reached boiling point.

At the same time, 99 per cent of visitors to LA can enjoy the fabulous beaches, the madcap architecture, the excellent museums, and generally soak up the sun-kissed LA life-style without ever exposing themselves to anything more dangerous than exceeding their credit limit in one of the world's greatest consumer paradises.

Around the skyscrapers of Downtown, the historic El Pueblo de Los Angeles, Chinatown and Little Tokyo sit at the core of this enormous city. To the east of Downtown, East LA occupies miles of urban sprawl and houses the bulk of LA's vast Latino population.

LA, as most visitors envisage it, stretches 16 miles west from Downtown, taking in Hollywood, Beverly Hills and Westwood before reaching the coast at Santa Monica.

South of Santa Monica, Venice Beach, Manhattan Beach, Hermosa Beach and Redondo Beach occupy the low-lying land that soon rises into the tall bluffs of the Palos Verdes peninsula, LA's southwestern extremity.

East of Palos Verdes, San Pedro and Long Beach sit on the LA harbour, south of Downtown and separated from it by the run-down and dangerous South Central LA.

The sun sets over Santa Monica

LOS ANGELES

No designer has arrived on the world scene until he or she has an outlet on Beverly Hills' Rodeo Drive, between Santa Monica and Wilshire boulevards.Everything here carries a prized name – Cartier, Hermes and Gucci just three of many – at a price few can afford.

Guided tours are a good way to get initial bearings of LA For general sightseeing and stars' homes, contact Gray Line (tel: (800) 538 5050) or Starline (tel: (800) 463 3131). The Los Angeles Conservancy (tel: (213 623-CITY) offers walking tours of historical areas; Grave Line Tours (tel: (310) 392 5501) run a hearse ride around the sites of Hollywood scandals; and Gondola Getaway (tel: (310) 433 9595) offers gondola rides around the waterways of Long Beach.

▶ ▶ ▷ **Beverly Hills**
When you see rows of open-topped Rolls-Royces waiting at traffic lights and immaculately groomed poodles being exercised along thoroughly scrubbed pavements, then you know you are in Beverly Hills.
From the 1920s, LA's movie idols followed the lead of Douglas Fairbanks and Mary Pickford and colonised the hills and canyons above Hollywood, soon making Beverly Hills a byword for glamour and mind-boggling wealth.
The stately and secluded hillside homes of the rich and famous still fill Beverly Hills, although it is around the designer-label stores on Rodeo Drive that you are most likely to spot the 'big names', even though today's Beverly Hills residents (whose average yearly income of $100,000 is four times the national average) are as likely to be plastic surgeons as film stars.

▶ ▷ ▷ **Century City**
On the one-time backlot of 20th Century-Fox studios, the metal and glass high-rise towers of Century City form LA's most anodyne district. The sterile mood is only eased by the cinemas and theatres of the ABC Entertainment Center, and the Century City Shopping Center – and the chance to peek at the New York street set that featured in the 1960s film, *Hello Dolly!*

▶ ▶ ▷ **Chinatown**
Pagoda-shaped buildings and dozens of ornamental fire-breathing dragons were among the things LA's sizeable Chinese community acquired when it was relocated to present-day Chinatown in the 1930s to make way for the building of Union Station. See the live poultry shops, sniff the aromatic herbs, and come back at night when the restaurants are at their liveliest and the neon decorations glow, and you will find one of LA's major ethnic communities at its least Americanised. (See also pages 119–20).

Chinatown has retained a distinct identity

■ **A vibrant (and sometimes violent) pot-pourri of races, religions, languages and cultures, Angelenos are a much more ethnically varied bunch than the well-off Anglo-American stereotype would seem to suggest.** .....■

From Mexico Though visible all over LA, the vast majority of the city's 2.5 million Hispanic residents – most of whom are Mexican – live in East LA, the third largest Mexican community in the world. For a taste of local life, stroll round the exotic pet shops and botanicas (supplying the implements of the voodoo-like *Santeria*) of Brooklyn Avenue, and drop into the lively El Mercado indoor market at 3425 E First Street.

From Asia Many Chinese rail labourers settled in LA around the turn of the century. To make way for Union Station in the 1930s, the original Chinatown was moved a short distance north to the present Chinatown (see page 118) along North Broadway. Crowds spill ceaselessly around the district's restaurants and shopping plazas, although many Chinese have moved from Chinatown to suburban life in the San Gabriel Valley.

LA's Japanese community also has a long history but was devastated in 1942 when almost all its members were forced into internment camps for the duration of the war. Now numbering 100,000 and probably the city's most prosperous ethnic group, Japanese LA's public face is within the traditional-Japanese-meets-modern-American architecture of Little Tokyo, where the Nisei Festival takes place each August and where the Japanese-American Cultural Center displays art and historical items.

Of the city's less populous Asian communities, many brightly painted buildings decorate the expanding Koreatown, based on Normandie Avenue, just south of Wilshire Boulevard; Vietnamese enclaves can be found within Chinatown and in Westchester; and a large Cambodian community is centred on Long Beach's Anaheim Street.

From Europe Armenians, Russians and Hungarians are evident around the Fairfax section of Wilshire Boulevard, also the heart of the US's second-largest Jewish community, and many Greeks have settled in the area around St Sophia's Greek Orthodox Church, close to Koreatown.

From Africa Within the depressed sprawl of South Central LA, the bulk of the city's African-American population is notoriously terrorised by violent gang warfare.

Less well known are the area's many successful community projects, and another positive aspect of South Central Los Angeles life has been the worldwide success of its rap musicians (see pages 132–3).

The precise American-English meanings of the terms Chicano, Latino and Hispanic have become blurred with use (and misuse) and you are likely to hear any one of them used to describe people or a person of Latin American origin or descent. Derived from the Aztec name for Mexico, 'Chicano' was first adopted by some US citizens of Mexican origin during a 1970s political movement. Literally, 'Hispanic' means 'derived from the Spanish', although many so-called Hispanics are actually of Indian blood. A more accurate term is 'Latino', which refers to all people of Latin American origin.

119

El Pueblo

■ **Hard to believe it may be, but the origins of unrelentingly modern LA go back to 1781 and a farming community growing food for California's Spanish missions. The 44-strong group of original settlers – a mix of Indians, blacks, Spanish, mestizos and mulattos – relocated twice before basing themselves close to what is now El Pueblo State Historic Park, on the northern edge of Downtown. .....■**

The Old Plaza Funded in part by donations of cattle and whisky, work on the **Plaza Church**, on Main Street facing the **Old Plaza**, commenced in 1818 but was not finished until 40 years later. Greatly modified over the decades, the church's plain exterior hides an interior rich with paintings and sacraments of the Catholic faith. Also by the Old Plaza, the Italianate **Pico House** was the finest hotel south of San Francisco when it opened in 1870. The hotel was financed by LA's last Mexican mayor, Pio Pico, who, so the story goes, sat on a bench outside the building (currently being transformed into a French restaurant) and wept after failing to meet the $30,000 mortgage repayments.

No trace remains of LA's time as one of the West's most lawless towns – when cockfights were common along its shabby streets, and blood ran as freely as alcohol in its saloons – through the early days of US rule.

Olvera Street Running off the Old Plaza, Olvera Street was once the scene of much of the carnage. It has earned an honest living since the 1930s, however, as a would-be Mexican street market, where south-of-the-border arts and crafts are sold, and Mexican food is consumed from hole-in-the-wall cafés.

Once uncharitably described as 'the first Disneyland', Olvera Street is none the less enjoyable to stroll along, and at no 10 enough remains of the 1818 **Avila Adobe** to justify its claim as the oldest house in LA – inside, reconstructed fittings suggest the local life-styles as they were in the 1840s.

Film show To learn more about El Pueblo, watch the free film show in the information centre on Olvera Street, or join the walking tour from the Visitor Information Center, Sepulveda House, 622 N Main Street, facing the Old Plaza.

A street market in El Pueblo State Historic Park

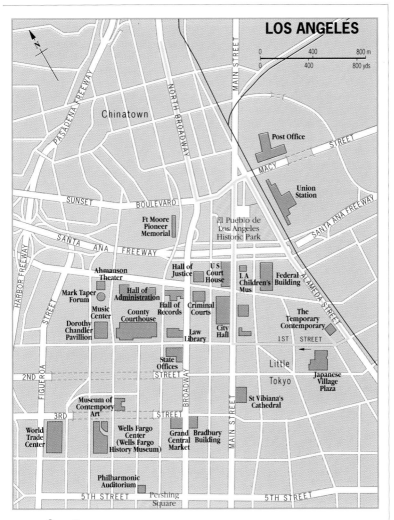

LOS ANGELES

Chinatown

Post Office

Union Station

Ft Moore Pioneer Memorial

El Pueblo de Los Angeles Historic Park

Ahmanson Theater

Hall of Justice

U S Court House

LA Children's Mus

Federal Building

Mark Taper Forum

Hall of Administration

Music Center

County Courthouse

Hall of Records

Criminal Courts

The Temporary Contemporary

Dorothy Chandler Pavillion

Law Library

City Hall

1ST STREET

State Offices

Little

Tokyo

Japanese Village Plaza

Museum of Contemporary Art

St Vibiana's Cathedral

World Trade Center

Wells Fargo Center (Wells Fargo History Museum)

Grand Central Market

Bradbury Building

Philharmonic Auditorium

5TH STREET

Pershing Square

5TH STREET

Walk Downtown sights of Los Angeles

From the Japanese Village Plaza Mall go west along First Street, turning into Main Street for City Hall.
The observation level of the 1928 **City Hall** is a great place for views across LA, if the smog allows.

Go north along Main Street for El Pueblo de Los Angeles (see page 120). Turn left into Macy Street then right into Broadway for Chinatown. From El Pueblo; cross Alameda Street for Union Station.

Union Station has welcomed rail passengers to LA since 1939.

Walk south along Alameda Street, turn right on to First Street and right again along Central Avenue for the Temporary Contemporary.
The **Temporary Contemporary** is a former police garage filled with oversized modern-art works.

Return to First Street and turn right for Japanese Village Plaza Mall.

■ **It may lack the tradition of European cities, but when it comes to architecture LA is no slouch. From playful gingerbread homes of the early 1900s to textbook examples of modernism, the city is filled with ingenuously designed buildings which, in some cases, are the finest examples of their kind.....■**

As famous architects dotted the city with their masterworks and mistakes, one of LA's most enduring structures was being painstakingly assembled by an unknown tilesetter called Simon Rodia. Between 1921 and 1954, Rodia's 100-foot high Watts Towers (1765 E 107th Street, Watts) evolved from bedsteads, bottletops and 70,000 shells. Working entirely alone and never giving any explanation for his creation, Rodia was to die in obscurity. Public support has, however, helped the towers survive several demolition threats, and recently restored, they remain as majestic and as mysterious as ever.

LA architecture, Downtown style

Early structures LA's earliest buildings were flat-roofed, single-storey adobe (or mud-brick) structures. The heavily restored 1818 Avila Adobe in El Pueblo de Los Angeles is one example, though a broader sense of the style is given by Rancho Los Cerritos and Rancho Los Alamitos in Long Beach.

Many of the settlers from the eastern US who arrived in LA at the start of the 20th century brought with them a liking for elaborate ornamentation. The desirable residences of the time were groups of richly decorative Queen Anne and Eastlake homes; the more turrets and twirls such a wood-built dwelling had, the more desirable it was. A group of handsome survivors can be seen on **Carrol Avenue**, just west of Downtown.

California Bungalows Plainer wooden houses – the city's first low-cost urban housing – sprang up in a medley of styles but, characterised by balconies, porches and overhanging roofs, they became collectively known as California Bungalows. An expensive adaptation of the California Bungalow appeared in the suburb of Pasadena. Here, the firm of Greene & Greene took their inspiration from England's arts and crafts movement and made their definitive statement with the 1908 **Gamble House** (see page 159), where highly polished teak emphasises the wood's natural pattern, joints are exposed and exaggerated, and every piece of furniture – from the tables and chairs to the lampshades – originated on the Greene & Greene drawing-board.

Plentiful though the California Bungalows in their various guises were, it was the thick walls, open courtyards, arches and plushly landscaped gardens of the Spanish Colonial Revival which became more strongly associated with LA, and all of Southern California, the region taking on Mediterranean looks to match its climate.

The successes and excesses of the movie industry inspired further large and sometimes ludicrous imitations of European architecture. The symbol of LA's emergence as a modern city, however, was the art deco explosion of the late 1920s, and the following decades' spin-off, Streamline Moderne, whose aerodynamic contours, porthole windows and projecting wings were exuberant monuments to the technological age.

LA's outstanding Streamline Moderne buildings were the Pan Pacific Auditorium (only the façade remains, 7600 Beverly Boulevard), the **May Co Department Store** (6067 Wilshire Boulevard), and the **Coca-Cola bottling plant** (1334 S Central Avenue), thinly disguised as an ocean liner, complete with ship's bridge, hatch covers and portholes.

As low-grade art deco and weak Spanish Colonial Revival swamped the city, influential maverick Frank Lloyd Wright arrived and looked back to pre-Columbian times. In 1917, his **Hollyhock House** (4800 Hollywood Boulevard) was an ambitious fusing of California Bungalow and Aztec temple. Unloved by its owner, the house and its grounds (the present Barnsdall Park) were given to the city. Wright refined his ideas and, in 1924, completed the **Ennis House** (2607 Glendower Avenue). Wright's assistant, the Austrian Rudolph Schindler, established his own modernist credentials with his own home of concrete slabs and interlocking indoor and outdoor spaces in West Hollywood (833 N Kings Road). Encouraged by Schindler, fellow-Austrian Richard Neutra arrived from Europe. In 1929, Neutra's **Lovell House** (4616 Dundee Drive), with its suspended balconies projecting from the hillside above Griffith Park, become LA's most acclaimed example of the International style.

More new styles From 1945 to 1964, the Case Study Program of experimental house building solidified LA's reputation as a centre of innovative architecture though, by definition, the city's staggering post-war growth restricted new projects – as have the preservation orders that protect its architectural past.

In the mid-1970s, the glass silos of the **Bonaventure Hotel** (404 S Figueroa Street) heralded a spate of new development in Downtown, unfortunately marred by the surrounding clutter. Downtown holds a distinguished recent addition to the city's architecture: Arata Isozaki's red sandstone mating of East and West, housing the **Museum of Contemporary Art** (250 S Grand Avenue).

Striking designs can be seen among the skyscrapers

Fear that the city's Spanish-Mexican architectural heritage might disappear encouraged a librarian, Charles Fletcher Lummis, to start the country's first preservation programme in 1895, which saved LA's outlying Spanish missions (San Fernando Rey in the San Fernando Valley and Mission San Gabriel Archangel in the San Gabriel Valley) from destruction.

The Gene Autry Western Heritage Museum

Index of Museums in and around LA
Aerospace Museum
Open: daily, 10.00–17.00hrs. Free. (See page 127.)
Afro-American Museum
Open: daily, 10.00–17.00hrs. Free. (See page 127.)
Armand Hammer Museum of Art and Culture Center
Open: Tuesday to Sunday, 12.00–19.00hrs. Entry fee. (See page 136.)
Cabrillo Marine Museum
Open: Tuesday to Sunday, 10.00–17.00hrs. Free. (See page 134.)
California State Museum of Science and Industry
Open: daily, 10.00–17.00hrs. Free. (See page 127.)
Gene Autry Western Heritage Museum
Open: Tuesday to Sunday, 10.00–17.00hrs. Entry fee. (See page 126.)
Hollywood Wax Museum
Open: Friday and Saturday, 10.00–14.00hrs; Sunday to Thursday, 10.00hrs- midnight. Entry fee. (See page 128.)
Hollywood Studio Museum
Open: Tuesday to Friday, 11.00–16.00hrs; Saturday 10.00-16.00hrs. Entry fee. (See page 128.)
Huntington Art Gallery
Open: Tuesday to Sunday, 13.00–16.30hrs. Free. (See page 155.)
J Paul Getty Museum
Open: Tuesday to Sunday, 10.00–17.00hrs. Free. (See pages 154–5.)
LA County Museum of Art
Open: Tuesday to Friday, 10.00–17.00hrs; Saturday and Sunday, 10.00–18.00hrs. Entry fee. (See pages 138–9.)
Laguna Beach Museum of Art
Open: Tuesday to Sunday, 11.00–17.00hrs. Free. (See page 157.)
Los Angeles Maritime Museum
Open: Tuesday to Sunday, 10.00–17.00hrs. Free. (See page 134.)
Max Factor Museum
Open: Monday to Saturday, 10.00–16.00hrs. Free. (See page 128.)
Museum of Contemporary Art 250 S Grand Avenue.
Open: Tuesday to Sunday, 11.00–18.00hrs; Thursday,to 20.00hrs. Entry fee. Top-ranking temporary exhibitions.
Museum of Natural History
Open: Tuesday to Sunday, 10.00–17.00hrs. Entry fee. (See page 127.)
Newport Harbor Art Museum
Open: Tuesday to Sunday, 11.00–17.00hrs. Donation requested. (See page 154.)
Norton Simon Museum
Open: Thursday to Sunday, 12.00–18.00hrs. Entry fee. (See page 155.)
Pacific Asia Museum
Open: Wednesday to Sunday, 12.00–17.00hrs. Donation requested. (See page 159.)
Richard M Nixon Birthplace and Library
Open: Monday to Saturday, 10.00–17.00hrs; Sunday, 11.00–17.00hrs. Entry fee. (See page 156.)
Southwest Museum
Open: Tuesday to Sunday, 11.00–17.00hrs. Entry fee. (See page 158.)

■ In the realm of spectator sport, the work hard, play hard ethic ingrained in LA life becomes watching hard, with an avid interest taken in the exploits of the city's numerous sports teams. .....■

National favourites LA has seven professional teams, two each for American football, baseball and basketball, and one for ice hockey.

The numerous college teams – the major ones being the Trojans (USC) and the Bruins (UCLA) – should not be considered second-rate. Many student athletes are on sports scholarships and destined for the professional sides.

One of the biggest sporting events in LA, in fact, is the New Year's Day football clash between the student champions of the West and mid-West at Pasadena's 104,000-seat Rose Bowl stadium.

The season's fixtures are listed in the phone book. Only tickets for major games, and any game by the LA Lakers, will prove elusive; use the phone numbers given below for detailed information.

American football With their season running from August to December, the city's professional football teams are the LA Raiders, based at the Memorial Coliseum by Exposition Park (tel: (310) 322 5901), and the LA Rams, who play at Anaheim Stadium, in Anaheim (tel: (310) 277 4748).

Baseball From April to October, the LA Dodgers play baseball at Dodger Stadium, on the edge of Elysian Park (tel: (213) 224 1306), while their Orange County counterparts, who go by the name of California Angels, appear at Anaheim Stadium, in Anaheim (tel: (714) 634 2000).

Basketball Most tickets to watch the fabled LA Lakers basketball team, who play at the Great Western Forum in Inglewood (tel: (310) 419 3182), are snapped up before the November to April season even starts. An alternative are the LA Clippers, who appear at the Sports Arena, just south of Exposition Park (tel: (213) 748 8000).

Ice hockey The sole professional ice hockey side, the LA Kings, bully off at the Great Western Forum (tel: (310) 673 6003) in a season lasting from November to March.

Horse-racing Horse-racing is LA's other major spectator sport. Major meetings are held at the LA County Fairgrounds in Pomona in September and October (tel: (714) 623 3111); at Hollywood Park in Inglewood from April to July and during November and December (tel: (310) 419 1574); and at Santa Anita Park in Arcadia from July to September and from December to April.

In 1838 a law was passed in Los Angeles banning the seranading of women without a licence.

125

The strapping football players of the University of California

[Map of Griffith Park area showing locations including North Hollywood, Ventura Freeway, Burbank Studios Ranch, NBC Color Television, Disney Studio, "Traveltown" Rail Transportation Museum, Burbank Studios, Forest Lawn Memorial Park, Universal Studios, Universal City, Cahuenga Peak, Gene Autry Western Heritage Museum, Los Angeles Zoo, Griffith Park, Mount Hollywood, Bird Sanctuary, Greek Theater, Observatory & Planetarium, Hollywood Lake, Pilgrimage Play Theater, Ferndell Nature Museum, Hollywood Bowl, Grauman's Chinese Theater, Tussauds Hollywood Wax Museum, CBS Studio, Columbia Studio, ABC TV Studio, etc.]

Drive A tour around Griffith Park

Enter the park at the Western Canyon Road gate for the Ferndell. A peaceful glade with a natural spring, the **Ferndell** *is recommended for picnics.*

Drive two miles further, then turn right along Observatory Drive for the observatory.
Griffith Park Observatory allows the public access to its heavens-scanning telescopes every night;

Griffith Park Observatory

daytime views with the naked eye can also be spectacular here. Other attractions include laser and star shows, and simulated space trips.

Descend from the observatory and turn right on to Western Canyon Road, continuing for a mile.
Pass the **Bird Sanctuary** on the left and the Greek Theater on the right.

At Vermont Avenue, turn left on to Commonwealth Canyon Road and then follow Vista Del Valle for six miles, turning left on to Griffith Park Drive and then right on to Zoo Drive for the Gene Autry Western Heritage Museum.
The **Gene Autry Western Heritage Museum** earns its spurs by cogently portraying the settlement of the western US. Close by, the **LA Zoo** is another busy attraction.

Drive back along Zoo Drive and head west along Forest Lawn Drive, leaving the park and crossing over the Hollywood Freeway to Mulholland Drive and Laurel Canyon Boulevard (see page 129).

Exposition Park

■ **At various times an open-air market, a site of horse- and camel-racing, and host (at the majestic Coliseum Stadium) of the Olympic Games in 1932 and 1984, Exposition Park is now best known for its museums and proximity to the USC campus. .....■**

Second only in size to the Smithsonian Institution in Washington DC, the **California State Museum of Science and Industry** grapples with the fundamentals of physics and chemistry with hands-on and interactive exhibits that can provide hours of fun for keen button-pressers of all ages.

The museum's Ahmanson Building stores several major large-scale working models, most impressively an almost too realistic simulation of a major earthquake; if the shaking building sets your pulse racing, give yourself a quick medical check-up in the Hall of Health.

A must for aviation and space fanatics, the **Aerospace Museum** is none the less an anticlimatic collection, mostly of intricate models of planes, satellites and space capsules suspended from the ceiling.

The echoing halls and galleries of the Spanish Renaissance-style **Museum of Natural History** reveal a substantial collection of pre-Columbian artefacts, a multitude of fossils, and the inevitable reconstructed dinosaur skeletons. Equally interesting is the museum's outline of California's development from the time of European discovery, and its stock of weird and wonderful vintage cars.

Bordering Exposition Park, the University of Southern California (USC) campus will consume any time you have left over after visiting the museums. The oldest building here (Widney Hall) dates from the 1880s; do not be misled by the cloistered courtyard and leering gargoyles of the Mudd Hall of Philosophy, intended to evoke a sense of medieval European academia.

Note, too, the George Lucas Film School, named for just one of its blockbuster-director graduates – Steven Speilberg is another.

The Coliseum Stadium, Exposition Park

Exploring an avenue of social history rarely well covered by more mainstream museums, the **Afro-American Museum**, presents a varied range of exhibitions relating to African-American life in the US and throughout the world, and is perhaps the park's most thought-provoking collection.

Given the number of accomplished novelists from all over the world who have arrived in Hollywood to try their hand at screenwriting, it is perhaps surprising that few have written about Hollywood itself as well or as caustically as Nathaniel West, whose 1935 *The Day of the Locust* remains the classic satire of Hollywood in the boom years. Interestingly, the run-down rooming house in which West lived at the time of writing still stands as shabbily as ever in the centre of Hollywood, at 1817 N Ivar Street.

▶ ▶ ▶   Hollywood

LA without Hollywood is impossible to imagine. For eight decades it has been the scene of the city's most public triumphs, disasters, scandals and decadent extravagances – in short, it is everything that the city is famous for.

The beginning Hollywood as the world knows it began in the 1910s when a bunch of hard-up but ambitious film-makers came west in search of a warm climate, free natural backdrops, and an escape from the patent laws hindering their activity on the East Coast.
Within a decade, Hollywood seethed with directors, stars, would-be stars, and opportunists, and all of Los Angeles became indelibly marked by the film industry as the unsophisticated early days grew into the prosperous decades of the 1940s and 1950s.

Seedy streets To today's Angelenos, however, Hollywood does not mean movies (all but one of the major studios have moved out) but seedy, low-rent neighbourhoods and streets that are best avoided after dark.
Hollywood's boundaries are hard to define but you will know you have arrived when the **Walk of Fame** appears beneath your feet: nearly 2,000 star-shaped brass plaques embedded in the Hollywood Boulevard sidewalk, each embossed with the name of an entertainment industry notable who did not mind paying $3,500 for the privilege.
Opened by Sid Grauman in 1927, the **Chinese Theater** (6925 Hollywood Boulevard) draws 2 million gawping visitors a year, not for the intricacies of its mock-oriental architecture but for the hand- and foot-prints of screen idols who literally made their marks here when they were arriving for celebrity-packed movie premières during the glory years. Some of them improvised: look for Betty Gable's leg-print, and the hoof-print of Gene Autry's horse.
Five years earlier, Grauman had celebrated the discovery of King Tut's tomb by erecting the **Egyptian Theater** (6704 Hollywood Boulevard), a plaster replica of the Temple of Thebes that has aged poorly but in its time was among Hollywood's great kitsch excesses.
More high camp than kitsch, the **Max Factor Museum** (1666 Highland Avenue) fills part of Factor's original premises with an entertaining assemblage of the lotions, potions, and bizarre gadgetry employed to keep movie idols looking beautiful.

Famous foundations As Factor supplied the make-up, Frederick's of Hollywood (6608 Hollywood Boulevard) supplied the high-fashion bras and corsets that held the famous flesh in place – numerous celebrity-donated examples are displayed in the shop's Lingerie Museum.
The **Hollywood Wax Museum** (6767 Hollywood Boulevard) is popular but predictable; a better place to visit is the **Hollywood Studio Museum** (2100 N Highland Avenue), inside the barn where Cecil B De Mille directed *The Squaw Man* (Hollywood's first feature film) in 1913.

Sign of a Golden Age?

Just across Highland Avenue, the **Hollywood Bowl**, summer base of the LA Philharmonic, has staged music under the stars since the 1920s.

Cowboy queues There is more movie lore south of Hollywood Boulevard. From the 1910s, scores of would-be screen cowboys queued as the junction of Sunset Boulevard and Gower Street for bit-parts in B westerns – the modern Gower Gulch shopping plaza, thinly disguised as an Old West frontier town, is the only memorial to them. The Hollywood Athletic Club (6525 Sunset Boulevard) served as a watering hole for the likes of John Wayne and Charlie Chaplin.

The end The shady **Hollywood Memorial Cemetery** (6000 Santa Monica Boulevard) provides a final resting place for Tyrone Power, Douglas Fairbanks and Rudolph Valentino among many others. Immediately south, Paramount Studios is the last major film company remaining in Hollywood.

As Sunset Boulevard crosses West Hollywood – packed with hip nightspots and fashionable restaurants, and the power base of LA's gay community – it briefly becomes the Sunset Strip, where enormous 'vanity boards' tout new films, new records and new faces.

Above Hollywood Laurel Canyon Boulevard and Mulholland Drive twist through the canyons of the Hollywood Hills where, over the years, innumerable stars have bought rambling mansions and gazed down on the Los Angeles sprawling beneath their balconies.

It is seldom possible to catch more than passing glimpses or distant views of the most interesting homes (by the roadside, vendors sell photocopied and often out of date locator maps for the star's homes), but among the highlights are Rudolph Valentino's 'Falcon Lair' (1436 Bella Drive), Harold Lloyd's 'Greenacres' (1740 Green Acres Place), and Errol Flynn's 'Mulholland House' (3100 Torreyson Place).

129

Erected in 1923 and illuminated with thousands of flashing light bulbs to advertise land sales in Beachwood Canyon (in the Hollywood Hills), the 50-foot high Hollywood sign (which originally read 'Hollywoodland') became famous throughout the world as the movie-making area's most enduring marker. Unhappy actress Peg Entwhistle committed suicide by jumping off it in 1932, but the closest anyone can get to the sign (without an arduous hike) today is Beachwood Drive, which ends about 100 metres from its base.

Walk Long Beach circular walk

Begin on the Promenade, beside the Long Beach Mural.

Long Beach is now California's fifth-largest city. It grew rapidly in the 19th century as its popularity as a resort increased. Boat cruises to Catalina Island depart from the end of Golden Shore Boulevard and from Pier J (see later in this walk). Funded by the Depression-era Federal Arts Project, the **Long Beach Mural** depicts 1930s Long Beach.

Walk south to Shoreline Park and turn left for Shoreline Village (on Shoreline Village Drive).

With souvenir shops, speciality stores and lively restaurants, **Shoreline Village** stretches along the waterfront. There is a restored carousel and, from time to time, live entertainment on the boardwalk.

Walk through Shoreline Park and cross the Queensway Bridge, turning left along Queens Highway to Pier J. This is where the *Queen Mary*, the last word in ocean-going luxury in the 1930s, is berthed (although at time of publication its future is uncertain, with its sale a distinct possibility). The geodesic dome, nearby, housed the *Spruce Goose*, before it left California at the end of 1992, bound for Oregon. (Finished in 1942, the *Spruce Goose* is the world's largest wooden plane.)

Return to the Promenade.

▶ ▶ ▶ **Santa Monica**

Groomed as a beachside resort from 1875, Santa Monica enjoys cleaner air and cooler temperatures than the rest of LA, and has earned a reputation as the stamping ground of unconventional writers, artists and left-wing politicians. Santa Monica's pride and joy, however, despite pollution problems, is a white-sand beach wide enough to accommodate thousands of cyclists, joggers, sunbathers and swimmers. On the beach itself, the wooden **Santa Monica Pier** has been around almost as long as the town, and proves as much with a collection of fading monochrome snaps from its youth. Along the pier are snack-stands and a 70-year old carousel – you may have seen it alongside Paul Newman in *The Sting* – that still gives 50 rides.

Away from the beach, the **Third Street Promenade** attracts a weekend procession of buskers and painters, and has trendy sidewalk cafés. Near by, Angel's **Attic** (516 Colorado Avenue) stores an amazing collection of antique toys inside an 1894 home, and plies callers with tea and cakes.

▷ ▷ ▷ **Venice**

Do not expect a quiet oceanside stroll in Venice (the name is all that remains from a doomed turn-of-the-century attempt to reclaim marshland and re-create the canals of the Italian city). **The beachside boardwalk** is a menagerie of fire-eaters, escapologists, tap-dancers and fortune-tellers, milling among the wackiest of LA's sun-and-surf worshippers who propel themselves on skateboards, rollerskates or (the latest hip accessory) roller blades. Oblivious to it all, musclemen pump iron in the open-air gym on **Muscle Beach** and look ready to kick sand in the faces of passers-by. Be aware that Venice is extremely dangerous at night, and visits should be only be made during daylight hours.

Santa Monica at night

When the beachside action becomes too much, seek out the many murals that decorate Santa Monica and Venice. Along Ocean Park Boulevard in Santa Monica are the *Whale Mural* and the 600-foot long *Unbridled*, depicting horses escaping from the carousel on the pier. In Venice, look along Windward Avenue: inside the post office there is a large *trompe-l'oeil*, and, on the junction with Ocean Walk, the *Rebirth of Venus* is a witty parody of Botticelli.

131

For views over Santa Monica, visit the Camera Obscura next to the Senior Recreation Center, or take the path through palm-lined Pacific Palisades Park, climbing the brow of the crumbling bluffs that run north from the town towards distant Malibu.

■ **These days it is not would-be film idols who walk the streets of Hollywood but long-haired, leather-clad wanna-be rock stars clutching guitar cases and demo tapes. .....■**

Mike Love of the Beach Boys

Home of rock The base of several major record companies, LA is a magnet to aspiring rock musicians from all over the US. Every night, hundreds of venues pulsate to the latest bands, and the city's place in rock history is only slightly less formidable than its role in the rise of the movies.

The first native Angeleno to make it big was Richie Valens (real name Richard Valenzuela), a 17-year old Hispanic boy from East LA whose 'La Bamba' topped the charts in 1958 (tragically, Valens died a year later in a plane crash).

Home of famous groups Predictably, it was not Valens' impoverished East LA but the idyllic surfing and hot-rodding life-styles of the coastal communities, eulogised from the early 1960s by The Beach Boys, Jan & Dean, and a host of imitators, that gave the the record-buying public a lingering image of LA.

Home of the hippies Later, while San Francisco was the undisputed flower-power capital of the world, many of the psychedelic era's most influential bands were based in LA.

One was Buffalo Springfield (their line-up including future solo stars Neil Young and Stephen Stills) whose début single, 'For What It's Worth', in 1967, was a response to the 'Sunset Strip riot', when baton-wielding police attempted to move the hippies – hundreds of whom were arriving in the city – intent on making the Sunset Strip, then a collection of up-market supper clubs, their own.

Other seminal LA groups included Iron Butterfly and Love, but it was The Doors who garnered the most vociferous response, thanks in no small part to their iconoclastic singer, Jim Morrison, whose lyrics were considered poetry and whose drinking exploits around the LA bars became legendary.

As the hippies flooded Sunset Strip, the musicians retreated to Topanga Canyon, a patch of wild country in the hills just a few minutes' drive from the city's clubs and studios. The canyon saw many night-long parties and star-studded jam sessions, and one resident band, The Byrds, used the stables at the head of the canyon's horse trails on the cover of their 'Notorious Byrd Brothers' album.

Home of commercialism By the early 1970s, the idealism had waned and the profit-motivated music industry had, after earlier doubts, decided there was a fortune to be made from the embryonic rock culture.

The showcase clubs of the city became dominated by

The Doors in their heyday

record company approved acts, and the easy-listening rock of commercially mega-successful bands such as The Eagles and Fleetwood Mac, and singer-songwriters such as Jackson Browne, became the standardbearers of a cosy and complacent LA rock scene.

Home of innovation With many of the most creative names of the 1960s gaining weight and drug habits in the Hollywood Hills, and music business executives too worried of losing their privileged positions to take risks, an artistic void had opened up by the mid-1970s, into which stepped the first LA punk bands – among them The Zeroes, The Plugz, The Dils, and X.
In a city where façade has traditionally counted for more than content, it was little surprise that the 1980s were dominated the rise of glam-metal and the emergence of made-up ear-crunchers such as Poison and Mötley Crüe.

Home of success The biggest success story, however, is the hard-rocking Guns 'n' Roses, carrying the rock-star-as-outlaw myth as far it would go and becoming the role model for thousands of bandana-wearing hopefuls.
Away from the Hollywood rock scene, Los Lobos grew out of the bars of East LA and found an international audience appreciative of their mixing of *corridos* (Mexican folk songs) and rock and roll. The band also acknowledged their roots by appearing as Richie Valen's backing band in the movie, *La Bamba*, in 1987.
Lately, the strongest sounds have emerged from the least likely quarter, the black ghettos of South Central LA, which have spawned globally-acclaimed rap acts such as Ice-T and NWA.

Drive Coastal route from Marina del Rey to San Pedro

See map on page 135.

Begin at Fisherman's Village in Marina del Rey.
Owners and crews of the private yachts berthed in **Marina del Rey** fill the pricey seafood restaurants of **Fisherman's Village**, facing the world's largest artificial harbour.

Drive the quarter-mile from Fisherman's Village to Vista del Mar and turn left, continuing south to Manhattan Beach.
Nets on the sands signify **Manhattan Beach's** place as the home of beach volleyball, a strenuous sport whose professional participants can often be seen honing their skills here.

Drive south along Highland Avenue to Hermosa Beach, turn left into Pier Avenue.
This quintessential quiet LA coastal community of **Hermosa Beach** honoured a local surfer of the 1960s with a statue at the end of Pier Avenue.

Continue south along Highland Avenue to Redondo Beach.
In **Redondo Beach, Fisherman's Wharf** holds souvenir shops, eateries, and stalls selling fresh seafood. Adjacent, the white-sanded **Redondo State Beach** is popular with surfers.

Continue south, turn right along Palos Verdes Drive West, rounding the Palos Verdes peninsula.
Rising above the ocean, the tree-covered **Palos Verdes peninsula** has numerous secluded beaches, often only reached by steep footpaths down the cliff face.

Continue on Palos Verdes Drive South.
On the left, Lloyd Wright's 1946 **Wayfarer's Chapel** is a monument to 18th-century Swedish mystic, Emmanuel Swedenborg, its glass

walls allowing it to merge into a redwood grove on the hillside.

Continue to the end of Palos Verdes Drive South, turn right into Paseo Del Mar for Point Fermin Park.
A launchpoint for hang-gliders, **Point Fermin Park** also has a 19th-century **lighthouse**.

Drive to the end of Paseo Del Mar and turn right along Stephen Wright Drive for the Cabrillo Marine Museum.
Well-stocked aquariums, large collections of shells, and informative displays on marine ecology fill the **Cabrillo Marine Museum** (*open*: Tuesday to Friday, 12.00–17.00hrs; weekends, 10.00–17.00hrs).

<< Santa Monica's pier is easily the best of the bunch that exist along the coast around here, a classic seaside addition dating from 1909. Further south, Manhattan Beach's barren strip of concrete deserves an award for dullness; Hermosa Beach's pier draws the thickest concentration of patient anglers, while the Redondo Sportfishing pier is the departure point for fishermen with a more substantial catch in mind. The quaintest pier in the LA area, however, belongs to Avalon on Santa Catalina. **>>**

Turn left into Pacific Avenue and enter San Pedro.
Originally a small fishing community, San Pedro quickly grew as the Port of Los Angeles was developed. Much of the seafaring flavour of bygone times remains strong around the short streets of **Old San Pedro**, and the **Los Angeles Maritime Museum** documents the growth of the town and the port. Close by, the overrated **Ports O'Call Village** has souvenir shops and restaurants.

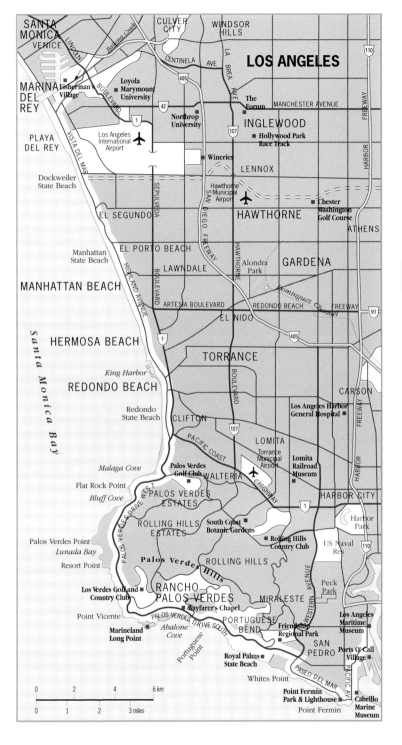

LOS ANGELES

SANTA MONICA
VENICE
CULVER CITY
WINDSOR HILLS
CENTINELA AVE
LA BREA AVE
110 FREEWAY
MARINA DEL REY
Fisherman's Village
Loyola Marymount University
405
42
The Forum
MANCHESTER AVENUE
INGLEWOOD
Northrop University
107
Hollywood Park Race Track
HARBOR FREEWAY
PLAYA DEL REY
1
Los Angeles International Airport
Wineries
LENNOX
Dockweiler State Beach
SEPULVEDA
SAN DIEGO FREEWAY
Hawthorne Municipal Airport
HAWTHORNE
Chester Washington Golf Course
ATHENS
EL SEGUNDO
HAWTHORNE
Manhattan State Beach
EL PORTO BEACH
LAWNDALE
Alondra Park
GARDENA
135
MANHATTAN BEACH
HIGHLAND AVENUE
SEPULVEDA BOULEVARD
ARTESIA BOULEVARD
Dominguez Channel
REDONDO BEACH FREEWAY
91
EL NIDO
405
HERMOSA BEACH
1
TORRANCE
Santa Monica Bay
King Harbor
REDONDO BEACH
BOULEVARD
CARSON
Redondo State Beach
CLIFTON
107
Los Angeles Harbor General Hospital
Malaga Cove
PACIFIC COAST
LOMITA
Palos Verdes Golf Club
WALTERIA
Torrance Municipal Airport
Lomita Railroad Museum
HARBOR FREEWAY
Flat Rock Point
WEST
PALOS VERDES ESTATES
Bluff Cove
PACIFIC COAST HIGHWAY
1
HARBOR CITY
Palos Verdes Point
PALOS VERDES DRIVE
ROLLING HILLS ESTATES
South Coast Botanic Gardens
Harbor Park
Lunada Bay
Resort Point
Rolling Hills Country Club
US Naval Res
Palos Verdes Hills
ROLLING HILLS
WESTERN AVENUE
Peck Park
Los Verdes Golf and Country Club
RANCHO PALOS VERDES
MIRALESTE
Point Vicente
Wayfarer's Chapel
PALOS VERDES DRIVE SOUTH
PORTUGUESE BEND
Friendship Regional Park
Los Angeles Maritime Museum
Marineland Long Point
Abalone Cove
SAN PEDRO
Ports O' Call Village
Portuguese Point
Royal Palms State Beach
PACIFIC AV
PASEO DEL MAR
Whites Point
Point Fermin Park & Lighthouse
Cabrillo Marine Museum
Point Fermin

0   2   4   6 km
0   1   2   3 miles

LOS ANGELES

Outside cinemas in Westwood, and to a lesser extent in other parts of LA, you may by offered free tickets to a 'sneak preview' of a new movie. These are offered only to people who appear to be members of the social group expected to be interested in the film. After viewing, you will be given a questionnaire to fill in, which is used to help plan the marketing of the movie.

▶ ▶ ▷   **Westwood**

Planned as a Mediterranean-style shopping village in the 1920s, the narrow streets of Westwood are laden with book, T-shirt and souvenir stores, and a variety of informal restaurants catering for the crowds who flock to the neighbourhood's first-run cinemas, eager to see films still fresh from the studios' editing suites. Movie buffs might like to pay a visit to the Westwood Memorial Park, where Marilyn Monroe is buried.

Westwood is one of the few places LA intended for walking in, although it is also favoured by adolescents and students (many from the adjoining UCLA campus) for bumper-to-bumper car cruising; the evening traffic can be intense, although a free minibus eases some of the strain.

A recent addition to Westwood is the **Armand Hammer Museum of Art and Culture Center,** displaying the ample fruits of 50 years of collecting by the extremely rich oil magnate. The main gallery reads like a Who's Who of European fine art, while a separate gallery is devoted to the *Codex Hammer*, pages from the notebooks of the 15th-century genius, Leonardo da Vinci.

Westwood, a Los Angeles village

▶▶▷ **UCLA**

The Romanesque brick buildings around the central quadrangle of the University of California at Los Angeles (UCLA) form the heart of the oldest and most respected of LA's academic institutions, founded in 1929. The buildings are full of character and, together with their carefully tended gardens, they provide a welcome break from the corporate towers that fill much of the surrounding area.

There is plenty to see on the campus but to find your way around it is essential to pick up a free map at one of the entrances.

Stop first at the **Powell Library**, for its grand staircase and imposing rotunda, and then enjoy the diverse stash of folk art inside the neighbouring **Fowler Museum of Cultural History**. Cutting-edge American art is usually on show at the **Wright Art Gallery**, outside which the five-acre jacaranda-shaded **Franklin D Murphy Sculpture Garden** provides surprises of all shapes and sizes – not least works by Rodin and Matisse.

Non-academic Angelenos appreciate UCLA most of all for the Bruins, the university's sports teams whose huge success is recalled by wall-to-wall trophies glinting inside the **Athletic Hall of Fame**.

Have a look, too, at UCLA's oddest item: the Inverted Fountain, where 10,000 unseen gallons of recycled water recreate the sounds of a mountain stream.

▷▷▷ **Wilshire Boulevard**

Bearing the name of H Gaylord Wilshire, the socialist entrepreneur who, in the 1880s, purchased a row of bean fields and marked out its route, Wilshire Boulevard passes through 16 miles of ethnic diversity, landmark architecture, and the city's major art collection, between Downtown and the coast.

At the turn of the century, the shovel of one-time gold prospector and future multi-millionaire, Edward L Doheny, struck oil and much of Wilshire Boulevard disappeared beneath a forest of oil derricks.

Royce Hall, on the UCLA campus

Flowers, shrubs and trees fare surprisingly well in this city of freeways and smog in several caringly nurtured gardens. To escape the mad metropolis, take a packed lunch to one of the following: the Rose Garden in Exposition Park; the grounds of Greystone Park (905 Loma Drive, Beverly Hills); the gardens of UCLA; the South Coast Botanical Gardens (26300 Crenshaw Boulevard in Rancho Palos Verdes); the Ferndell section of Griffith Park; or the Japanese Garden of the CSULB campus in Long Beach.

Miracle Mile As it turned out, the oil reserves were soon exhausted and a longer-lasting boom came in the 1920s and 1930s when Wilshire Boulevard acquired the fabulous art deco department stores of the Miracle Mile – the first department stores in (what were then) the LA suburbs, and the first step on the way towards the city's decentralisation and dependence on the automobile; uniquely for the period, the stores were designed with their own car-parks.

Officially, the Miracle Mile extends from La Brea and Fairfax avenues but the finest example of the eye-pleasing art deco that dominates it is just east, with the **Bullocks Wilshire Department Store** (No 3050). Many of the other structures have aged less gracefully and are now surrounded by busy food shops serving one of the most racially varied quarters of the city: a melting pot of predominantly Mexican, Filipino and Korean settlers.

A forerunner of the Miracle Mile, the Ambassador Hotel (No 3400) cost a staggering $5 million and occupied 23 acres when it opened in 1921. Closed in 1989 and facing an uncertain future, the Ambassador's place in LA history is assured: besides the tales of Hollywood celebrities making fools of themselves in its legendary Cocoanut Grove nightclub, it was here in 1968 that Senator Robert Kennedy was killed by an assassin's bullet.

The buildings of the Miracle Mile could hardly have a less architecturally inspiring neighbour than the the **Los Angeles County Museum of Art** (No 5905). Within the vast museum's stern 1960s exterior, however, centuries' worth of European painting and sculpture, influential contemporary American works, and countless treasures among the Asiatic collections, provide several hours of enjoyable viewing.

Be certain to tour the museum's newest addition, the Japanese Pavilion, whose beautiful Edo-period paintings are greatly enhanced by the light-spreading qualities of the purpose-built pavilion.

Next door to the Museum of Art, several fibreglass mastodons partially sunk in tar frame the grounds of the **George C Page Museum** (No 5801), which informatively annotates the fossils and reconstructs the skeletons of many of the creatures that came, literally, to a sticky end 2 million years ago in the **La Brea Tar Pits**. The tar, once used by Indians to waterproof their homes, still seeps to the surface of streets in the area.

The **Craft and Folk Art Museum** (No 5814) has entertaining small temporary exhibitions of old and new folk art, and in a rough neighbourhood just south of Wilshire Boulevard, the **St Elmo's Village Art Center** is an off-the-beaten-track art discovery: the downtrodden community's success in creating and maintaining the mural-enshrouded art centre is celebrated in May with the Festival of the Art of Survival, which gets bigger and better with each passing year.

Community area The Fairfax Avenue section of Wilshire Boulevard passes through one of the US's largest Jewish communities. Inside the Jewish Community Building (No 6505), the **Martyr's Memorial and Museum** of the Holocaust has stark reminders of

Getting stuck into it at the George C Page Museum

the horrors of Hitler's concentration camps, and emotive paintings by some of those interned in them.

Also close to Fairfax, just south of Wilshire Boulevard, the Farmer's Market began when a small group of farmers, poverty-stricken by the Depression, were allowed to sell their produce for free from a patch of open ground. Nowadays, it has grown into a curious mix of groaning fruit and vegetable stalls, tacky souvenir shops, and food stands offering plenty of options if you fancy a cheap, tasty snack.

LA's contemporary art can be found at: LA Artcore (652 S Mateo Street); Los Angeles Contemporary Exhibitions (1804 Industrial Street); or Cirrus (542 S Alameda Street). Latino art is shown at the Palmetto Gallery (1370 Palmetto Avenue) and Galeria Nueva (912 E Third Street).

Shopping

Melrose Avenue

Some 30,000 people a day weave around the cut-rate food stalls of the indoor Grand Central Market (317 S Broadway), where the din is not for the nervous.For insomniacs and very early risers (the action is over by 09.00hrs), sweet smalls and bright colours abound at the Flower Market, between Seventh and Eighth streets.

Mountainous piles of fruit and vegetables from the state's farms are unloaded at the Produce Market (on Eighth and Ninth streets close to Central Avenue).

Consuming passions run high in LA, and shopping is the city's favourite pastime. Several areas, such as Farmer's Market, Fisherman's Wharf and Ports O'Call Village, are noted for their tourist appeal but actually offer little beyond standard souvenirs. However, there are many better and more interesting places – from luxury malls to thrift stores – in which to discover the LA art of acquiring.

Something for everyone Few cities can equal LA's state-of-the-art shopping malls, gigantic air-conditioned shrines to consumerism. Two of the flashiest are the The Beverly Center (bordered by Beverly and La Cienega boulevards), packed with stylish, refined shops that attract the affluent of West LA, and the Century City Shopping Center (10250 Santa Monica Boulevard), which includes LA's best mall bookstore – Brentano's – and the high-quality ethnic fast-food stalls of The Market.

Elsewhere, two smaller malls reflect contrasting ethnic groups. LA's Japanese are the main customers at Little Tokyo's Japanese Village Plaza Mall (Central Avenue between First and Second streets), with numerous outlets for Japanese goods, food and clothes. Meanwhile, Latino East LA does its shopping at the lively El Mercado market (3425 E First Street), accompanied by strolling mariachi street musicians.

Up-market department stores All over the city, department stores such as I Magnin, Nordstrom, Neiman-Marcus and Saks will dependably fulfil most sartorial needs, though for top-of-the-range clothes, the ultra-expensive designer stores of Beverly Hills' Rodeo Drive and the Rodeo Center (see page 118) are the places to exercise your credit cards.

Cheap clothing Substantially less expensive good quality clothing can be found in Downtown's Garment District (centred on Los Angeles Street, between Seventh Street and Washington Boulevard), where a rake through the immense stocks of the Cooper Building (860 Los Angeles Street) will turn up many bargains. A few miles south, another outlet for top-name togs at wholesale prices is the Citadel (5675 E Telegraph Road). Second-hand clothes with interesting pasts turn up at A Star is Worn (7303 Melrose Avenue). The stock is donated by film and TV celebrities for charity. The clothes racks filling the city's numerous thrift stores, such as Goodwill Industries (342 San Fernando Road), offer great finds, especially for women.

Accessories For a hat to do more than keep the sun off, visit Elizabeth Marcel's Hat Gallery (5632 Melrose Avenue), which is packed with inventive creations from traditional materials. For the finest hand-made gloves, call on Gloves by Hammer of Hollywood (72100 Melrose Avenue).

The remnants of Downtown's once-thriving jewellery district are the best places to seek out wearable gems at the right price: try the Vincent Jewellery Center (650 S Hill Street), or the International Jewellery Center.

Alternatively, radical jewellery is a speciality of Sculpture to Wear (8441 Melrose Avenue), offering an eye-catching range of contemporary designs.

For the antique collector Searching for antiques and collectibles in this futuristic city may seem perverse, but the Antique Guild (8800 Venice Boulevard) has around 40,000 items culled from the manor homes of Europe, which contrast strongly with the kitsch Americana period-pieces of Off the Wall (7325 Melrose Avenue). Fine artefacts from Mexico and the ancient cultures of the Southwest fill Territory (6907 Melrose Avenue), and rock music fans should find something to tempt in the memorabilia-packed Rock Store (6817 Melrose Avenue).

For the book lover It is said that Angelenos lack the attention span necessary to read books, but this is not something borne out by the size of the city's second-hand bookstores. The long-established Larry Edmunds (6658 Hollywood Boulevard) leads the field in movie and theatre books and posters, although the Collector's Bookstore (1708 Vine Street) is fast catching up.
For fiction, and everything else, allocate a day for scrutinising the endless shelves of Acres of Books (240 Long Beach Boulevard). Hard-to-find art and architecture volumes turn up in Arcana Books on the Arts (1229 Third Street Promenade, Santa Monica).
To turn browsing into meditation, visit the Bodhi Tree Bookstore (8585 Melrose Avenue), packed with New Age, healing, medicine, psychology, religious and philosophical titles.

A few of the basic essentials of life which are on hand for Beverly Hills shoppers

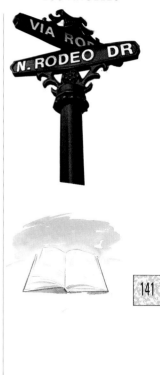

141

Food and Drink

International flavour Gastronomically speaking, LA is at the crossroads of the world. Coffee shops, delis and burger joints are as common here as anywhere else in the country (if often in unusual forms, such as gourmet hot-dog stands and 1950s-themed diners), but overall American food is less prevalent than the scores of ethnic cuisines offered at anything from roadside stalls to reservation-only restaurants.

Angelenos and visitors alike enjoy a culinary choice that few cities can better. What is more, you do not need to be rich to indulge.

Even the famously bizarre concoctions of LA's world-class chefs soon filter down from the temples of fine dining to affordable street-level outlets. Designer pizza, for example, with its exotic gourmet toppings, was born in the exclusive Spago's, but is now an accessible dish, plied to the masses through the branches of California Pizza Kitchen.

The fresh fruit and vegetables raised on the state's farms heighten the nutritional value of many dishes, and salads are often full meals in themselves, with strawberries, orange quarters and grapes alongside the more usual ingredients.

Having the Pacific Ocean for a neighbour enables LA's seafood restaurants to boast of the freshness of their fare which includes abalone, tuna, swordfish and fist-sized shrimps. Innumerable cafés along the coast offer tasty fishy snacks as refreshments to accompany a day's tanning.

On average, you should budget for about $6 to $8 for breakfast in Los Angeles; $8 to $10 for lunch; and around $12 to $15 for dinner. Despite the reasonable prices, most establishments serve up enormous helpings at mealtimes.

Mexican Among the ethnic cuisines, Mexican food not only offers unbeatable value but is also far healthier than the authentic stuff south of the border.

All Mexican dishes are based on variations of the tortilla, a doughy pancake made from cornmeal or wheat, which can be baked or fried and then rolled or folded around food, or laid flat beneath it. Mashed or refried beans, rice, chillies, beef and cheese are the other staple ingredients. Fish tacos, and the melted-cheese-filled tortilla called a *quesadilla*, are a couple of the meat-free alternatives.

Bowls of tortilla chips and spicey salsa are laid out as free hors-d'oeuvres in Mexican restaurants; tortilla chips with melted cheese, known as nachos, make a good side dish or snack.

LA's Mexican menus also include the burrito – a large flour tortilla filled with beef, cheese, chillies and beans – which you will not find at all in Mexico; it was invented in LA primarily for in-car consumption.

Oriental Not as cheap as Mexican but very enticingly priced, Japanese cuisine has been a feature of the city since *sushi* bars became the rage in the 1970s. There are Japanese restaurants all over the place, but the most interesting are in Little Tokyo, where curry dishes are the latest craze and steaming jugs of *sake* are always on hand to help down the food.

Chinese food in its various forms comes best, not surprisingly, in the hundreds of restaurants filling Chinatown, and Korean cuisine is making steady headway from its Koreatown base.

Italian food is not hard to come by in LA

European and North African The many sailors who have settled in San Pedro give rise to a globe-spanning group of eateries, including Greek, Yugoslav, Moroccan, and Eastern European, in the small harbour-side town.

Italian Italian cooking is hard to miss. Pasta and pizza (always crustier and chewier than its European counterpart) stops are everywhere and in the classier places, top Italian chefs are inspired by the similarities in climate and natural produce between their homeland and southern California.

Drinks These are dispensed as eagerly as food. Droughts permitting, a glass of iced water will be poured the instant you sit down, and rare is the coffee shop or diner that does not keep your coffee – choose between regular and de-caff – cup filled to the brim. Tea as a hot drink only appears in herbal forms, although iced-tea is common and is the ideal coolant on a hot day; refills are usually free.

Most restaurants are fully licensed and some are regarded as places to drink as much as places to eat. Several Mexican eateries are better known for the strength of their margaritas – often available in fruit-flavoured forms beside the 'original' mix of tequila, triple sec and lime juice, with (optional) salt around the glass – than the quality of their food.

Listings of recommended LA restaurants begin on page 274 of the Directory.

The ultimate drive-in...Hard Rock Café

You could spend months exploring nocturnal Los Angeles and still only scratch the surface of the city's nightlife. For the latest on what's happening where, the best option is to read the listings in the free *LA Weekly* newspaper.

Bars There are few of the smoky bars that predominate in many US cities, although anyone seeking local colour should try Barney's Beanery, 8447 Santa Monica Boulevard (tel: (213) 654 2287), with its pool tables and dozens of imported brews, or Gorky's, 536 E Eighth Street, Downtown (tel: (213) 627 4060), supplying home-brewed beer to a bohemian crowd.

Hotel choice More typically, LA watering holes are the cocktail bars of hotels. Among the most distinctive are the Biltmore Hotel's Grand Avenue Bar, 506 S Grand Avenue (tel: (213) 612 1595), decorated with marble columns and Mies van der Rohe chairs, the revolving Bonavista Lounge of the Westin Bonaventure Hotel, 404 S Figueroa Street (tel: (213) 624 1000), and the most famous place in town for an overpriced tipple, the Polo Lounge of the Beverly Hills Hotel, 9641 Sunset Boulevard (tel: (213) 226 2751).

Jazz, rock and R&B These are the main fare of the city's innumerable live music venues.
The Troubador, 9801 Santa Monica Boulevard (tel: (310) 276 6168), made its name as a folk venue and now features rock acts; the Roxy, 9009 Sunset Boulevard (tel: (310) 276 2222), has hopeful new bands; and Gazzari's, 9039 Sunset Boulevard (tel: (310) 273 6606) is the archetypal LA hard rock club.
The Mint, 6010 W Pico Boulevard (tel: (213) 937 9630), and King King, 467 La Brea Avenue (tel: (213) 934 5418), are intimate spots to hear R&B and blues; for similar music from bigger names in a ritzier setting, pay a visit to the art deco Cinegrill ballroom of the Hollywood Roosevelt Hotel, 7000 Hollywood Boulevard (tel: (213) 466 7000).
Noted for their knowledgeable audiences and constantly good shows, the pick of the jazz clubs include: At My Place, 1026 Wilshire Boulevard, Santa Monica (tel: (213)

451 8596); Nucleus Nuance, 7267 Melrose Avenue (tel: (213) 939 8666); and Birdland West, 105 W Broadway, Long Beach (tel: (310) 436 9341).

Cabaret, comedy and magic These are all in plentiful supply in LA. The Comedy Store, 8433 Sunset Boulevard (tel: (213) 656 6225) is the main stage for proven comics; the Improvisation, 8162 Melrose Avenue (tel: (213) 651 2583), features acts on the rise; and Café Largo, 432 N Fairfax Avenue (tel: (213) 852 1073), presents comedians on some nights, but you are just as likely to discover poetry readings or performance art at this innovative cabaret venue.

Conjuring connoisseurs will love the Magic Castle, 7001 Franklin Avenue (tel: (213) 851 3314), a building devoted to trickery and illusion where the strange happenings are not limited to the stage. The Castle is for members only but your hotel receptionist should be able to arrange entr for you.

Theatre, dancing and music If you simply want to dance, go to the Crush Bar at the Continental Club, 1743 N Cahuenga Boulevard (tel: (213) 462 9156), for its 1960s grooves; Miami Spice, 13515 Washington Boulevard, Venice (tel: (310) 306 7978), where Salsa sounds percolate across the dance floor; or, for reggae music, Kingston 12, 814 Santa Monica Boulevard (tel: (310) 451 4423).

The trendiest nightclubs have steep cover charges, but if you want to pose among the city's fashionable faces, try the China Club, 1600 N Argyle Agenue (tel: (213) 469 1600), or Twenty/20, 2020 Avenue of the Stars (tel: (213) 933 2020).

Activity in the classical field centres on the Music Center, 135 N Grand Avenue where the Dorothy Chandler Pavilion is the venue for the Joffrey Ballet (tel: (213) 972 7211), the Los Angeles Master Chorale (tel: (213) 972 7200), the Los Angeles Opera (tel: (213) 972 7211), and the Los Angeles Philharmonic (tel: (213) 972 7211). The Philharmonic also play a summer season at the Hollywood Bowl, 2301 N Highland Avenue (tel: (213) 850 2000).

The Music Center has drama, too. The Mark Taper Forum (tel: (213) 972 7373) runs contemporary plays, and the Ahmanson Theater (tel: (213) 972 7337) hosts Broadway blockbusters.

One of LA's more popular theatres is Tamara, 2035 N Highland Avenue (tel: (213) 851 9999), where the audience join the cast for dinner in an Italian Villa and then follow the action from room to room as a murder mystery unfurls.

Nightlife in Sunset Boulevard

Accommodation

Be it a jacuzzi-equipped luxury suite, a dependable no-frills motel room, or simply a budget-priced bed in a youth hostel dormitory, there is no shortage of accommodation in LA.

Book in advance Wherever you plan to stay and however much you plan to spend, it is wise to book as far in advance as possible. Many hotels have toll-free 800 phone numbers enabling you to call them free of charge from anywhere within the US.

If you do not have a reservation, any of the visitor information offices listed on pages 149 can help with finding a place to stay; each has shelves laden with hotel, motel and hostel brochures, which sometimes offer a few dollars discount on the regular price.

Getting around LA is near impossible without a car, which means location is of less importance when seeking accommodation than ease of access to the city's freeways; being close to one can save valuable sightseeing time. If you are not using a car, spread your stay across several areas to avoid long hours riding the LA buses. Location does make a difference to costs, however, and you should also note that in very few parts of LA is it safe to walk after dark.

LA's Bonaventure Hotel

A price to suit every pocket Downtown accommodation spans everything from skid row flophouses to the architecturally inventive hotels ready to pamper jet-setting business travellers. Between these extremes, a growing number of hotels ($45 to $70) in

The Hotel Beverly Wilshire

restored buildings offer solid value and make a good base for exploring the area – a rare instance of an LA district suited, in daylight, to walking.

Moving west, central Hollywood, holding the main remnants from the movie industry's golden years, has a dozen or so comfortable hotels ($70 to $95) close to Hollywood Boulevard; just south, numerous motels ($50 to $85) of varying quality can be found along Sunset Boulevard.

Standards and prices rise in unison as you continue west into West Hollywood, Beverly Hills and Westwood. It is here that you will find plush hotels with built-in gymnasiums and roof-top tennis courts intended to help visiting entertainment-industry moguls unwind. Prices begin at around $130 and increase swiftly; this is a very refined area in which to stay, and several sections are safe for evening strolling.

At the coast Shabby but serviceable motels (around $50) neighbour swanky resorts (upwards of $120) in Santa Monica. To the south, through rowdy Venice Beach and on to the quieter communities of Manhattan Beach, Hermosa Beach and Redondo Beach, there is a good range of medium-priced hotels and motels ($40 to $80). A money-saving trick here is to seek out accommodation a few blocks inland where it is often $10 or $20 less than a hotel facing the beach.

Around the Palos Verdes peninsula San Pedro has a good mix of modern chain hotels and trusty motels (from $80 and $50 respectively), as does, to a lesser extent, nearby Long Beach.

Flying in very late or flying out very early are the only reasons to opt for one of the pricey hotels surrounding the airport. Many hotels in other areas provide free airport transportation; even if they do not, airport shuttlebuses are plentiful.

Listings of recommended LA accommodation begin on page 273.

Youth hostels are much less expensive than hotels and motels, and there are several of them: one each in Hollywood, San Pedro and Santa Monica; as well as a number of backpacker-patronised hostels in and around Venice Beach, where nightly stays in small dormitories cost from $10 to $15.

Not surprisingly, this sprawling metropolis has no campsites within its boundaries, although some of the most atmospheric accommodation is offered by a tiny band of Bed and Breakfast Inns ($75 to $150) scattered across the city, usually graciously appointed Victorian homes with a limited number of guest rooms. To stay in one of these popular hideaways, you will need either a lot of luck or a six-month advance booking.

*Los Angeles
International Airport*

Arriving by plane All international flights and most domestic flights land at Los Angeles International Airport (LAX), 15 miles southwest of Downtown and a mile east of the coast. The airport is a large and efficiently run facility, although getting through immigration can take an hour.

To get from the airport to other parts of the city, use one of the shuttle buses (there are dozens, run by private firms) which collect passengers from the airport concourse and deliver them to almost any address in LA. The shuttle buses charge according to how far you travel: most fares are between $10 and $20. Local buses (see below) are cheaper, but LA's bus network is bewildering for first-time arrivals. Taking a taxi from the airport is likely to cost in excess of $30.

Airlines All the major transatlantic airlines have several offices around LA, their main phone numbers are: American Airlines (800) 424 7225; British Airways (800) 247 9297; Continental (800) 525 0280); Delta (213) 386 5510; Northwest (800) 328 2216; TWA (213) 484 9311; United (800) 633 8825; Virgin (800) 862 8621.

Arriving by bus or train All long-distance buses into LA stop in Downtown at 208 E Sixth Street (tel: (213) 620 1200); some services also run to Hollywood, 1409 Vine Street (tel: (213) 466 6381) and Santa Monica, 1433 Fifth Street (tel: (310) 394 5433).

LA's railway terminal is Union Station, 800 N Alameda Street in Downtown (tel: (213) 624 0171).

In the spring of 1992 the social, economic and racial tensions which have long been apparent in Los Angeles exploded into riots, looting and violence. An uneasy calm returned to the city after a few days, but though visitors are unlikely to face danger if they act sensibly, the city has yet to solve its deep-seated problems.

Currency exchange Other than the airport, the only place to change foreign currency into dollars is at the Bank of America, 555 S Flower Street, Downtown (tel: (213) 228 2721).

Getting around As mentioned earlier, it is easiest to get around LA by car. The bus system, however, is comprehensive and taxis are common.

Car hire – if you have arranged car hire ahead of arrival, your car can be collected at the airport, just look for the appropriate car-hire firm's desk. You can also hire on arrival at the airport, or elsewhere in LA, by phoning one of the numerous car-hire firms (whose offices are spread all over the city) on one of the following numbers: Alamo (800) 327 9633; Avis (213) 615 4300; Budget (213) 649 7500; or Hertz (800) 654 3131.

Local buses – contrary to popular opinion, LA has the largest bus service in the US. Given the sheer size of the city, however, getting from place to place by bus can be extremely time consuming.

Most services are run by the RTD (for information, tel: (213) 626 4465), and have a flat single journey fare, payable with exact money when boarding.

Buses run roughly every 10 minutes (less frequently at night) along the main streets linking Downtown and the coast, passing through Hollywood and Beverly Hills before reaching Santa Monica or Venice. Useful routes are 1 (along Hollywood Boulevard); 2 (along Sunset Boulevard); 4 (along Santa Monica Boulevard); 11 (along Melrose Avenue); and 20, 21, and 22 (along Wilshire Avenue).

Taxis – LA's taxis charge a fee for stopping and then a further fixed charge per mile. They need to be phoned for rather than flagged down from the kerb: Checker Cab (tel: (213) 654 4800) and LA Taxi (tel: (213) 627 7000) are two major firms; others are listed in the phone book.

Useful phone numbers Dentist referral service: (213) 481 2133; doctor referral service: (213) 483 6122; emergency services: 911; talking clock: (213) 853 1212; traveller's aid: (213) 686 0950; weather: (213) 554 1212.

Visitor information The biggest source of general tourist information in the city is the Visitor Information Center, 695 S Figueroa Street, Downtown (tel: (213) 689 8822).

Smaller but equally useful offices in other areas include: Beverly Hills Visitors and Convention Bureau, 239 S Beverly Drive, Beverly Hills (tel: (310) 271 8174); the Janes House, 6541 Hollywood Boulevard, Hollywood (tel: (213) 461 4213); Visitor Information Kiosk, 1400 Ocean Avenue, Santa Monica (tel: (310) 393 7593); Long Beach Visitor and Convention Council, 180 E Ocean Boulevard, Long Beach (tel: (310) 436 3645); and San Pedro Chamber of Commerce, 390 W Seventh Street, San Pedro (tel: (310) 832 7272).

AROUND LOS ANGELES

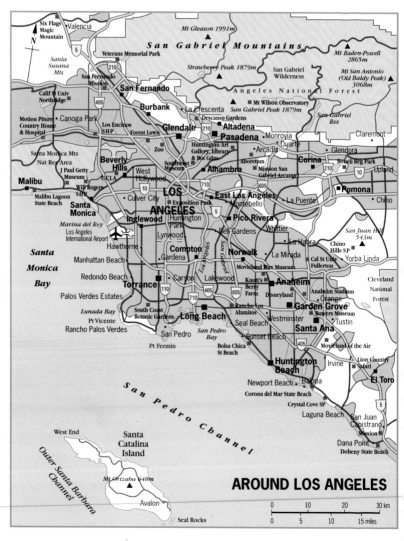

Mt Gleason 1991m

San Gabriel Mountains

Six Flags Magic Mountain · Valencia

Santa Susana Mts

Veterans Memorial Park

Mt Baden-Powell 2865m

Strawberry Peak 1879m

San Fernando Mission

San Gabriel Wilderness

Mt San Antonio (Old Baldy Peak) 3068m

Calif St Univ Northridge

San Fernando

Angeles National Forest

Burbank

La Crescenta

Mt Wilson Observatory

San Gabriel Peak 1879m

San Gabriel Res

Motion Picture Country House & Hospital · Canoga Park

Los Encinos SHP

Descanso Gardens

Claremont

Forest Lawn

Glendale

Altadena

Monrovia

Duarte

Santa Monica Mts Nat Rec Area

Zoo

Pasadena

Arcadia

Glendora

J Paul Getty Museum

Beverly Hills

West Hollywood

Huntington Art Gallery, Library & Bot Gdns

Arboretum

Covina

Boheli Reg Park

Malibu

UCLA

Southwest Museum

Alhambra

Mission San Gabriel Arcangel

Upland

Will Rogers SHP

LOS ANGELES

East Los Angeles

La Puente

Pomona

Malibu Lagoon State Beach

Santa Monica

Culver City

Exposition Park

Montebello

Chino

Marina del Rey

Inglewood

Huntington Park

Pico Rivera

Los Angeles International Airport

Lynwood

Bell Gardens

Whittier

San Juan Hill 543m

Hawthorne

La Habra

Chino Hills SP

Yorba Linda

Santa Monica Bay

Manhattan Beach

Compton

Gardena

Norwalk

La Mirada

Cal St Univ Fullerton

Redondo Beach

Movieland Wax Museum

Cleveland National Forest

Palos Verdes Estates

Carson

Lakewood

Knott's Berry Farm

Anaheim

Torrance

Disneyland

Anaheim Stadium

Orange

Lunada Bay

South Coast Botanic Gardens

Rancho Los Alamitos

Bowers Museum

Pt Vicente

Long Beach

Westminster

Tustin

Rancho Palos Verdes

San Pedro

Seal Beach

Garden Grove

Santa Ana

Pt Fermin

San Pedro Bay

Sunset Beach

Movieland of the Air

Bolsa Chica St Beach

Huntington Beach

Irvine

Lion Country Safari

Newport Beach

Balboa

El Toro

Corona del Mar State Beach

Crystal Cove SP

Laguna Beach

San Juan Capistrano Mission

San Pedro Channel

Dana Point

Doheny State Beach

West End

Santa Catalina Island

Outer Santa Barbara Channel

Mt Orizaba 648m

Avalon

Seal Rocks

AROUND LOS ANGELES

| 0 | 10 | 20 | 30 km |
| 0 | 5 | 10 | 15 miles |

Fifty years of frantic growth has seen Los Angeles spread across hills, through valleys, and along the coast, absorbing entire communities and turning former farmland into a uniform suburbia stretching as far as the eye can see.

A few older towns have retained their character in this commuter-dominated territory, and it is also around LA that some of the state's very best art collections are stashed. Here, too, Disneyland continues to set the pace for theme parks throughout the world, and the coastline spans everything from broad sandy beaches to towering rocky bluffs.

Beside the ocean just north of LA, Malibu has for years exerted a magnetic appeal to visitors in search of California's rich and beautiful faces. Much more apparent, however, are the surfer-dominated sands and, just inland, rugged canyons which shelter secluded hamlets and provide boundless scope for wilderness hiking.

To the south, the Orange County shoreline is sculptured into numerous coves and inlets, along which several distinctive and personable communities stand in marked contrast to inland Orange County, a network of look-alike middle-class suburbs pock-marked by theme parks – most famously Disneyland – the only reason for most people to penetrate the neighbourhood's blandness.

Beyond the hills on LA's northern edge, an immense population fills the dead-flat floors of the San Gabriel and San Fernando valleys. The luckiest of the valley dwellers live in long-established settlements such as Pasadena and several significant historical sites are also located there.

The beauty of Malibu: a beach near by, on the Pacific Coast Highway.

Centre of glamour and riches: Malibu

Malibu

Many of LA's – and the world's – richest and most glamorous people own million-dollar homes in Malibu, immediately north of Santa Monica. However, it is the dramatic Malibu hills, twisting canyons and inviting beaches that impress.

A century ago, a well-off settler called Frederick H Rindge bought up the Mexican rancho which then covered Malibu. As LA expanded, Rindge (and later his widow, Mary) fought tooth and nail against state plans to put a road through their land, only to be defeated in the Supreme Court and subsequently to see their fortune vanish in the Wall Street Crash.

The Malibu Beach Colony From the 1920s, a secluded beachside enclave of Hollywood notables, which included Clara Bow, Barbara Stanwyck and Gloria Swanson, began turning Malibu into a desirable address. Even today, Malibu's rock stars, TV personalities and sports stars, carefully (if illegally) prevent public access to the beaches close to their homes.

Approaching Malibu from the south brings you first through Pacific Palisades, where the **Will Rogers State Park** holds the former home of the 'Cowboy Philosopher' whose homespun wisdom and one-line witticisms kept Americans amused through the 1920s and 1930s. Old-West artefacts are piled high inside the humorist's former home and the 187-acre grounds include numerous picnic spots and walking and hiking trails, and a still-used polo field where Rogers indulged in his favourite pastime.

A mile to the north, the **Self-Realisation Fellowship**, founded by an Indian Mystic in 1950, seeks to express the universality of the world's major religions. Arranged around a swan-filled lake, the fellowship evokes a suitable mood of serenity and contemplation, and a replica Dutch windmill conceals a small, atmospheric chapel.

Mystical matters are also pursued in neighbouring **Topanga Canyon**, a base for exploring the inner self and the leading of alternative life-styles since a hippie colony arrived here in the psychedelic 1960s.

Between March and August on nights following high tides, small fish called grunion come ashore for a frantic three-hour bout of spawning and egg-burying known as the Grunion Run. Seeing the beach crawling alive with thousands of these squirming fish, the only kind to lay their eggs on land, is an amazing sight that pulls big crowds. Any beach in the LA area is a likely vantage point for this only-in-California phenomenon.

Health and nature Currently, it is the vibrations of the New Age movement (see page 17) which permeate the numerous health-food restaurants, handicraft shops and ramshackle bookstores. Untamed nature is another facet of Topanga Canyon. A network of hiking trails weaves across the chaparral-covered slopes of the 9,000-acre **Topanga State Park**, emerging to breathtaking views of ocean, mountains and sprawling LA.

Similar terrain fills **Malibu Creek State Park,** a few miles north, once used by 20th-Century Fox as the setting of M*A*S*H among many film and TV productions, and where wild flowers brighten the spring meadows.

The town of Malibu is surprisingly bland, and it has been the local beaches that have pulled the crowds since Surfrider Beach provided the setting for the low-budget beach party movies of the late 1950s.

Surfrider Beach, now renamed Malibu Lagoon State Beach, has been overlooked for 90 years by the 700-foot **Malibu Pier.** Besides making a prime vantage point for watching the surfers, the pier (built by Frederick Rindge to unload supply ships) also marks the site of the **Adamson House**, inhabited by one of the Rindge family until 1964. Touring the house, whose Spanish colonial design is enhanced by the colourful ceramics known as 'Malibu tiles', and the adjoining museum, gives an intriguing peep into Malibu's past.

Las Tunas and Corral beaches are noted for their scuba-diving, Paradise Cove is ideal for beachcombing, the picnic tables and snack-stands of Zuma Beach attract thousands of San Fernando Valley dwellers every weekend, and **Leo Carillo State Beach** (which takes its name from the actor who played Poncho in the *Cisco Kid* TV series) is split in two by Sequit Point, a bluff through which wave action has gouged a large tunnel.

By the light of the silvery surf

Surfing, swimming and sunbathing are not the only activities enjoyed along the LA area's coastline. From Malibu in the north to San Clemente in the south, there are ample opportunities for snorkelling and scuba-diving. Explorable underwater caves are plentiful, rich kelp beds attract shoals of brightly coloured fish, and the deep water on the ocean side Santa Catalina (see page 162) has several submerged wrecks. Equipment hire outlets are easy to find anywhere where conditions are suitable.

153

■ **Easily the most opulent of three exceptional, but very different, art museums within the LA area, the J Paul Getty Museum of Art – the world's richest museum – sits high above Santa Monica Bay in an elaborate replica of the Villa dei Papiri, an Italian villa buried by the eruption of Vesuvius 2,000 years ago. .....■**

After 1995, it is intended that only the classical antiquities will remain at the villa, and the rest of the Getty collection will move to a building being erected by architect Richard Meier on an expansive hilltop site in West Los Angeles.

The J Paul Getty Museum of Art

A treasure-trove of art Getty, the controversial and immensely rich oil tycoon, opened the museum in 1974 to show off an already substantial art collection. His major passion was Greek and Roman statuary, a fact borne out by the stunning array of ancient marble, terracotta and bronze figures which fill the villa's ground floor. The highlights include the 2nd-century *Lansdowne Herkales* and the 3rd- to 4th-century *Victorious Athlete*. Almost as impressive are two small items from 2500BC: a Cypriot female figurine and a Cycladic harpist.
If time is tight (as it may well become when viewing this vast hoard), pass over the strong stock of paintings – many of which have been acquired since Getty's death – in favour of the rooms of French decorative art: a remarkable stash of intricately crafted furniture, ceramics, silverware and carpets, from the early years of Louis XIV's reign to the end of the Napoleonic period.

A fascinating array Illustrated manuscripts of the Middle Ages are another recent addition to the museum: the bright, colourful works which adorned religious and other texts make for absorbing viewing. The museum's drawings, too, can be exceptional: a red chalk etching of a nude woman posing as Cleopatra by Rembrandt, and Albrecht Dürer's bizarre *Stag Beetle* being especially eye-catching.
More striking images are found among the photography – from the 1840s on – shown on rotation, and including works by Nadar, Man Ray and August Sander.

The Norton Simon Museum It may be less famous and much less rich, but the quality of the paintings within the Norton Simon Museum in Pasadena surpasses those of the Getty. Here, Rubens, Rembrandt, Raphael and Breughel delight among the Old Masters; Cézanne, Renoir and Van Gogh shine out in well-filled Impressionist and Post-Impressionist galleries; a Degas collection includes a set of small, sculptured dancers; and the 20th-century stock features Picasso, Matisse and the German Expressionists.

Yet the great names (and great works) of Europe are matched by the museum's stunning Asian collections, spanning 2,000 years of North Indian Buddhist art and Hindu sculpture, and South Indian, Himalayan and Southeast Asian art.

The Huntington Art Gallery After encountering such Asian treasures in an LA suburb, discovering an extraordinary stock of English 18th-century portraiture and 19th-century landscapes inside the Huntington Art Gallery, just a few miles east of the Norton, should come as no surprise.

In the former home of railway tycoon Henry E Huntington, who instigated LA's first (and last) efficient mass transit system during the early 1900s, the ornately furnished gallery rooms hold works by Hogarth, Turner and Constable, and lead to the prized exhibits: Gainsborough's *Blue Boy*, Sir Thomas Lawrence's *Pinkie*, and Reynolds' *Mrs Siddons as the Tragic Muse*.

Other sections of the house contain Renaissance paintings and 18th-century French sculpture, and the adjoining Virginia Steele Scott Gallery shows American art from colonial times to the present, and includes a section on the architectural firm of Greene & Greene.

Rare books and manuscripts Elsewhere on the Huntington estate, 2 million manuscripts and 300,000 rare books are housed in the **Huntington Library** – among them a 15th-century manuscript of Chaucer's *The Canterbury Tales* and some early editions of Shakespeare.

Inside the Paul Getty Museum of Art, the wealthiest museum in the world

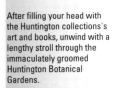

After filling your head with the Huntington collections's art and books, unwind with a lengthy stroll through the immaculately groomed Huntington Botanical Gardens.

Balboa Beach

Made entirely of glass, save for its white steel trusses and wooden fittings, the multi-million dollar Crystal Cathedral (12141 Lewis Street, Garden Grove) was built in 1980 at the behest of TV evangelist Robert Schuller. In 1955, Schuller's preaching career began in a disused drive-in cinema, later moved to the world's first drive-in church, and now centres on showbiz-style sermons delivered from the Crystal Cathedral's pulpit, which are broadcast live on cable TV.

Orange County

Aside from cutting inland to visit Disneyland and a few other theme parks, the best way to take in Orange County – characterised by plain shopping malls, identical houses and freeway interchanges – is by sticking to its coast.

One place warranting a detour deep in the throes of suburbia, however, is the **Richard Nixon Birthplace and Library** at Yorba Linda, which records in a lavish (and entirely uncritical) manner the extraordinary career of the nation's 37th president.

The first of the coastal towns, **Huntington Beach** has been a surfing hot-spot since the 1920s when California's earliest surfing contests were held beside its pier. In the evening, the action moves ashore with dozens of impromptu barbecues held around the beach's fire-rings. By contrast, champagne-drinking yacht owners make neighbouring **Newport Beach** a shrine to money-laden living, with only the three-mile long **Balboa Peninsula** offering any inducement to visitors.

A fine-sanded beach lines the peninsula, whose southern end holds the wooden Balboa Pavilion, a ritzy dance hall from 1905 that is now filled with souvenir shops and amusement arcades. Pleasure craft cruise the harbour from the nearby marina (see page 151), and another short boat trip is the 20¢ ride offered by the Balboa ferry, which has plied the almost jumpable gap between the peninsula and Balboa Isle – an artificial island packed with expensive homes – since 1909.

Away from the beach, local life revolves around the high-fashion clothing outlets of the primly landscaped Fashion Island shopping centre, and the **Newport Harbor Art Museum**, justly acclaimed for its displays of contemporary southern Californian art.

South of Newport Beach, **Crystal Cove State Park** has a refreshingly unkempt and under-used beach, while hiking trails through the inland section of the park lead into the San Joaquin Hills, once a grazing place for the cattle of Mission San Juan Capistrano.

Powdery-sanded beaches, rocky outcrops and secluded inlets make the **Laguna Beach** shoreline the most attractive in Orange County. Such visual appeal has also turned the town into an artists' colony, with a liberal reputation not shared by its Orange County neighbours.

Art galleries and handicraft stalls line Laguna's short streets. Dropping into the **Laguna Beach Museum of Art** reveals the best works of the local artists, and during July and August, thousands flock to the Pageant of the Masters arts festival (see page 158). South of Laguna Beach, the dramatic headland of **Dana Point** rises high above the ocean. It was named after Richard Henry Dana, who described how cow hides were flung over the cliffs to be loaded onto boats below in *Two Years Before the Mast*, his 1840 classic of pre-pioneer writing.

At the southern tip of Orange County, **San Clemente** is a likeable if unexciting resort town, with a cliff-walled beach. To Californians, the town is best known as the location of Richard Nixon's 'Western White House', where the disgraced ex-president sat out his post-resignation years on an estate overlooking the ocean.

Mission San Juan Capistrano was completed in 1806; its **Serra Chapel** is believed to be the state's oldest building. A replica of the original Great Stone Church, destroyed by earthquakes, stands to the north along El Camino Real and serves the local Catholic community. Follow El Camino Rea south downhill and turn right into Verdugo Street to see the **Capistrano Depot**, still the railway terminal, with Spanish arches and decorative tiles. Near by, on Los Rios Street, is the **O'Neill Museum**, which shows the locations of 19th-century adobe homes in the adjacent **Los Rios Historic District**.

Since Spanish times, swallows have nested at Mission San Juan Capistrano and legend (and a hit song of the 1930s) has it that they return from their winter migration each 19 March, St Joseph's Day. In fact, the swallows return throughout the spring, with numerous factors influencing their timekeeping. Nonetheless, crowds of visitors arrive on 19 March for the Fiestas de la Golondrinia, a welcome-home carnival which takes place with or without the swallows, and October's Adios de las Golondrinias, a smaller event marking the swallows' winter departure.

157

Mission San Juan Capistrano

The New Year's Day Tournament of Roses parade in Pasadena is a famous prelude to the play-off between respective champions of the West and mid-West college football leagues at the Rose Bowl Stadium. From mid-July, the six-week Festival of the Arts and Pageant of the Masters in Laguna Beach sees fanciful recreations of famous works of art; alongside, the Sawdust Festival shows and sells local craftwork. Tucked away in the Santa Monica Mountains, there are six weeks of medieval-themed happenings beginning in mid-April at the Renaissance Pleasure Faire in Agoura Hills.

San Gabriel Valley

In the 1920s, the San Gabriel Valley was a verdant landscape of walnut, orange and lemon groves, dotted with small settlements to which Angelenos decanted to improve their health. Today, the valley communities have blurred into an almighty slab of suburbia and suffer in the summer from the infamous LA smog, often thick enough to obscure the nearby mountains and poisonous enough to warrant health warnings being issued.

Conditions permitting, the best base for seeing valley is **Pasadena**, within easy reach of the Gamble House, the Norton Simon Museum and the Huntington Art Gallery, and a section of Colorado Boulevard which has been transformed into a very attractive 'Old Town'.

A few miles south, the first fixed settlement in the valley grew up around **Mission San Gabriel Arcangel** (537 West Mission Drive, San Gabriel), founded in 1771, and whose citrus groves, livestock and high-yield vineyards, made it the most prosperous of the California missions.

Within the five-foot-thick buttressed walls, the mission's original altar remains, and an engrossing museum documents mission life. Unfortunately, earthquakes have regularly caused damage and currently the mission's interior is closed for structural repair.

Reminders of the valley's green past are provided by the **LA Arboretum** (301 N Baldwin Avenue, Arcadia), filling 127 acres of a former Mexican rancho with an exotic array of over 30,000 plants collected from every continent, and by **Descanso Gardens** (1481 Descanso Drive, La Canada), which, aside from more flowers, boasts an oriental teahouse dispensing refreshments.

One place not to be missed is the **Southwest Museum** (just off the Pasadena Freeway at 234 Museum Drive, Highland Park), the brainchild of Charles Lummis, an early protector of LA's architectural heritage (see pages 122–3). Together with a reconstruction of an 1850s adobe building, typical of Mexican California, the museum offers a record of American cultures.

San Gabriel Mountains, seen from Pasadena

Drive The San Gabriel Valley

Begin at the Southwest Museum in Highland Park. Drive north on the Pasadena Freeway, exiting on to Arroyo Boulevard and continuing north to the Rose Bowl Stadium.
The **Rose Bowl Stadium** has staged the New Year's Day Rose Bowl football fixture since 1923.

Go along Rosemont Boulevard and follow signs for the Gamble House.
The **Gamble House** is a definitive example of the California Arts & Crafts architectural movement.

Drive half a mile south on Prospect Street before turning left on to Colorado Boulevard, continuing for six miles to Santa Anita Racetrack.
Birthplace of the photo-finish, the **Santa Anita Racetrack** is a famous horse-racing venue.

Backtrack briefly and turn south on to Rosemead Boulevard. After three miles exit west on to Las Tunas Drive, following signs for Mission San Gabriel Arcangel.
Once the only permanent settlement in the valley, the heavily restored **Mission San Gabriel Arcangel** is now engulfed by suburbia.

Walk Pasadena

Begin at the public library, 285E Walnut Street.
The Renaissance-style **public library** was completed in 1927.

Walk south along Garfield Avenue for Pasadena City Hall.
The courtyard of the Spanish baroque-style **City Hall** surrounds a fountained garden, and a staircase provides access to the dome.

Continue along Garfield Avenue, shortly turning right along Colorado Boulevard and crossing Raymond Avenue for the 'Old Town'.
Pasadena's **'Old Town'** has numerous restored shop façades from the 1910s and 1920s.

Continue along Colorado Boulevard for the Norton Simon Museum (see page 155). Backtrack along Colorado Boulevard to Los Robles Avenue, turning left for the Pacific Asia Museum.
Housed in a 1924 re-creation of a Chinese palace, the **Pacific Asia Museum** exhibits the arts of the Far East and Pacific Rim.

Continue along Los Robles Avenue to Walnut Street, turning left to return to the library.

■ **In a fine example of LA's contrasts and extremes, the city's environs not only contain three world class art collections (see pages 154–5) but also three enormously popular theme parks, including Disneyland, the biggest and best of them all. .....■**

Sleeping Beauty Castle, Disneyland

Disneyland More than 300 million people have visited Disneyland (1313 South Harbor Boulevard, Anaheim) since it opened in 1955 and very few of them have left disappointed. Be it shaking hands with Mickey Mouse or flying through space with R2D2, Disneyland offers escapism at its most innovative and brilliant in a multitude of constantly updated rides and shows.

Extraordinary though it may seem now, visionary animator Walt Disney had to struggle to convince his business partners of the viability of Disneyland, which he described as 'a place for people to find happiness and knowledge'. Disney had the last laugh when a million visitors arrived in the first seven weeks and the park paid off its $9 million debts inside a year.

The jungle of tourist hotels and restaurants which now surround it are proof that Disneyland is never deserted, but being selective about when you come may well save hours of queueing for the most popular attractions: if possible, aim for a mid-week day between mid-September and mid-June.

In the park, head first for **Tomorrowland**, which holds the most imaginative and popular rides. Here you can go into orbit on a Saturn rocket, venture under water on the Submarine Voyage, watch a 3D Michael Jackson save a planet (in the *Captain EO* film), and fasten your seatbelt for Star Tours, a space trip based on the *Star Wars* film.

Many of the early animated Disney characters appear in the less hair-raising **Fantasyland**. Among the rides here are Snow White's Scary Adventures, Peter Pan's Flight, Mr Toad's Wild Ride, and Pinocchio's Daring Journey.

A four-course banquet inside a mock 11th-century castle, complete with javelin-throwing contests, sword-fights, and jousting knights on horseback, is just the ticket after a day spent wandering through a theme park. And that is precisely what is offered at Medieval Times (7662 Beach Boulevard, Buena Park). Reservations are a good idea (tel: (800) 438 9911).

Aiming to capture the spirit of pioneer-period America, **Frontierland** lets you escape death aboard the runaway train of Big Thunder Mountain Railroad, and next door, beneath the iron balconies of New Orleans Square, you can cast off with the Pirates of the Caribbean or be tickled by the cobwebs in the Haunted Mansion.

When you tire, take a ride on the **Disney monorail**, looping from the entrance to Tomorrowland and back, or on the Santa Fe & Disneyland Railroad which circles the park, negotiating the Grand Canyon on the way.

Knotts Berry Farm Smaller and far less slick than Disneyland, Knotts Berry Farm (8039 Beach Boulevard, Buena Park) grew from an 1848 gold rush town re-created during the Depression by farmer John Knott to entertain customers arriving for his wife's 65¢ dinners.

The ghost town section still remains, although millions of dollars have been pumped into the park since Knott's time. One expensive recent addition is the impressive **Kingdom of the Dinosaurs**, a trip back to a time when the earth was roamed by creatures looking vaguely similar to the electronic robots roaming here. Elsewhere, **Camp Snoopy** lets youngsters stave off boredom in the company of the characters of the *Peanuts* cartoon strip.

Six Flags Magic Mountain (26101 Magic Mountain Parkway, Valencia) is almost entirely devoted to scaring people witless, with a complex of roller-coasters and other attractions set across 200 acres of hills and woodlands.

Looping the loop at Knotts Berry Farm

AROUND LOS ANGELES

At Six Flags, the Colossus is believably claimed to be the fastest and biggest wooden roller-coaster ever built: a 110-foot drop is just the start of this exciting ride, which climbs to 9,000 feet before gravity takes over. Not to be outclassed, the Revolution dips and dives on its steel tracks before hurling its white-knuckled passengers around a vertical loop, and the aptly named Shock Wave lets you experience high-speed twists and curves while standing up.

▶ ▶ ▷ Santa Catalina

The best day-trip in the LA area starts with an hour-long ferry crossing to Santa Catalina, an island 26 miles off the Orange County coast. An enticing mix of romantic holiday hideaway and wild backcountry, Catalina also holds the only city (Avalon, population 2,000) in California where nobody travels by car.

History A 4,000-year occupancy of the island by the Gabrieleño Indians was ended in the early 1800s when white fur-trappers arrived and the tribe was forcibly resettled on the mainland. Catalina then became a haunt of smugglers and pirates until William Wrigley Jr (of the Wrigley chewing-gum dynasty) bought it in 1911, discovered a loophole in the state's anti-gambling laws, and opened the Avalon Casino to entice moneyed mainlanders.

With its art deco features restored to their original glory, the casino is now known as the **Avalon Ballroom** and demands to be toured. After which, more of the island's curious history can be gleaned inside the adjacent **Catalina Museum**.

Besides the casino and museum, Avalon also has an enjoyable pier, glass-bottomed boat trips, a small sandy beach, whimsical residential architecture galore, and the curious sight of islanders weaving around on electrically-powered carts (to avoid pollution, cars are as good as banned).

Outside Avalon To see the rest of Catalina, you will need to venture into the pristine interior. The only road, actually a narrow track, runs to the island's airport, passing the flat-topped **Mt Orizaba**, Catalina's highest point with fabulous views of the ocean, and slopes

Several sailings to Santa Catalina depart daily from San Pedro, Long Beach and (in summer) Newport Beach and Redondo Beach. A return trip costs from between $25 and $30. Operators are Catalina Cruises (tel: (800) 888 5939), Catalina Express (tel: (213) 519 1212), and Catalina Passenger Service (tel: (714) 673 5245). Once ashore, zip around Avalon by bicycle or an electrically-powered cart, both available from stands on Crescent Avenue. Other than with a tour, trekking into the interior requires a permit from the Visitor Information Center, facing the pier.

Santa Catalina

where buffalo and antelope roam.

William Wrigley Jr ploughed some of the casino's profits into the Santa Catalina Conservancy, which has restricted commercial development and protected much of the island's unique flora and fauna – including an extraordinary variety of wild flower – easily appreciated at the **Wrigley Botanical Gardens** (1400 Avalon Canyon Road).

The former Wrigley mansion (on Wrigley Terrace Drive), a summer home of the family, is now a guest house, as is the pueblo-style former dwelling of Western author Zane Grey (The Zane Grey Hotel, 199 Chimes Tower Road), who arrived in Catalina for the filming of his book, *The Vanishing American*, and liked it so much he never left. Both ex-homes can be toured.

San Fernando Valley

The ultimate dormitory community for the ultimate metropolis: 1.8 million people fill the 177 square miles of the San Fernando Valley, occupying a vast expanse of identical stuccoed bungalows and doing their shopping in malls haunted by the legendary Valley Girls, responsible for adding titbits such as 'gag me with a spoon', and 'bag your face' to the rich lexicon of LA street-speak.

Like the San Gabriel Valley to the east, white settlement in the San Fernando Valley began with a Spanish mission and later, through the Mexican period, was divided into gigantic land holdings roamed by herds of cattle.

Expansion Not until water began pouring along the Owens Aqueduct in 1913 and San Fernando Valley joined itself administratively to LA, did growth truly begin. Film companies arrived to escape the high rents and confined spaces of Hollywood, heavy industries followed, and the advent of freeways made the valley a viable LA commuter base.

The sights All that most tourists see of the valley are the film and TV-studio tours in North Hollywood and Burbank (see panel), the roller-coasters of the Six Flags Magic Mountain theme park (see page 161–2), or Glendale's Forest Lawn Cemetery (see page 165). Yet while first appearances may suggest otherwise, the San Fernando Valley does a pretty good job of preserving its past.

Now unceremoniously skirted by freeways, the focal point of valley life at the turn of the 19th century was Mission **San Fernando Rey** (15151 San Fernando Mission Boulevard), whose church, bell-tower and monastery have been completely rebuilt and many of the original workshops and storerooms re-created to give visitors a sound grounding in the fundamentals of mission life.

In Brand Park, facing the mission, plants and shrubs from California's other missions are grown and, a few streets away, the San Fernando Historical Society mounts temporary exhibitions inside the Indian-built **Andres Pico Adobe** (10940 Sepulveda Boulevard), LA's second-oldest home, dating from 1834.

The stunt-filled Universal Studios Tour (tel: (818) 508 9600), which lays on a saloon bar shoot-out, a meeting with Jaws and the parting of the Red Sea for its visitors, is the most spectacular of the film and TV studio tours available in the San Fernando Valley. To learn about actual production techniques, reserve a place on the Warner Brothers Studios VIP tour (tel: (818) 954 1744), which includes visiting in-use sound stages and editing suites.
Aficionados of American TV might prefer the 75-minute glimpse behind the scenes offered at NBC Studios (tel: (818) 840 3537).

163

Half a mile long and still growing, the *Tujunga Wash* mural is the longest such artwork in the world, and the account of California history it depicts does not spare the murkier episodes staining the state's back pages. You will find the mural, a collaborative project overseen by the Venice Arts Center, on Coldwater Canyon Boulevard, between Burbank Boulevard and Oxnard Street.

Encino Several further points of historical appeal lie in Encino, a leafy well-to-do district on the western side of the valley. Here, the nine-acre **Los Encinos State Historic Park** is filled with eucalyptus trees and contains a natural spring which quenched the thirst of a Spanish discovery party in 1769, and the nine-room Osa Adobe built 1849. A less expected sight in the park is a limestone French-style house, the work of two Basque brothers in 1872.

Calabasas The cobwebs are kept off two more ageing homes in Calabasas, an Old West flavoured town making much of its past as a stagecoach stop. The **Leonis Adobe** (23537 Calabasas Road) had its second storey added by Miguel Leonis, a smuggler turned sheep-farmer, in imitation of the Monterey-style in vogue during the 1840s. The **Plummer House**, dating from 1879, now forms the entrance to the Leonis Adobe and has displays on the valley's rancho period.

At the northern end of the valley, the mansion and grounds of the hilltop **William S Hart Park** (24151 Newhall Avenue), belonged to a silent-era movie cowboy, who became the role model for all subsequent celluloid western heroes. Packed with Old West furnishings and ornaments, and intriguing bits and pieces from Hart's acting career, the home is set at the heart of a 260-acre park, and watched over by the grazing bison.

Forest Lawn

■ **Forest Lawn cemetery has several branches around LA but the most famous of them – and the one which inspired Evelyn Waugh's satirical novel *The Loved One* – fills a 300-acre hillside site on the edge of the San Fernando Valley (1712 S Glendale Avenue, Glendale). .....■**

A unique concept Founded in 1917, the idea of Forest Lawn was to create a fusion of art and landscaping to uplift the living as much as to remember the dead. To this end, the cemetery boasts almost 1,000 pieces of classical statuary, including replicas of all of Michelangelo's most noted works, a huge stained-glass replica of da Vinci's *The Last Supper*, and a 500-square-foot mosaic based on the *Signing of the Declaration of Independence*.

Forest Lawn's small amount of original art is no less grandiose. In the **Hall of the Crucifixion-Resurrection**, Jan Styka's 195 foot by 45 foot *Crucifixion* is claimed to be the world's largest religious work on canvas, and it partners Robert Clark's only slightly smaller *The Resurrection*. Meanwhile, funeral services (and, surprisingly perhaps, a large number of weddings) take place in the cemetery's churches:

painstaking re-creations of 10th- and 14th-century English and Scottish originals.

Last stop for the rich and famous

The fame of the cemetery itself tends to eclipse the stature of the many movie idols spending eternity within its midsts. The tombs of Clark Gable, Carole Lombard, Jean Harlow and W C Fields are inside the **Great Mausoleum**, while Clara Bow, Chico Marx, Alan Ladd and Nat King Cole are among those interned in the **Freedom Mausoleum**, just outside of which lies Errol Flynn – allegedly sharing his coffin with six bottles of whisky.

The other main branch of Forest Lawn is in the Hollywood Hills on the edge of Griffith Park (6300 Forest Lawn Drive) where, besides another batch of imitation European sculpture, the roll-call of the deceased includes Buster Keaton, Stan Laurel, George Raft and Liberace.

Forest Lawn statuary

SAN DIEGO

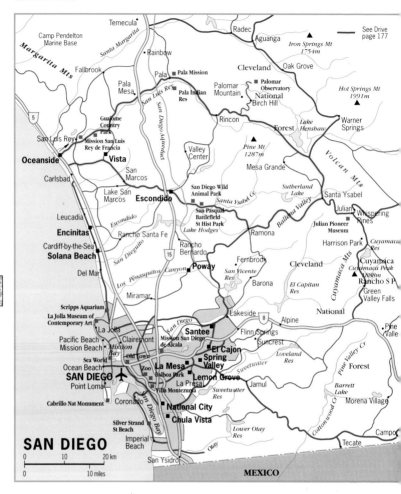

See Drive page 177

SAN DIEGO

```
0          10          20 km
0          10 miles
```

MEXICO

Affluent, comfortable and bathed daily in sunshine, San Diego is as close to the ideal holiday destination as it is possible to get. While lacking the romance of San Francisco and the glamour of Los Angeles, San Diego is free of the smog and the inner-city social problems that blight its northerly rivals, and nobody who lives there – whether they are basking on the best beaches in California or making their fortune in the city's international banking market – would trade California's second-biggest city for any other.

Landing in 1542 on Point Loma, a rugged peninsula sheltering San Diego Bay, Juan Cabrillo became the first European to set foot on Californian soil. Yet it was not until the building of California's first mission in 1769 that San Diego's settlement began, in what is now the Old Town, six miles northwest of today's Downtown.

Downtown itself only came into being a few decades after US rule was established, the centre of a classic spit-and-sawdust frontier town. San Diego did itself a power of good by staging the 1915 Panama-California

Exposition. This brought international prestige, and turned Balboa Park – a mile north of Downtown – into a nationally known showcase of Spanish-style architecture and landscape gardening.

Another economic boost came in the 1940s when San Diego became the base of the the US Navy's Pacific fleet. Aircraft carriers and frigates became a common sight, and the military presence fuelled the city's reputation for conservatism.

Today's San Diego knows how look after itself. Restoration programmes have kept many historic areas intact and accessible, numerous parks and waterways are set aside for recreational use, and the investment of $165 million in a sparkling new Convention Center evinces the city's intention to be among the nation's most up-to-date and user-friendly cities.

Around San Diego There is a sharp distinction between the heavily populated suburban communities lining the coast and the sleepy rural towns dotting a sparse inland area, which is flanked by pine-coated hills.

San Diego is also on Mexico's doorstep: the city's public transport runs to the border, and Tijuana, just over it, can easily be toured as a half-day excursion.

A San Diego street

Entry to almost all the Balboa Park museums is free on the third Tuesday of every month, otherwise admission ranges from free to $4. Buying a Balboa Passport allows you into any four museums on any one day. Most of the museums are closed on Mondays.

The 500-seat Globe Theater (in Balboa Park), an approximate replica of London's 15th-century original, is one of three theatres forming the Simon Edison Complex for the Performing Arts. To find out what is playing, tel: (619) 239 2255.

Music-maker in Balboa Park

▶ ▶ ▶   Balboa Park

Leasing a section of the rattlesnake-infested scrubland on the northern outskirts of late-1800s San Diego paid off for the local authorities. Planting trees in lieu of rent, a local botanist started what officially became Balboa Park in 1911 – 1,000 green acres of lush, tropical landscaping only a mile from Downtown. A host of Spanish baroque-style buildings, erected for the Panama-California Exposition of 1915 and the California-Pacific International Exposition 20 years later, catch the eye in Balboa Park, and they hold one of the largest groupings of museums in the US.

In the northern half of the park, the San Diego Museum of Art, draws its ample stocks from near and far: floors of European Old Masters adjoin rooms of squatting Buddhas and gleaming jewels from all points east, and vigorous American Pop Art fills the final spacious halls.

The smaller **Timkin Gallery** is more selective, with an outstanding grouping of Russian icons taking pride of place. Near by, the **Art Institute Gallery** carries low-key exhibitions of local artists, and the temporary exhibitions at the **Museum of Photographic Arts** are rarely dull.

Away from art, there are entertaining and informative hands-on exhibits in the **Museum of Natural History**, and at the **Reuben H Fleet Space Theater and Science Center** the IMAX films, projected on to a gigantic screen, make the movie shows – ranging from space trips to assaults on mountains – breathtakingly realistic.

The **Museum of Man** reveals a little of the native American cultures of the southwest and the efforts of anthropologists to examine them, though the overall effect is slightly shallow. The **Museum of San Diego History** is more enjoyable, recording the rise of the city.

In the centre of Balboa Park, the open-air Spreckels Organ Pavilion houses the world's largest pipe organ (there is a free recital each Sunday afternoon), and each of the cottages of the House of Pacific Relations has a few cultural knick-knacks from various foreign countries. At the southern section end of the park (reached by foot or aboard a free trolley-bus), the **Aerospace Historical Center** will keep anyone remotely interested in flight and fliers amused for hours with collections from the beginnings of manned flight to the conquest of space. Next door, the **Automative Museum** does a less thorough job for land-based transport, showing off rows of the streamlined autos that cruised across the US in 1940s and 1950s.

▶ ▶ ▷   Coronado

Across the curling Coronado Bridge from Downtown, and also accessible by the ferry from San Diego Harbour, the tidy community of Coronado grew up around the **Hotel Del Coronado**, a whimsical Victorian pile of wooden turrets and towers built to lure wealthy, ailing Easterners to the balmy southern climate.
The hotel has been spoiling its guests since the 1880s, the most notable of whom – including the future Edward VIII and Mrs Simpson, who allegedly met here in 1920 – are remembered inside the hotel's small museum. You will also spot memorabilia from the 1950s movie, *Some Like It Hot*, which found Marilyn Monroe, Jack Lemmon and Tony Curtis cavorting around the hotel's grounds.
Other than the hotel, there is little else to see in Coronado, though the Trackless Trolley finds enough to fill a 20-minute narrated tour; it leaves from the ferry dock and includes a stop at the hotel.

The Hotel Del Coronado

Festivals are two a penny in San Diego but the following are the most enjoyable: the Mexican Cinco de Mayo (5 May) celebration in the Old Town; the Cabrillo Festival, centred on Point Loma, a re-enactment of the first European landing in California (late September); the Michelob Street Scene, open-air rock music in Downtown's Gaslamp Quarter (September); and the Over-The-Line softball tournament contested by 1,000 teams on the city's beaches every July. Around San Diego, the major event is the Del Mar Fair, a three-week long recreation of an old-time state fair, running from mid-June.

169

■ Few Californian cities have been as careful or as successful as San Diego in protecting and restoring their architectural heritage. Be it the squat adobe homes of pioneer settlers or the streamlined office blocks of contemporary San Diego, the city's buildings are seldom individually striking, but collectively they provide a lucid insight into the community's development. .....■

Old Town Many cramped but comfortable adobe homes were built in what is now the Old Town, their thick mud-brick walls keeping the rooms cool in summer while improvised carpets of straw softened the rough floors. Several good examples remain, their survival largely due to the relocation of the city to the present Downtown during the late 1800s.

<< Tijuana is only 23 miles from San Diego and a visit does give a taste of south-of-the-border life. There are no customs or immigration formalities but to re-enter the US, passport holders who require a visa for entry into the US will need to meet the usual requirements (see page 256). >>

Santa Fe railway depot, a fine example of Spanish-Moorish style

The Gaslamp Quarter In Downtown, the boom years are remembered by the tidied up, turn-of-the-century commercial brick buildings of the Gaslamp Quarter, whose owners grew rich and secreted themselves in picturesque Queen Anne homes, many of which still stand a few miles north in the bohemian Hillcrest area.

Expo Although San Diego originally grew around a Spanish mission, it was not until 1915 that the city made a fuss about its roots, erecting half a dozen Spanish baroque-style buildings in Balboa Park for the Panama-California Exposition. Few of these buildings were intended to last, but the success of the Exposition in putting San Diego on the map, and the popularity of the buildings – with their elaborate façades and sculpture-filled courtyards – among local people was impossible to ignore. Strengthening and rebuilding took place, and a second Exposition was held in 1935, this time signalling the city's emergence from the Depression. The spacious Spanish-Moorish Santa Fe railway depot, on Broadway in Downtown, was also designed for the 1915 Expo and continues to be a pleasing sight for rail passengers. Recently, however, the station has become overshadowed by the black, bronze and silver exteriors of Broadway's numerous new office blocks, rising up to proclaim the city's present-day role as a centre of US-Far East high finance.

Mission Beach broadwalk

 Downtown

A frantic swirl of bankers, beggars, and fast-food vendors, Downtown San Diego's easily walked **Gaslamp Quarter** should not be missed. It comprises 16 short blocks lined by restored buildings just south of Broadway between 4th and 6th avenues.

Patterned red-brickwork and other Romanesque revival trimmings decorate many of the district's structures, which went up between the 1860s and 1920s, though the best place to begin is at the William Heath Davis House (410 Island Avenue; also the departure point for walking tours at 10.00hrs on Saturdays), a simple wooden dwelling dating from 1850.

 Mission Bay

The marshland which once filled the gap between Downtown and Mission Beach is now the sculptured lagoons and beaches of Mission Bay Park, offering rich pickings for watersports enthusiasts. Mission Bay is also the home of **Sea World**, where theatrical shows by killer whales and dolphins draw thousands of people, and the penguin and shark exhibits are among the best of their kind. However, Sea World attracts plenty of criticism for its training of intelligent creatures for human amusement; marine conservationist Jacques Cousteau is just one who refuses to visit.

 Old Town and Mission Valley

From 1769, California's first Spanish mission sat on the hilltop overlooking what is now the Old Town, where San Diego began. Half a decade on, the mission was moved six miles north, and the Old Town almost disappeared when the new San Diego (the present Downtown) was founded.

The restored buildings of the Old Town merit a stroll, though few match the reconstructed **old mission** for atmosphere, still serving a spiritual function but now in the urban sprawl of Mission Valley (10818 San Diego Mission Road). Its museum is well stocked too.

San Diego in the late 19th century was better known for its saloons and whorehouses than its culture. Endeavouring to change things, a band of wealthy settlers clubbed together and built an irresistible mansion – the Villa Montezuma (1925 K Street) – to lure a renowned English-born aesthete and entertainer, Jesse Shepard, to the fledgling city. Shepard's effect on the community, and his penchant for stained glass and spiritualism, can be assessed on guided tours of the lovingly restored abode.

SAN DIEGO

One way to reach the Old Town is aboard an Old Town Trolley, one of several buses which link the Old Town with Balboa Park, Coronado and Downtown, on a two-hour loop route. It is a stress-free way to see the city, and the amusing spiel of the drivers will keep you entertained and informed. Tickets can be used repeatedly all day (for details, tel: (619) 469 6944).

▶ ▶ ▶ **Old Town**

San Diego's first permanent settlement mostly comprised presidio (the military fort protecting the mission) personnel and their families living at the foot of the hill beneath the mission. Within the Old Town State Historic Park, several of San Diego's earliest buildings have been restored and many more are devoted to preserving the memory of bygone times.

The adobe structures of the early 1800s are by far the most interesting buildings. The largest of them, the labyrinthine **Casa de Estudillo**, belonged to José Estudillo, the first commander of the presidio. Following Estudillo's death, the structure proved large enough to accommodate Estudillo's son, his wife, and their 12 children.

José Estudillo's son-in-law, Juan Bandini, was another significant figure in early San Diego, who turned his home – Casa de Bandini – into a noted social gathering place. When Bandini fell on hard times the house was sold and turned into a hotel; it is now an enjoyable Mexican restaurant.

San Diego came under US rule in 1846, an era evoked by several things: the single-classroom Mason Street School; the Western memorabilia inside the Seeley Stables; the San Diego Union Building, where the first edition of what is still the city's main newspaper was assembled in 1868; and the Whaley House Museum (just outside the park at 2482 San Diego Avenue), San Diego's first brick-built house, stuffed with the fixtures and fittings typical of a well-to-do settler of the 1850s.

Taking a break at the Bazaar del Mundo, San Diego's up-market version of a Mexican street bazaar

One edge of the park is consumed by Bazaar del Mundo, an entertaining if up-market imitation of a Mexican street bazaar, whose tiled courtyard is lined with restaurants and craft shops.

▶ ▷ ▷ Presidio Park
In a faithful reconstruction of the original mission, and close to its original site at the crown of Presidio Park, the Junípero Serra Museum provides a modest insight into Spanish mission life in California. More dramatically, the contrast of early photos and the current view through the windows make plain the incredible recent growth of the city: quiet orange groves becoming traffic-clogged freeways in a just a few decades.

▶ ▶ ▶ Point Loma
Wealthy residential areas, naval bases, thick woodlands, and coastal bluffs reminiscent of the state's Central Coast, characterise the 10-mile long Point Loma peninsula which divides San Diego Bay from the Pacific. At Point Loma's southernmost point, the unspectacular **Cabrillo National Monument** marks the landing of Juan Cabrillo, a Portuguese adventurer who, in September 1542, became the first European to arrive in California. The view over the bay to the San Diego skyline is sufficient reason to come here, however, and there is also a 19th-century lighthouse to explore and footpaths leading to the tidal pools beneath the bluffs.

▷ ▷ ▷ San Diego Harbour
The departure point for numerous sailings and the site of two sea-linked museums, San Diego Harbour is where the city displays its nautical connections. The pick of three vintage vessels moored in the **Maritime Museum** is the *Star of India*, a fully equipped three-mast sailing ship that plied the seven seas from 1863.
Adjacent, a disused warehouse now stores the **America's Cup Museum**, telling the story of the yachting event that has been whipping up local passion since 1987, when the San Diego Yacht Club brought the cup back from Australia, and more recently when San Diego hosted the America's Cup in 1992.
From the harbour, the **Embarcadero** walkway winds around the bay front, passing joggers and roller-skaters, to **Seaport Village**. Here there are some entertaining souvenir shops, but they are aimed at the tourist.

▶ ▶ ▶ San Diego Zoo
To the north of Balboa Park, San Diego Zoo got started with animals left over from the 1915 Panama-California Exposition. It has since grown into a one of the world's leading zoos, specialising in re-creating a range of habitats – from deep canyons to equatorial rainforests. Wherever possible, moats and other natural obstacles are used in preference to bars.
Among nearly 4,000 inhabitants across 128 acres of plushly vegetated grounds are the US's largest gathering of koalas, some flourishing Galapagos turtles (like koalas, an endangered species) and an excellent collection of primates. Many other smaller, strokeable creatures reside inside the Children's Zoo.

San Diego Zoo

Whenever schedules permit, the US Navy berths one or more of its vessels at the end of Broadway Pier for free public viewing. Close by are the departure points for civilian ferries and pleasure boats, such as the San Diego Bay Ferry (also called the Coronado Ferry) to Coronado, numerous sightseeing trips around the bay, and all-day cruises to the Mexican coastal town of Ensenada.

■ **San Diego is great news for sea and sand addicts. Whether you want to surf, swim, sunbathe, snorkel, or strip off completely you will find the perfect spot somewhere along the 70 miles of coastline in and around the city.....■**

In a city almost surrounded by water, it should be no surprise that watersports are big news in San Diego. Yachting is favoured by the smart set, but it is surfing that captures the imagination and there is no better place in the state to try your luck. Boards can be hired for around $8 from any of the numerous shops around Ocean Beach and Mission Beach. If you do not fancy making a fool of yourself, watch accomplished exponents of the art in action at Tourmaline Surfing Park and Windansea Beach in La Jolla.

Imperial Beach Quiet and secluded (not least because of fears of sewage spills from Mexico), Imperial Beach is an inauspicious beginning at San Diego's southern extremity, but its northern edge meets the more promising Silver Strand State Beach, a 15-mile long sliver of sand dividing San Diego Bay from the Pacific Ocean.

Silver Strand State Beach Parts of Silver Strand are high-grade beachcombing territory (indeed, its name is derived from the millions of tiny silver seashells which wash up on it), while other sections, equipped with picnic tables and fire rings, fill at weekends with families. Silver Strand also provides the sole link between the mainland and Coronado, where a lack of strong currents makes Coronado Shores Beach an ideal base for sea swimming.

Ocean Beach Across the bay, sheer-sided cliffs are typical of the Point Loma shoreline. A notable exception, though, is Ocean Beach, a haunt of surfers and beach revellers, if much less the all-out party venue today than it was a few years ago. At the nearby northern end, in a very Californian gesture, Dog Beach is reserved for untethered canines and their owners.

Mission Beach Do not come to San Diego and miss Mission Beach. Seething with surfers and barely covered tanning flesh, and buzzing with impromptu games of beach volleyball, Mission Beach is a perfect example of the southern California beach strip. Beside the actual beach a vintage carousel began turning again in 1991 and the smart shops and fitness centre of Belmont Park replaced what used to be a crumbling funfair. These things have brought more families to Mission Beach but have done little to dent the pervading sense of youthful hedonism.

Mission Beach – an archetypal California beach

Blue sea, white sands...Mission Bay

Pacific Beach Directly north of Mission Beach, Pacific Beach is calmer and more refined. Nevertheless, it holds most of the bars and discos favoured by Mission Beach revellers after dark. It also eases the transition from San Diego proper into wealthy La Jolla, where Tourmaline Surfing Park and Windansea Beach are legendary among skilled surfers (novices are only welcome as spectators). Also in La Jolla, the crystal-clear waters of La Jolla Cove cover a marine park and a series of caves, which are enjoyable to explore with the aid of a snorkel.

For a complete tan, make for the soft sands of Black's Beach, a few miles north of La Jolla, where all-nude volleyball games are played (although nudity was outlawed in 1971). Perhaps the authorities turn a blind eye since the beach is shielded from prying eyes by 1,000-foot high sandstone cliffs, with the beach accessible only by a treacherous pathway.

Star-spotting This plays a key part of the activity on Del Mar Beach, though often the film, TV and sports celebrities who live in the town take the rays from the privacy of their poolside. A few miles north, Solana Beach has a more egalitarian mood, as does Moonlight State Beach, between Leucadia and Encinitas, the start of a surfer-dominated strand stretching for 10 miles to Carlsbad, where the classic Beach Boys' songs still ring true and board-clutching blond hunks appear whenever the surf is up. The bars and diners surrounding the beaches also retain a laid-back 1960s ambience.

Camp Pendleton Marine Base Total contrast comes at the perimeter of San Diego County with the enormous Camp Pendleton Marine Base. Save for a nuclear power station, no buildings blot the landscape and three untainted beaches offer what is generally acknowledged as the best surfing in the entire US.

The much-loved California gray whales head south from the Arctic Ocean to the warm waters off Baja California from mid-December to March. With luck, you will catch sight of them from the viewing platforms close to the Cabrillo National Monument on Point Loma, or from Whale Point in La Jolla. For a closer look, numerous companies run boat tours, advertised along San Diego Harbour.

▶ ▷ ▷   Carlsbad

Among the more distinctive of the coastal communities in the San Diego hinterland, Carlsbad is also one of the nicest in which to stroll. The tourist-friendly shops of the downtown area include the **Alt Karlsbad Haus Gift Shop**, which doubles as the entrance to a small museum recording the stroke of luck that allowed the town to prosper from the late 1800s: a natural well, the waters of which became famous for their health-improving qualities.

▷ ▷ ▷   Chula Vista

Striving to forge an identity of its own within the metropolitan San Diego area, Chula Vista benefits from a bayside location: its enjoyable harbourside walk meanders beside a multitude of yachts and fishing boats, and the **Nature Interpretive Center** provides a solid introduction to the ecology of California's wetlands; some of the 130 species of bird which inhabit them can be spied from the observation tower.

▶ ▷ ▷   Cuyamaca

Often neglected by visitors making for the neighbouring Anza-Borrego Desert, Cuyamaca and its enormous **Cuyamaca Rancho State Park** offers landscapes ranging from forests of oak and pine to upland meadows riven by mountain streams. It is a place best appreciated by hiking and camping: this is easily done, as hundreds of miles of trails span the park's 26,000 acres and campsites are plentiful.

Near the information centre, there is also a small museum recording the resistance of the local Indian tribes to 19th-century white settlers' attempts to plunder the area's tree stocks.

Indian tribes' museum, Cuyamaca

The tall bluffs which divide La Jolla from Del Mar are covered by the 1,000-acre Torrey Pines State Preserve, holding one of the world's two surviving stands of the Torrey pine tree. Owing to salty soil, the pines here grow as little as 10 feet in 100 years, while ocean winds force them into strange, stumpy shapes that make any of the short walking trails a memorable undertaking.

▶ ▷ ▷   Del Mar

Actor Bing Crosby and singer Pat O'Brien took a shine to the seaside resort of Del Mar during the 1930s and pumped money into the local racecourse, which soon became a palm-lined architectural masterpiece and helped solidify the town's reputation as a playground for Hollywood's rich and famous. Household names still have holiday homes here, though the real draws are the beach and shops and restaurants along 15th Street.

Drive Highway-76 and Highway-78

(See map on page 166.)

Leave Oceanside on Highway-76; drive for five miles to San Luis Rey.
On the left, **Mission San Luis Rey de Francia** dates from 1798, and is the largest of the California missions (see page 180). The ruins of the no less sizeable guards barracks are on the right.

Continue for three miles.
On the right, the **Guajome Adobe** was at the centre of Rancho Guajome (see panel, this page), a major land-holding during Mexican rule in the 19th century; it now sits at the heart of the 500-acre **Guajome County Park**.

Continue on Highway-76, entering the Pala Indian Reservation.
On the left, the small **Pala Mission** was founded in 1816 and serves the spiritual and educational needs of reservation dwellers. The interior of the **chapel** is decorated by Pala Indian murals (see page 180).

Continue for 24 miles and turn left along Road S6 for the Palomar Observatory.
Since the 1940s, the **Palomar Observatory**'s 200-inch telescope has tracked and photographed galaxies at the edge of the known universe. The museum has photos and explanatory displays, and the mighty telescope can be viewed from the visitors' gallery.

Return to Highway-76 and continue for 30 miles to the junction with Highway-78 at Santa Ysabel.
Just before the junction, the tiny **Mission Santa Ysabel** stands on the left, with a one-room museum and a large Indian cemetery.

Drive west for 32 miles on Highway-78, passing Ramona and San Diego Wild Animal Park, to Escondido.
Escondido is best known as the home of light entertainer Lawrence Welk, whose museum, recording

<< Following Mexican independence from Spain, large chunks of mission-owned land were granted to Spanish-Mexican settlers, the so-called *Californios*, for farming. One of these major farms became Rancho Guajome, at the centre of which was the 20-room Guajome Adobe, now rated as one of the finest examples of the period's domestic architecture. Eight miles from Oceanside on Highway-76, the adobe is best appreciated by joining the guided tour (for further details, tel: (619) 565 3600). **>>**

the growth of his 'champagne music', and golf-based resort consume the northern edge of town.

Continue for 24 miles on Highway-78, to Carlsbad.
Carlsbad's surfer-packed beach is typical of San Diego's coastal towns, but a curious past as a spa resort makes it one of the more historically distinguished (see page 176).

The Palomar Observatory

Bernado Winery,
near Escondido

The comparatively cool climate and fertile soils found in the foothills of the mountains dividing San Diego County from the inland deserts, allow the cultivation of apples, peaches, pears and other fruit which are otherwise in short supply. Drive anywhere close to Julian and you will find roadside stalls offering locally grown fruit and jam, and each October the town lets its hair down for the month-long Apple Harvest Festival.

▷ ▷ ▷ **Escondido**

A quiet and comfortable residential community, Escondido is also the home of MOR entertainer Lawrence Welk, whose **Lawrence Welk Village**, containing a dinner theatre and a museum devoted to his career, sits on the edge of town.

Close by are a couple of commendable wineries – Bernardo and Ferrara – both of which offer free tastings and tours, though a bigger attraction is the expansive **San Diego Wild Animal Park**, six miles east. Taking up where the San Diego Zoo leaves off, the park recreates African and Asian terrains and fills them with the appropriate creatures.

▶ ▶ ▶ **Julian**

First settled by gold miners in the 1860s, Julian swiftly became one of the biggest towns in San Diego County. The present population is just 500, with locals being outnumbered at weekends by visitors enjoying Julian's setting in thickly forested mountain foothills. Many San Diegans also come to Julian during the winter for their first sight of the snow. The **Pioneer Museum** forges a strong impression of the town's rough-and-ready early days.

Inside the **Julian Cider Mill**, a right turning off Main Street, you can inspect the process of turning apples into cider, see peanut butter being made and sample honey produced by the mill's own beehive. Across Main Street and B Street, the **Julian Hotel**, founded by freed slaves, has been offering accommodation since 1899, but keeps its quaintly furnished interior for viewing by guests only. Back along Main Street and to the right along C Street are the **Old Miner's Trail** and the **Eagle Gold Mine Museum**, which stores the last vestiges of Julian's gold-mining industry in a series of claustrophobic tunnels.

■ **San Diegans are noted for their bulging bank accounts, but those with more money than most buy homes on the hibiscus-lined lanes of La Jolla (pronounced 'La Hoya'), a hillside community rising high above the Pacific directly north of the city. .....**■

Chic and non-conformist With its showpiece streets, Prospect Street and Girard Avenue, filled with trendy art galleries, expensive boutiques, members-only fitness centres and chic top-notch eateries, La Jolla is a place with pretensions. However, it is also a place with a streak of non-conformity stemming from its many resident artists and writers, and its proximity to the sprawling campus of the University of California.

The town, whose name either means 'the jewel' (from the Spanish) or 'cave' (from Indian legend) depending on who tells the tale, also boasts a picturesque coastline, a fine modern art museum, and fancy wrought-iron benches that are a welcome sight for visitors in need of a breather.

Modern art After admiring the contours of the coast from Scripps Park, a small and tidy green patch flanked by palm trees above La Jolla Cove, call into the Museum of Contemporary Art, which specialises in modern works from the California minimalist and Pop Art genres. Most of the museum itself is a modern work, too, designed by renowned San Diego architect Irving Gill, although its origins go back to 1915 and an oceanside villa belonging to Ellen Browning Scripps, wealthy sister of a publishing magnate who poured money into La Jolla throughout her life.

Marine research Scripps is to be thanked for keeping much of La Jolla free from developer-led devastation, most spectacularly the Torrey Pines State Preserve (see page 176). Furthermore, her money financed the **Scripps Oceanographic Institute and Scripps Aquarium**, in which stunning re-creations of

marine habitats illuminate the mysteries of the deep, and the **Salk Institute**, an extremely well-equipped biological research centre occupying an imposing concrete structure (intended to stimulate original thought) perched above the ocean.

Folk art One further sight of note in La Jolla, though oddly placed in the University Town Center shopping mall, is the **Mengei International Museum of World Folk Art**, whose stimulating exhibitions are drawn from native cultures around the globe.

A university campus sculpture

One of southern California's most exclusive communities lies five miles inland from Solana Beach on Road S8. Here in the 1920s, Hollywood's favourite couple, Douglas Fairbanks and Mary Pickford, bought a ranch and soon turned the area into a millionaires' playground. Many fabulous hillside mansions are obscured from public view by trees, though anyone can walk around the town's ultra-smart Rancho Santa Fe Inn in the hope that some of the glamour may rub off on them.

▷ ▷ ▷ Oceanside

The town has a decent strip of beach and fishermen line the wooden pier, but most of Oceanside is dominated by the marines from the neighbouring Camp Pendleton base, the US military's main centre for amphibious-landing training, and the reason why 125,000 acres along the coast north from Oceanside are totally free of development.

Surfers are partial to the sea here, however, and there is a Landing Vehicle Track Museum inside the base that is open to the public, where you can learn more about the tricks of the amphibious landing trade than you thought it was possible to know.

▷ ▷ ▷ Pala

The tiny community of Pala sits just inside the Pala Indian Reservation and holds the only mission in California still serving Indians as a place of worship and education.

Built in 1816 as a branch of Mission San Luis Rey, the **Pala Mission** (known formally as Mission Assistencia de San Antonio de Pala) had suffered considerable deterioration by the time the Cupeño tribe was forcibly moved to the area in 1903. Some parts have been finely restored and the interior walls of the chapel are covered with intriguing frescos, but the bumpy brick floors and the splintered beams give the mission a rustic appearance; something matched by the hand-made wooden crosses marking the tombs of the Indian cemetery, just outside.

The Mission of San Luis Rey de Franca – occupied by Franciscan monks since 1893

▷ ▷ ▷   San Luis Rey

Once described as the 'the most beautiful, most symmetrical, and the most substantial mission in California', the **Mission of San Luis Rey de Franca** had 3,000 native Americans under its jurisdiction during the early 1800s, and even today is an impressive sight as it emerges from the anonymous suburbia that fills the five miles between it and Oceanside.

While only the 1807 church is original, the mission has been kept in good repair by the order of Franciscan monks who have occupied it since 1893. The museum gives an instructive account of mission-era life, and there are numerous pieces from the time of the mission's founder, Padre Fermin de Lasuen.

In mid-July, a fiesta based around the Blessing of the Animals ceremony takes place in the mission's grounds.

▷ ▷ ▷   Santa Ysabel

Most people visit Santa Ysabel, a community of a few hundred people around the junction of Highway-76 and Highway-78, only long enough to buy bread from **Dudley's Bakery**, where the choice of still-warm loaves spans jalopeño, onion, potato, Irish brown and German black.

However, a short way along Highway-76, the minuscule **Mission Santa Ysabel** is of historical significance, founded in 1818 as a branch of the San Diego Mission. The small church that stands here now dates from 1924, and is less interesting than the mission's one-room museum, packed with photos and objects, and carrying a text describing the mystery of the mission's missing bells. There is a honesty box inside for your dollar donation, and a sign reminds you to switch off the light when you leave.

If you are visiting in November, you will see the mission's Indian cemetery bathed in candle-light; traditionally at this time, a candle is placed on every grave.

From May to September, the hillsides of Encinitas, half-way between Del Mar and Carlsbad, are covered with a colourful carpet of blooming flowers – an indication of the town's place as a major flower-producing centre. To revel in the sights and fragrances, stop at the Quail Botanical Gardens (230 Quail Gardens Drive) and follow the self-guided walking tour.

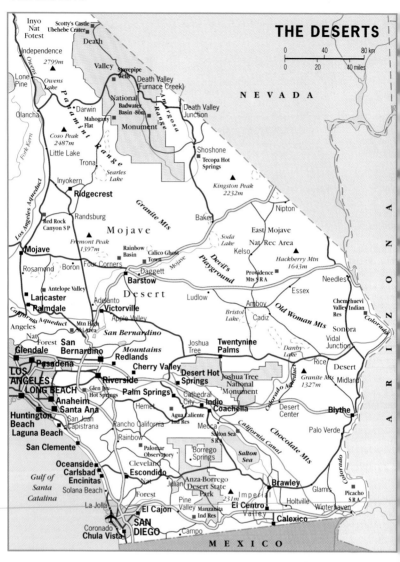

THE DESERTS

0   40   80 km
0   20   40 miles

NEVADA

ARIZONA

MEXICO

Far from being the barren wastelands many people expect, some of the most striking vistas in all of California are found within the three deserts which occupy the southern and eastern parts of the state.

Flora and fauna These climatically extreme but ecologically delicate regions teem with exotic plant and animal life, and contain often monotonous – but sometimes spectacular – landscapes of rippled sand dunes, weather-sculptured rocks, and eerily shaped trees, interspersed by palm-filled oases and bordered by snow-capped mountain ranges.

The high elevation of the northernmost desert, the Great Basin, pushing into the Owens Valley from Nevada, limits its vegetation to the bush shrub – making for the least interesting of the three deserts. Immediately south, the Mojave Desert promises more, holding two exceptional areas: Death Valley, one of the natural world's most remarkable places, and the more subdued but equally haunting scenery of the Joshua Tree National Monument.

South of the San Jacinto Mountains, the mild winters of the Colorado Desert enable a multitude of desert vegetation to thrive, best examined in the Anza-Borrego Desert, an area steeped in pioneer-period history and whose higher points give views to the Salton Sea, a vast inland lake created, bizarrely, by human error.

Ghost towns and ruined gold mines, particularly plentiful in the Mojave, are testament to the fact that desert life has never been easy (even today, desert travel involves risks, see the tips on page 194–5), although native American habitation of these fierce regions goes back thousands of years, and there are many markers to aboriginal culture – most impressively the ancient rock drawings called petroglyphs.

While large towns such as Riverside occupy the fertile lands on the extreme western edge of the deserts, other substantial communities have grown up as health resorts on the numerous natural hot springs. And in the oases towns of the Coachella Valley, most famously Palm Springs, desert living means luxury living for the nation's highest rollers.

The Anza-Borrego Desert

Colour in the wilderness: Anza-Borrego Desert

One-legged Thomas Long 'Pegleg' Smith was journeying across the Anza-Borrego Desert in the mid-1800s when he picked up several black stones, which turned out to be almost pure gold. Pegleg gradually embellished the story of his discovery until, by the time he died in 1866, he was claiming ownership of an entire gold mine. Every April, Pegleg's tall tales – and their place in desert folklore – are remembered by the Pegleg Liars Competition, held at the pile of stones beside Road 22 known as Pegleg's Monument.

▶▶▷ Anza-Borrego Desert

Named after Juan Bautista de Anza, a Spaniard who made the first recorded crossing of it in 1774, and for the bighorn sheep (or Borrego) who once roamed it in force, the 600,000-acre Anza-Borrego Desert is a mixture of sun-scorched lowlands and narrow, twisting canyons, and forms the largest state park in the US.

Holding the only accommodation (other than basic hikers' campsites), the mountain-ringed oasis town of **Borrego Springs** is an obvious base for touring Anza-Borrego – though even here, summer temperatures frequently rise above 100° F (38° C).

The park's visitor centre, set into the mountainside two miles west of Borrego Springs at **Palm Canyon**, carries essential maps and information, and mounts displays on desert history, geology and climate. Outside, a cactus garden and a simple nature trail will whet your appetite for what lies beyond.

Sandstone formations warped by millions of years of erosion are a common and evocative sight throughout the park, but the most striking views come at **Font's Point**, off Road S22, which overlooks the bone-dry creek beds and steep-sided ravines of the Borrego Badlands, a vegetation-free mass inhabited only by lizards and snakes.

Through the southerly sections of the park, 1840s gold-prospectors hacked out the only snow-free route into California, a trail later followed by the Mormon Battalion (on the journey that led to the founding of Salt Lake City) and the Butterfield Overland Mail company, whose stagecoaches carried passengers and post through these desolate scenes to the infant communities of Los Angeles and San Diego. From Box Canyon Monument on Road S2, a path leads to a lookout point above the old trail.

The barren vistas may suggest otherwise, but desert ecology is a fragile affair, and its subtleties are highlighted from March and May as wild flowers bloom across the Anza-Borrego hillsides, bringing tens of thousands of Californians to enjoy the colours and sweet smells.

By contrast, frustrated rally drivers power Off Road Vehicles (see page 185) over the dunes and dry river beds of the **Ocotillo Wells Recreational Area**, on the park's eastern edge.

▷▷▷ Barstow

Most visitors to Barstow are jackpot-dreaming bus passengers on their way to or from Las Vegas, or shoppers from LA driving out for the discounted designer-label clothes and goods sold at the town's **Factory Merchants' Outlet Plaza**. More edifying matter fills the **Mojave River Valley Museum**, including a variety of desert minerals and archaeological finds from Calico (see opposite).

▶▷▷ Big Bear Lake

High in the San Bernadino Mountains, the seven-mile long Big Bear Lake, formed by a dam in 1883, is a summer centre for watersports, horse-riding and hunting, and in winter becomes a popular ski-resort.

▷ ▷ ▷   Blyth

A minuscule town on the Arizona border, Blyth is slowly transforming itself into a desert health resort, although as yet local interest begins and ends with the giant-sized **rock drawings**, found on the Colorado River Indian Reservation, immediately to the northeast.

▶ ▷ ▷   Calico

Since 1968, archaeological excavations close to Calico have revealed more and more of a 'tool factory' claimed to be 200,000 years old. If such advanced age can be proven, this is both the oldest known site of human habitation in the US and one that overturns all the established theories concerning the earliest Americans. The dig-site can be viewed.

Less interestingly, the actual town of Calico flourished a century ago because of its silver and borax mines, but has now become a rather contrived re-creation of a gold-rush town, of which only the pervading heat seems at all authentic.

▶ ▷ ▷   Cathedral City

In the process of dropping the 'City' from its name, to avoid the popular but unflattering local abbreviation to 'Cat City', Cathedral is chiefly of interest for food and lodging at lower prices than its famous neighbour, Palm Springs.

A vision of the past: Calico rebuilt

Not everyone visits the desert to admire its scenery and delicate ecology; some people simply want to bounce over its dunes in Off Road Vehicles (or ORVs), such as dune buggies and customised four-wheel-drive jeeps. Any winter weekend finds the desert's natural serenity turned into great clouds of tossed-up sand and engine noise at several designated areas, one of the most popular being Glamis, on Highway-78 about 70 miles east of the Anza-Borrego Desert. Anyone concerned for desert conservation should keep well away.

185

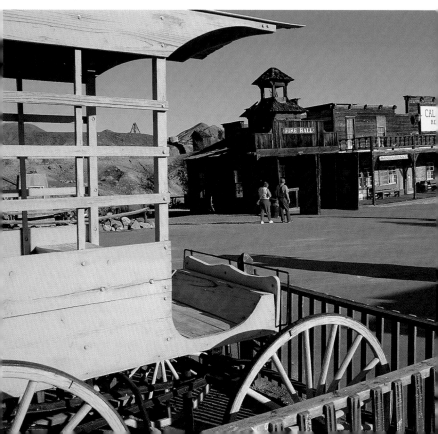

THE DESERTS

A one-time New York ballerina now on the wrong side of 60, Marta Beckett stages solo dance and mime performances every Friday, Saturday and Monday evening throughout the winter at the tiny Amargosa Opera House in Death Valley Junction near the junction of Road 127 and Road 190 (for more details, tel: (619) 852 4316).

▶ ▷ ▷ **Cherry Valley**

An unlikely find in apple-filled Cherry Valley, near San Bernadino, is a gathering of furniture and 17th- to 19th-century European and Asian art at the **Edward-Dean Museum of Decorative Arts** (9401 Oak Glen Road).

▶ ▷ ▷ **Daggett**

In Daggett, just east of Barstow, hundreds of mirrors protruding at odd angles from the ground are actually the heliostats of the **Solar One Power Plant**, busy producing energy from the sun's rays. A visitor centre explains the process. Also in town, the **Stone Hotel** has provided shelter for desert travellers since 1875.

▶ ▷ ▷ **Darwin**

Darwin is just one of several short-lived silver-prospectors' communities which now stand in ruins close to the junction of Highway-395 and Highway-190 on the approach to Death Valley. Following a dirt track south, however, leads to the secluded beauty of Darwin Falls, a waterfall fed by a natural spring.

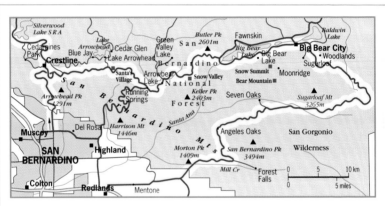

Drive 'The Rim of the World'

Drive north from San Bernardino on Road 18 to Crestline, and then join Road 138 for 10 miles to the Silverwood Lake State Recreation Area.
Picnicking, hiking, swimming and a varied birdlife are the primary attractions here.

Return to Road 18 and drive east for 15 miles to Lake Arrowhead.
LA's wealthy socialites pass leisurely weekends in luxury homes at **Lake Arrowhead**.

Continue three miles east on Road

18 for Santa's Village.
Santa's Village is a tacky but entertaining collection of amusement rides aimed at kids.

Continue for 30 miles on Road 18 for Big Bear Lake.
LA residents who cannot afford Lake Arrowhead make the most of **Big Bear Lake** (see page 184).

Continue east on Road 18 for 12 miles, joining Road 38 at Big Bear City and from there making a 50-mile winding descent to Redlands (see page 192–3)

Death Valley

■ Filled by a larger-than-life landscape of sand dunes, volcanic craters, salt flats and multi-coloured mountain walls, Death Valley is one of the hottest and driest places in the world – yet also one of the most misleadingly named. .....■

Life in Death Valley Death Valley's seemingly inhospitable environs actually support a rich diversity of life. A unique species of tiny fish lives in its ponds, wild asses and bighorn sheep roam the hillsides, and mesquite and bristleconed pines are among the 900 varieties of plantlife which take root here.
Signs of human habitation have been dated to 5000BC, when much of the valley was filled by a lake. The most recent permanent inhabitants were the Shoshone Indians, here during the 1880s when the first white men arrived to mine a rich strain of borax. A few hours of carefully planned driving will reveal sights to linger in the memory for years, although seeing all of Death Valley on anything less than a lengthy hiking expedition is impossible – and even short hikes should be undertaken with care (see pages 194–5).

Points of interest Signposted viewing points on the nine-mile **Artist's Drive** make clear the varying colours of the valley's rock walls, caused by the presence in the rock

Barren beauty in Death Valley

<< Chicago millionaire Albert Johnson ran short of funds following the Wall Street Crash, and lived in an unfinished Spanish-Moorish mansion at the northern edge of Death Valley until his death in 1948. Scot died six years after Johnson, and the folly is now open for tours. **>>**

of oxides, copper and mica. To the north, a turn-off leads to **Golden Canyon**, whose metallic tints make it live up to its name at sunrise and sunset. On the northern side of Road 198, just east of **Stovepipe Wells,** sand dunes form a 14-square-mile rippled yellow carpet. Deposited between 2 million and 12 million years ago, the mudflats of **Zabriske Point** (reached with Road 190) are legendary for the almost hypnotic effect they have on visitors. **Dante's View** (reached off Road 190), overlooks the entire valley and makes visible two of the highest and lowest points in the US: Badwater, 282 feet below sea-level and, 60 miles distant, 14,495-foot high Mount Whitney.

THE DESERTS

▶ ▷ ▷ **Desert Hot Springs**

In Desert Hot Springs, a health-resort community close to Palm Springs, **Cabot's Old Indian Pueblo Museum** has an intriguing collection of pioneer-era desert relics and Indian artefacts, including a 20-ton monument carved from a sequoia tree which fills the spacious four-storey former home of Cabot Yerka, one of the area's first settlers.

▶ ▷ ▷ **Indio**

The National Date Festival has been held each February in Indio since 1921, and the celebrations of the town's best-known product include ostrich and camel races. Meanwhile, the **Coachella Valley Museum and Cultural Center** fills a building only slightly younger than the date festival with bits and bobs spanning 70 years of local life.

▶ ▶ ▷ **Joshua Tree National Monument**

High and low desert meet in the 850 square miles of the Joshua Tree National Monument, whose name comes from the trees, a species of yucca growing up to 50 feet tall which were christened by the 1840s Mormon Battalion who saw their upraised branches as the arms of the prophet Joseph, pointing the route westwards.

The weird look of the trees and the huge quartz boulders near by endow the eastern section of the monument (the western half is best left to seasoned desert adventurers) with an eerie quality, particularly when bathed in the red glow of sunrise or sunset – it is easy to understand why many Californians attribute mystical qualities to the area.

More prosaically, the irregular formations of the granite slopes are prized by climbers, many hiking trails crisscross the wild landscapes, and there is plenty to be appreciated by car – but do not undertake any kind of visit without first picking up maps and advice from the visitor centre at Oasis, just south of Twentynine Palms (or from the other centres at Cottonwood and Blackrock Canyon).

Within the monument, **Key's View** is an essential stop: a high vantage point with panoramic views over the Joshua Tree area and, on a clear day, to Palm Springs and the Salton Sea, 40 miles away.

A signposted side road, nine miles south of the Oasis visitor centre, leads to the **Cholla Cactus Garden**, where a foot-trail passes a variety of plants, and usually quite a few of the creatures, which have adapted themselves for desert survival.

Joshua Tree National Monument

The Geology Tour Road runs through 18 miles of curious terrain, and a free brochure from the visitor centre aids understanding of the subterranean upheaval that gave rise to these spectacular scenes.

Gold mining flourished here from the 1880s and continued into the 1940s. Of the disused mines strewn across the area, the Lost Horse Mine, said to have produced $3,000 worth of gold a day, repays a 1.5-mile hike, while another, the Desert Queen Ranch, can be only be reached with a ranger-led tour, usually departing on weekends outside of summer.

Palm Springs, a 'desert community' with lush green acres and all the comforts you might need

▶ ▶ ▷ Palm Springs

The best-known and by far the nicest of half a dozen shoulder-to-shoulder towns (collectively known as the 'desert communities') lining Interstate-10 in the Coachella Valley, Palm Springs attracts 2 million visitors a year, many of them drawn by the glamorous reputation of the country's most famous resort.

The health-improving qualities of the local mineral springs saw efforts to market Palm Springs as a spa town as early as the 1890s, but it was not until actors Charlie Farrel and Ralph Bellamy founded the Palm Springs Racket Club in 1931 that Palm Springs really took off. They lured their Hollywood celebrity chums – Humphrey Bogart, Clark Gable and Marlene Dietrich among many – with the promise of relaxation far from the madding crowds.

Comedian Jack Benny's broadcasts from the town's Plaza Theater and the arrival of many more showbiz names (and later, political ones, including former president Gerald Ford whose wife, Betty, put her name to the nation's best-known detoxification clinic), helped cement the town's links with American high society.

Surprisingly perhaps, for all its up-market trappings, Palm Springs is a small (with only 30,000 residents) and very affable place, with street crime virtually unknown.

Known to locals as the 'lonesome triangle', the eastern Mojave desert lies mostly between Interstate-15, Interstate-40 and the Colorado River. One of the rewards for braving its 1.5 million acres of arid and unyeilding terrain is the Mitchell Caverns in the Providence Mountains State Recreation Area, about 80 miles east of Barstow. They are filled with strange limestone formations and their smoke-blackened walls indicate 500 years of native American usage.

THE DESERTS

Drive five miles from the centre of Palm Springs along South Palm Canyon Drive and you reach a toll-road leading into the Indian Canyons, once the domain of a large group of Cahuilla Indians. The easiest to explore is Palm Canyon, lined for its first seven miles by native Californian palms, their greenery providing a vivid counterpoint to the stark canyon walls. Beyond its car-park, Palm Canyon – like the other canyons – can be investigated further on foot or horseback.

Stunning views of a mountain landscape from the Aerial Tramway in Palm Springs

Strange territory Palm Springs has many curious features. Its dozens of golf courses are lubricated by a million gallons of recycled water per week; palm trees cover the tops of street lights to prevent their glare diminishing the clarity of the star-filled night sky; and the town's major landowners are the Agua Caliente Indians, from whom businesses rent land on 99-year leases.

Favourite Palm Springs pastimes are poolside tanning , shopping in the air-conditioned malls, and eating in the restaurants along Palm Canyon Drive, where micromist systems spray fine clouds of water to cool patio diners.

Other possible activities include exploring **Moorten's Botanical Gardens** (1701 S Palm Canyon Drive), a jungle-like collection of cacti and other imposing desert vegetation, whose creator also landscaped a section of Disneyland. Equally recommended is the **Desert Museum** (101 Museum Drive), which crowns its 20-acre sculpture-filled grounds with imaginative indoor exhibitions of desert-related art, natural history and anthropology, and fields a strong winter programme of performing arts in the adjoining Annenberg Theater.

Vestiges of Palm Springs' earlier times are maintained at the **Village Green Heritage Center** (221 S Palm Canyon Drive), where the 1884 McCallum Adobe and the 1893 Cornelia White's House can be visited, though more entertaining is a rake through the 1930s consumer durables inside the re-created Ruddy's General Store.

When the heat becomes too much, rise 6,000 feet up into cooler climes on the **Aerial Tramway**, watching the desert scene become an alpine one as you reach San Jacinto State Park. Even if you do not plan to use the park's 50 miles of hiking and horse trails, which become cross-country ski-trails in winter, the views alone make the ascent worthwhile.

Map

Desert Hot Springs
Kingdom of the Dolls
Cabot's Old Indian Pueblo Museum
Colorado River Aqueduct
Banning
White Water
North Palm Springs
Sky Valley
Cabazon
Snow Creek
10
▲ *Ranger Peak 1549m*
▲ *Black Mt 2369m*
San
Jacinto
Palm Springs
▲ *Edom Hill 492m*
Thousand Palms
Coachella Valley
San Jacinto Peak 3293m
Palm Springs Aerial Tramway
✈
Mount San Jacinto State Park
Pine Cove
Moorten Botanic Garden and Cactarium
Cathedral City
Valle Vista
San Jacinto
Idyllwild
Idyllwild Park
Saunders Meadow
Mountain Center
Rancho Mirage
Whitewater
Palm Canyon
Palm Desert
Living Desert Reserve
San Bernardino
Apache Peak 2306m
Santa Rosa Mts
Cahuilla Hills
Lake Hemet
Mountains
National Forest
▲ Palm View Peak 2177m
Asbestos Mt 1605m
Deep Canyon
Thomas Mt 2002m ▲
Garner Valley
Thomas Mountain
Alpine Village
Nightingale
Pinyon Crest
▲ *Cahuilla Mt 1718m*
Spring Crest
Cahuilla
Anza
Toro Peak 2657m

0 5 10 km
0 5 miles

191

Drive **Around Palm Springs**

Drive south from Palm Springs on Road 111 to Rancho Mirage.
Many of the wealthy who supposedly live in Palm Springs actually live among the golf courses and country clubs of **Rancho Mirage**; Bob Hope and Frank Sinatra are just two residents who have had streets named after them here.

Continue to Palm Desert.
The ultra-rich of the desert communities do their shopping along the pricey **El Paseo** in Palm Desert. A less costly stop is the 900-acre **Living Desert Reserve**, where a stroll along the foot-trails will reveal much about desert ecology.

From Palm Desert, take Road 74 and climb for 54 miles into the San Jacinto Mountains; at the junction with Road 243, turn right on to Road 243 for Idyllwild.
A mile high and surrounded by tall pines, **Idyllwild** is a mountain resort that is also noted for its School of Music and Arts.

Continue on Road 234 for 21 miles to Interstate-10; drive east on Interstate-10 for 12 miles before exiting on to Road 111 and returning to Palm Springs.

<< The first date palm seeds in North America arrived with the Spanish in the late 1700s, but not until this century did the US Department of Agriculture develop a strain that was suited to life in the California desert, the only place in the US where climate and soil are right. The most productive area is around Indio, where 4,000 acres of date palms annually produce $30 million worth of the fruit. >>

▶ ▷ ▷   Rainbow Basin

At the heart of the Rainbow Basin, 15 miles west of Barstow, you will find a steep gorge with colourful, striped sides – an effect caused by different layers of sediment. The rock walls are also packed with the fossils of three-toed horses, dog-bears, mastodons, and other prehistoric creatures which inhabited this once lake-filled area.

▶ ▷ ▷   Randsburg

Bad weather and human error led to the existence of the Salton Sea

Many buildings dating to the 1890s – when the discovery of gold brought the town a 3,000-strong population and made it a stop on the Santa Fe Railroad – have been carefully preserved in Randsburg, and the **Desert Museum** (161 Butte Avenue) is filled to its rafters with curious remnants from the mining times.

▶ ▷ ▷   Redlands

Earning its name from the colour of its soil, the diverting of water from Big Bear Lake in the 1880s enabled Redlands to flourish as a citrus farming centre. At the same time, the town found favour with wealthy wintering Easterners, whose money financed the ornately gabled and turreted wooden homes still standing along Olive Street, although these are outdone for grandeur by the chateau-style **Kimberly Crest** (1325 Prospect Street), which is open for tours.

In Smiley Park in the town centre, the Redlands Bowl auditorium is known throughout the state for its summer ballet and opera programmes, and, near by, the **Lincoln Shrine Memorial** ranks among California's most obsessive historical collections, completely devoted to President Abraham Lincoln and his role in the Civil War.

On the fringes of Redlands, the wide-ranging collections and displays of the **San Bernadino County Museum** (2025 Orange Tree Lane) provide an overview of the growth of the area, though more evocative of life in the early 1800s is the two-room museum at the restored **San Bernardino Asistencia** (26930 Barton Road), a branch of Mission San Gabriel Arcangel.

▷ ▷ ▷ Ridgecrest

The sole redeeming feature of Ridgecrest, a large community mostly composed of military personnel from the China Lake Naval Weapons Centre, is the **Mutarango Museum**, with a small but engaging collection of the native art and culture of the eastern Mojave, and a special display on the Indian rock inscriptions found in the China Lake area.

▶ ▶ ▷ Riverside

The California orange – the navel – was born in Riverside in the 1870s, and the town's resultant affluence saw the building of the **Mission Inn** (3649 Seventh Street), a Spanish-style exercise in luxury whose bedrooms, music rooms, terraces and patios were decorated by $1 million worth of antiques. Newly restored, the inn is often open for tours.

Now a busy industrial centre as well as an agricultural base, Riverside's past is recorded by copious relics in the **Municipal Museum** (3720 Orange Street). Close by, the **Museum of Photography** (3824 Main Street) has excellent temporary exhibitions.

Just east of the town, the local branch of the University of California looks after the 39-acre **Botanical Gardens**, which specialise in winter-blooming dry-climate plants and feature a formidable batch of cacti.

Wild cacti covers much of **Mount Rubidoux**, to the west of Riverside, the 1,300-foot summit of which can be reached by a twisting lane. At the top, the Serra Cross has been the venue for Easter sunrise services since 1909, and from it are impressive views.

▶ ▷ ▷ Salton Sea

One of the largest inland seas in the world, the Salton Sea resulted from a combination of an engineering blunder and a severe winter, which in 1905 led to the Colorado River breaching the canals directing it to the Imperial Valley, and flooding a dried-up lake bed just east of the Anza-Borrego Desert.

An enormous but very shallow body of water, the authorities added ocean fish to the Salton Sea when its water turned saline, and anglers (nowadays joined by watersports fans) were quick to take advantage of the marinas and campsites of the Salton Sea Recreation Area created on its eastern bank.

Meanwhile, birdwatchers arrive in search of herons and egrets, among a host of much rarer winged creatures, who are regular visitors to the Salton Sea Wildlife Refuge, on the Sea's southern edge.

▶ ▷ ▷ Twentynine Palms

Ignored by many travellers speeding through on their way to the nearby Joshua Tree National Monument (see page 188), a pause in Twentynine Palms gives the chance to inspect the Historical Society Museum (6136 Adobe Road), charting the origins and growth of this little desert settlement.

Seventy courses have earned Palm Springs and the desert communities the title of 'Golf Capital of America'. Many top tournaments are held here and famous names – be they golfers, entertainers or ex-presidents – are familiar figures on the fairways. Many courses are members only or very expensive, although local municipal courses (listed in the phone book) are always cheap and open to all. Interestingly, to conserve water, new courses have to be laid on a bed of tile; this enables the precious liquid to be collected after irrigating the greens and then recycled.

193

California's desert regions are sprinkled with hot springs, whose thermally heated mineral-rich water bubbles up through the earth's crust. Opportunities to sample the waters, and put their alleged health-improving qualities to the test, are numerous and range from the jacuzzi- and sauna-equipped spa resorts such as Murrieta Hot Springs, about 25 miles south of Riverside, to the free mineral baths at Tecopa Hot Springs County Park, close to Road 127, just east of Death Valley.

■   **By world standards, California's three deserts are lush and young, having formed 1 million to 5 million years ago, primarily through the inability of rain-bearing clouds to cross the Sierra Nevada mountains. Their landscapes are extremely varied, as is their flora and fauna, some of which are unique and all of which have been able to adapt to desert conditions in a variety of inventive ways. .....■**

You will not see any antelopes in Antelope Valley, but arrive between March and May and you will see millions of orange and purple wild flowers brightening the hillsides that rim the western edge of the Mojave Desert. And at the Antelope Valley California Poppy Reserve, 2,000 acres are set aside for the careful nurturing of California's state flower – the subtleties of which are explained inside a specially built, energy-conserving visitor centre.

Desert flora The cactus is the most obvious example of the succulent desert plant; one which stores water whenever it is available, using a shallow but extensive root system.

Some non-succulent plants can become dormant in the absence of water, others – such as the brittle bush and creosote bush – can reduce the size and constituency of their leaves to reduce water loss, and, when necessary, shed all their leaves and branches to protect their root system.

Other than the Joshua trees of the Joshua Tree National Monument, the plants that bring most people to the deserts are the springtime wild flowers. These grow from seeds which only germinate in response to a precise amount of rainfall, which ensures the survival of the plant.

Desert fauna Desert animals are no less inventive. The kangaroo rat never drinks but creates water inside its body after eating dry seeds, and is able to condense moisture while exhaling air; the red-spotted toad can absorb its own urine; and desert insects respond to unfavourable conditions by entering a form of suspended animation called aestivation.

Aside from cold-blooded reptiles such as lizards, which scamper from sunlight to shade to regulate their body temperature, and a multitude of birds ranging from turkey vultures to scrub jays, most desert creatures are nocturnal and spend time in the heat of the day sleeping behind rocks or plants.

Animals most likely to be encountered in the desert by humans are the chipmunk-like antelope ground squirrel and the large desert tortoises, most commonly found chewing on the grasses and wild flowers of springtime. With luck, training your binoculars on distant slopes will bring a glimpse of the rarely sighted bighorn sheep.

Desert travel tips Careful preparation will help you to experience the desert comfortably and safely – and may even save your life.

The only sensible time for desert travel is between November and April, when daytime temperatures are warm but bearable (though the nights can be freezing), and well short of the roasting heat of the summer, when tourist services – such as the all-important visitor centres – are likely to be closed.

Desert driving Before setting out, ensure that your vehicle is in perfect condition, and stock up with around five gallons of spare fuel – desert driving means fewer miles per gallon than on regular roads – and a similar amount of spare water for the radiator.

In the desert, never drive off the marked roads – doing so causes environmental damage. If you are intending to tour one of the isolated side roads, inform a park ranger, or other relevant authority, of your plans.

If your car breaks down, do not leave it. Wait until another car passes and signal for assistance. This may involve a long wait, so it is important to carry ample food and – most crucially of all – at least a gallon of drinking water per person per day.

Other useful accessories include a first-aid kit, a flashlight and waterproof matches.

Desert hiking and walking Many hiking and walking trails can be completed easily in a few hours, but do not embark on one without a detailed map or without carrying water.

Even on a short walk, be sure to drink regularly even if you do not feel thirsty. Keep in the shade whenever possible, and rest at the first sign of dizzyness.

Wear loose, light-coloured clothing, dark glasses and a wide-brimmed hat, and apply sunscreen liberally. On your feet, wear trainers with socks or walking-boots – do not wear sandals or go barefoot.

Be careful where you put your hands and feet, and be wary when turning over rocks. These precautions will help avoid potentially fatal contact with black widow spiders, scorpions and rattlesnakes, and the less harmful tarantulas and centipedes.

You should, however, ensure that you know what to do if bitten by a desert creature – details are available from any desert visitor centre or rangers' office.

The Cholla Garden, Joshua Tree National Monument

In the California of the late 1800s, gold mining was more glamorous but less lucrative than borax mining. Rich deposits of borax – used in the manufacture of glass and in glazes for ceramics – were discovered in Death Valley (see page 187). Getting the mineral out of the ground proved a lot easier than getting it out of Death Valley, however, and it took 20-strong mule teams 10 days to haul their loads to the nearest railway terminal. Nowadays, most of the world's borax comes from the Boron area, about 80 miles west of Death Valley.

195

SIERRA NEVADA

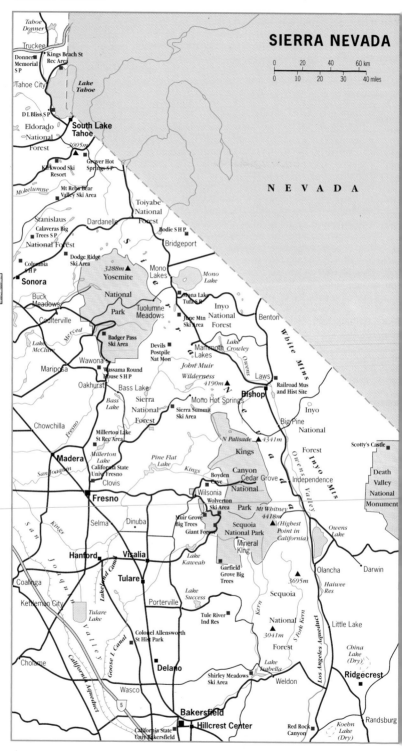

You might be a geological ignoramus when you arrive in the Sierra Nevada region but you will leave with a much surer knowledge of earthly forces and how they have shaped – and continue to shape – California.

An expanse of granite domes, pinnacles and ridges some 450 miles long and up to 80 miles wide, the Sierra Nevada mountains give the region its name and divide the state's fertile Central Valley from the arid eastern deserts.

Hot Stuff Yet, despite the feelings of permanence evoked by the colossal peaks, the Sierra Nevada is one of North America's most geologically volatile regions; the hot springs which litter the area are merely the most benign manifestation of the tensions lying deep underground.

Historically, the Sierra Nevada provided one of the major obstacles for would-be settlers approaching by land. Now, visitors still have to plan carefully how – and when – they tour the area.

Approaching from the west, it is tempting to make a beeline for the national parks – the world-famous Yosemite, and the less visited but equally worthwhile Sequoia and King Canyon – at the heart of the region, and not worry too much about pressing further east.

Eastern pleasures It is in the east, however, that the sheer-sided Owens Valley forms a slender and visually spectacular corridor, linking the Sierra Nevada's wealth of strange geological phenomena – such as eerie tufa formations and geometrically precise basalt columns – while giving access to scores of sparkling alpine lakes, including the stunning Lake Tahoe on the region's northern edge.

Unfailingly, the Sierra Nevada's natural sights exert greater appeal than its towns. A few bear witness to the region's pioneer days (and one, Bodie, is a genuine gold-rush ghost town) but most of the modestly sized settlements are geared to servicing the needs of the hikers and climbers who are the lifeblood of local economies.

In winter, mountain roads are closed and hiking routes are inaccessible, rendering the most pristine sections of the Sierra Nevada's magical icy landscapes off-limits. The bulk of the region's through traffic at this time are skiers, who turn Lake Tahoe and Mammoth Lakes into the country's busiest winter sports centres.

Winter transport in Mammoth Lake

SIERRA NEVADA

Research during the 1950s by Professor Edmund Shulman, of the University of Arizona, dated the oldest of the bristlecone pines at 4,600 years, the prelude to much hullabaloo over the discovery of the world's oldest living things. In 1980, however, the bristlecones were made to look like mere infants by a desert shrub, the creosote bush, one of which was found by a botanist to have lived to the ripe old age of 11,500 years.

▶ ▷ ▷ Bass Lake

A large reservoir in the pine-covered foothills on the western approach to Yosemite National Park (see pages 208–9), Bass Lake is one of the state's busiest recreational areas. Speedboats and water-skiers skim across the surface, anglers are tempted by the spiny-finned fish which give the lake its name, and a series of trails pick through the surrounding countryside, offering some respite from the crowds which pack the lakeside cottages and campsites throughout the summer.

▷ ▷ ▷   Big Pine

Like most Owens Valley towns, Big Pine offers little other than food, lodging and access to spectacular natural areas. Above the town, the Palisades Glacier – North America's most southerly ice sheet – pulls expert ice-climbers to its tricky slopes. Everyone else should spend a day familiarising themselves with the world's oldest living things at the **Ancient Bristlecone Pine Forest**, 12 miles east and reached by State Road 168.

The **Visitor Center at Schulman Grove** provides an introduction to the strange, warped forms of the 4,000-year old bristlecone pines, which dominate this extraordinary landscape, each one growing barely an inch per year and looking more dead than alive.

Alabama Hills, near Bishop

Bump over the potholes of Bodie Road, off Highway-395, 20 miles southeast of Bridgeport, and you will enter Bodie State Historic Park ghost town. A century ago nearly 10,000 people lived in the gold rush town; their buildings are now too rickety to enter, save for the Miner's Union Hall, which houses a museum. The last three miles of road may be closed in winter.

The most evocative section of the forest is 11 miles further on and 1,000 feet higher at **Patriarch Grove**, where a scattering of bristlecones bestow a weird beauty on an uncompromising terrain – an area selected by NASA for the testing of their lunar rover before it was sent to the moon.

▷ ▷ ▷   Bishop

Nestling among the motels, restaurants and adventure sports shops which fill Bishop, 15 miles north of Big Pine, the **Paiute Shoshone Indian Cultural Center** and Museum (2300 W Line Street) provides a welcome opportunity to discover something of the life-styles and handicrafts of the valley's native dwellers.

■ **The Sierra Nevada could be tailor-made for adventure sports enthusiasts. As elsewhere in the state, canoeing and white-river rafting are available wherever conditions are right, and thrill-seeking visitors will also find skiing, climbing and mountain biking on offer in an area which fully lives up to its reputation as California's most participant-sports crazy area. .....■**

Skiing A November to May snow covering facilitates some outstanding downhill skiing in the region, although high costs and long queues for ski-lifts have strengthened the popularity of cross-country (or Nordic) skiing; many free cross-country routes are operated by the various local Forest Services.

Venue of the Winter Olympics in 1960, Lake Tahoe has dozens of ski resorts, most of them pitched at the intermediate and advanced skier. Anyone embarrassed at falling over might fare better at the beginner-aimed Tahoe Donner (tel: (916) 587 9424).

Further south Mammoth Lakes is no less busy and activity centres on the enormous Mammoth Mountain Resort (tel: (619) 934 2571), while cross-country enthusiasts can follow a web of backcountry routes organised by the Tamarack Cross-Country Ski Center (tel: (619) 934 2442).

In Yosemite National Park, the gentle slopes of the Badger Pass Ski Resort (tel: (209) 372 1330) are considered ideal for novices. Also in the park, overnight and three-day guided cross-country trips to Glacier Point are organised by the Yosemite Cross-Country Ski School (tel: (209) 372 1244).

Climbing The sheer, near-vertical granite rock faces, such as Yosemite's El Capitan, which proliferate in the Sierra Nevada have forced the world's mountaineering fraternity to devise entirely new techniques to conquer them. The region's climbing schools pass on such skills, and also instruct raw beginners in the rudiments of rock and ice climbing.

The main climbing school bases are the Yosemite Mountaineering School (tel: (209) 372 1244) and the Palisades School of Mountaineering (tel: (619) 873 5037, September to May; (209) 372 1335, June to August).

An unusual way to soak up the beauty of the Sierra Nevada – and learn a great deal about what you are seeing – is on a pack trip, allowing a mule or a llama to carry your backpack while the guide (usually a qualified naturalist) provides a commentary. Many companies – widely advertised in the area – operate pack trips from the main trailheads. More information is available from the Eastern Sierra High Packers Association, operating through the Bishop Chamber of Commerce (tel: (619) 873 8405).

Mountain biking Provided your bum can stand the buffeting, a thrilling way to explore the ups and downs of the Sierra Nevada is by mountain bike. Many sports shops throughout the Owens Valley and around Lake Tahoe hire out the machines for a charge of around $15 a day.

Guided mountain-bike trips are run by the Bishop-based Mountain Routes (tel: (619) 873 8034).

SIERRA NEVADA

▶ ▷ ▷   Bridgeport

These days little more than a collection of supply stores, Bridgeport's voluminous 1880 County Courthouse reflects the community's boom years when it, as the county seat, grew wealthy from nearby Bodie's gold strikes. If you need proof of former glories, explore the Mono County Museum, inside the town's former schoolhouse, which stores artefacts from the halcyon decades.

▶ ▶ ▷   Grover Hot Springs

Set in a divine alpine meadow, the bubbling waters issuing from the earth at Grover Hot Springs State Park have been credited since California's pioneer days as a cure for whatever ails. More recently, the mineral-rich spring water has meant bliss for aching hikers, who can enjoy a soak in one of the park's two temperature-regulated bathing pools.

▶ ▷ ▷   Independence

Besides rest and nourishment, Independence, 28 miles south of Big Pine, offers the excellent **Eastern California Museum** (155 Grant Street), covering the geology, history and ecology of the region. The museum includes a striking collection of Paiute and Shosone Indian crafts, and a thought-provoking exhibit on Manzanar Camp, immediately southeast of the town, where 10,000 Japanese-Americans were interned following the outbreak of hostilities between the US and Japan in 1941.

Many of the town's older building have been moved to the museum's grounds and assembled as a pioneer village. One that has not been relocated is the former home of author Mary Austin (follow the signs from the museum), who lived in Independence from 1896, and described Owens Valley life evocatively in a book of essays, *Land of Little Rain*, published in 1903.

One of the gorier tales of early California concerns the Donner Party of 1846, a wagon-train of 89 men, women and children following the Emigrant Trail into California. A series of errors of judgement by their leader culminated in the party being trapped by snow and forced to spend the winter without supplies in what is now the Donner Pass, just west of Truckee. Only 47 people survived the ordeal, some of them having resorted to cannibalism to stay alive.

Looking across the meadow to Grover Hot Springs

Drive Sequoia and Kings Canyon National Parks

<< California's coastal redwoods may be taller, but in terms of bulk the giant sequoia tree – which grows only on the western slopes of the Sierra Nevada – is the world's largest living thing. The biggest of the trees, the General Sherman Tree in Sequoia National Park, boasts a circumference of 102 feet. The largest sequoias have lived for over 3,000 years, their longevity greatly aided by their fire-resistant bark. >>

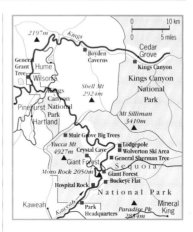

201

Enter Sequoia National Park on Highway-198.
Sequoia National Park is home to thousands of the world's largest living thing: the giant sequoia tree.

Continue on Highway-198, the General's Highway, to Giant Forest Village, turning right on to Crescent Meadow Road.
The road passes famous trees, such as the **Auto Log**, and foot-trails lead into the groves, one of which contains the largest, the **General Sherman Tree**.

Turn off Crescent Meadow Road for Moro Rock.
There are fantastic views from the top of **Moro Rock**.

Return to the General's Highway, continuing to Grant Grove.
At **Grant Grove** an excellent **Visitors' Center** describes the wondrous lives of giant sequoias.

From Grant Grove, join the Kings Canyon Highway and drive towards Cedar Grove.
Part of **Kings Canyon National Park**, the highway makes a spectacular, winding descent through Kings Canyon.

Turn off Kings Canyon Road for Boyden Caverns, signposted near

the canyon's floor.
See the fabulous stalagmites and stalactites inside the deep **Boyden Caverns**.

Continue along Kings Canyon Highway, passing Cedar Grove Village for Zumwalt Meadow.
A one-mile walking trail crosses the Kings River by a suspension bridge as it winds above and around **Zumwalt Meadow**.

Beyond Zumwalt Meadow, only hiking trails penetrate further into the Kings Canyon backcountry.

The giant sequoia tree

■ **You do not need to be in California long to realise that the state sits on a very fidgety portion of the earth's crust. Not only are earthquakes an almost daily phenomenon (fortunately, the vast majority of them are too small to cause concern), but natural forces are still moulding what may at first appear to be California's most solid geographical region: the Sierra Nevada mountains. .....■**

202

The formation of the Sierra Nevada Around 200 million years ago, the Pacific plate was slipping under the North American continental plate and what is now California began emerging from the ocean as immense pressures in the earth's crust caused the sea-bed to buckle and rise. This in turn formed the earliest outline of what were to become the Sierra Nevada mountains.

Between 250 million and 80 million years ago, the surface rock had eroded sufficiently to allow hot magma within the earth's crust to push upward (owing to the reduction of the pressure from above). This magma eventually burst through the surface as volcanoes or, more often, cooled beneath the surface to form as huge granite intrusions known as batholites.

Combining with minerals in liquid form on its upward journey, it was this molten rock that provided California with its deposits of gold, silver and other precious metals.

A subsequent process known as exfoliation, when surface rock expands as a result of underground heat, caused the outer layers of the granite monoliths to fracture and break away, eventually creating the bare domes which are characteristic of the Sierra Nevada ranges. Prime examples are El Capitan and Half Dome in Yosemite Valley.

Around 70 million years ago, the rising of the coastal mountains caused the Sierras to tilt westwards, a process which increased the erosive power of its rivers, which proceeded to carve great valleys through the hillsides.

Mountain bikes are ridden at breakneck speed up and down the tortuous terrain for which they were designed in the Silver Canyon Ultimate Kamikaze Downhill Mountain Bike Race, which push the machines and their riders to the limit. The event is held in the White Mountains' Silver Canyon area during July.

During three separate periods, the latest around 30,000 years ago, falling global temperatures caused glaciers to form in the Sierras. The moving ice sheets wore away the weaker rock leaving spindly towers and pinnacled ridges, smoothed the harder rock surfaces, and chiselled out the rock bowls which later filled with crystal-clear water and became alpine lakes.

Yosemite Valley's U-shape (river-formed valleys have a V-shape) was formed by the action of ice, while Lake Tahoe is the country's largest example of a glacial lake, with many smaller specimens lying close to Mammoth Lakes.

The Sierra Nevada today The eastern and western sides of the Sierra Nevada are markedly different nowadays. In the west, the forested foothills composed of older rocks rise steadily upwards from the immense flat expanse of the Central Valley towards the region's big peaks. In the east, however, the mountains fall off sharply, forming a spectacular wall to the slender corridor of the Owens Valley with a 400-mile long fault-line along their base considered by many experts to be the most geologically active place in the US.

An earthquake here in 1872, one of the strongest ever in North America (8.3 on the Richter scale), demolished the town of Lone Pine and instantly added 13 feet to the height of the surrounding ridges. Evidence – often bizarre, and often beautiful – of violent upheaval is everywhere, from the columns of cooled lava at the Devil's Postpile Monument to the valley's innumerable hot springs.

Curiously, though, while the Sierra side of the Owens Valley is a comparative infant, the White Mountains, which form the valley's east wall, are composed of some of California's oldest rock and dotted by the world's oldest living things, the bristlecone pine.

As geysers gurgle far below, the Palisades Glacier continues to creep steadily through the mountain canyons above Big Pine, a constant reminder of the region's geological extremes – and the fact that the formation of the Sierra Nevada is a process that is far from complete.

The clear alpine lakes of the Sierras were formed when glaciers scooped valleys out of the rocks

The highest point in the continental US, 14,494-foot Mount Whitney can be seen from many places, but its summit can only be reached by trekking up a stiff 10-mile trail from the end of the Whitney Portal Road, which branches from Lone Pine. The trail is usually snow-free only for a few weeks in summer, when hundreds of visitors jam the car park at the trailhead before commencing the climb.

SIERRA NEVADA

Native Americans – some of them pre-dating known tribes – carved colourful figures, or petroglyphs, on to many of California's hillsides. Just outside Laws, a 50-mile Petroglyph Loop Trip through the Chalfont Valley has six marked stops where some of these curious – and dateless – works can be seen.

▶ ▷ ▷ Laws

Being a stop on the railway was a blessing for any small community during the frontier days, when Owens Valley farm produce needed transporting to the state's mining areas. One such place was Laws, six miles from Bishop, which has been partly re-created in its 1880s form as the **Laws Railway Museum and State Historic Site**. The rail terminal is an impressive restoration, as are several of the town's other early buildings: your tour around them might well be in the company of local history enthusiasts, dressed in period garb and dispensing endless historical anecdotes.

▶ ▶ ▷ Mono Lake

Almost a million years old and 9,000 feet above sea-level, few of the many haunting sights in the Sierra Nevada can match the other-worldly vistas of Mono Lake.

Gazing across the 13-mile wide saltwater expanse (often called California's Dead Sea), the eye comes to rest on the bizarre **tufa formations**, mostly on the south side, which sprout above the surface in mysterious shapes, each one a pillar of limestone created by the alkaline lake water mingling with fresh spring water.

The tufa formations have existed for thousands of years but only broke surface when the lake level fell owing to the draining of its tributary rivers to provide water for Los Angeles (see panel on page 206).

Eerie tufa formations reflected in the waters of Mono Lake

The falling water-level has also greatly affected a finely balanced ecosystem for which the lake is the linchpin. One consequence has been to turn Nigret Island, in the centre of the lake, into a peninsula, allowing hungry coyotes to reach what was previously a secure nesting place for California gulls, where 90 per cent of their population breed.

Situated immediately west of the lake in Lee Vining, the **Mono Lake Visitor Center** explains the lake's evolutionary history and the various threats that it is currently facing.

Lake Tahoe

■ **Fringed by thick forests and overlooked by snow-capped mountain peaks, Lake Tahoe holds enough water to flood the entire state. To most Californians the lake means a weekend of watersports, skiing or gambling (the eastern third of the lake lies in Nevada, where, unlike in California, gambling is legal). .....■**

Commercialism Such is the scale of recreational tourism that the area's natural beauty is constantly threatened by motels, fast-food outlets, and ski-lifts. It is most pronounced at South Lake Tahoe, an eight-mile sprawl of hotels and restaurants beside Highway-50, which merges into the Nevada town of Stateline, dominated by high-rise casinos.

Enjoyable lake cruises These are a more positive feature of South Lake Tahoe, and the **Lake Tahoe Historical Society Museum** (3058 Highway-50) gives background on the lake's formation and its cultures. The prettiest section of the lake is the southwestern corner, where the steep, conifer-lined and boulder-strewn slopes of **Emerald Bay State Park** (on State Road 89) reach down to a secluded inlet. Here, a mile-long trail leads to **Vikingsholm**, an approximation of a 9th-century Nordic castle designed in the 1920s by a Swedish-born architect, whose brief was to create a 38-room lakeside home without disturbing a single tree. Another short trail leads to the cascading **Eagle Falls**. Thirty miles north, **Sugar Pine Point State Park**, holds some enjoyable sandy beaches and the 1903 **Erhmann mansion**, built of local wood and stone for a San Francisco banker now serves as the visitor center. Similar properties are being renovated at the **Tallac Historic Site Estates**, near Fallen Leaf Lake. North of Lake Tahoe, **Truckee** appeared with the building of the transcontinental railway in the mid-1800s, which linked the rest of the US to Sacramento, 80 miles west. The difficulties that the local terrain presented to travellers prior to the railway are outlined inside the **Emigrant Trail Museum**, at Donner Memorial State Park, a few miles west of Truckee on Interstate-80.

<< The *Tahoe Queen* (tel: (916) 541 3364), operates a ferry service and by night hosts a dinner -dance cruise. The MS *Dixie* (tel: (702) 588 3508), makes a sightseeing run from Zephyr Cove as far as Emerald Bay. **>>**

205

Drive Mammoth Lakes

Leave Highway-395 between Lee Vining and Bishop, taking State Road 203 until you come to Mammoth Lakes.
With a population of 4,000 and hotel beds for 40,000, **Mammoth Lakes** is one of the US's most popular skiing areas.

Continue on State Road 203 for three miles to the Mammoth Lakes Visitor Center.
The volatile geology of Mammoth Lakes is explained inside the excellent **Visitor Center**.

Continue on State Road 203 for eight miles, reaching the Minaret Vista Picnic Area.
Jagged peaks and ridges rise high above the **Minaret Vista Picnic Area**; while far below, the San Joaquin River negotiates a deep canyon.

Continue on State Road 203 for 14 miles, for the Devils Postpile Monument.
The extraordinary hexagonal basalt columns of the **Devils Postpile Monument** formed as molten lava flow cooled and was polished by passing glaciers.

Retrace your route along State Road 203, after 17 miles turning right on to

<< The Owens Valley Aqueduct was completed in 1913 to siphon water from the Owens Valley to the growing metropolis of Los Angeles. Despite the harm the scheme caused to the valley, the aqueduct was extended to Mono Lake in 1941, and a second aqueduct was built in 1970. **>>**

Lake Mary Road and continuing for six miles to the Lake Mary Loop Road.
The Lake Mary Loop Road circles **Lake Mary**, the largest of several glacial lakes in the vicinity.

Return to State Road 203 and turn left, after a mile turning right to come on to the Mammoth Scenic Loop.
Constructed in the 1970s as an evacuation route in the event of a major earthquake, the **Mammoth Scenic Loop** passes several examples of volcanic upheaval, including the water-filled **Inyo Craters**, to the left.

Continue on the Mammoth Scenic Loop to rejoin Highway-395 eight miles north of the State Road 203 junction.

Walks and Lakes

■ **Excellently laid-out and well-maintained short walks put some of the Sierra Nevada's most unforgettable scenery within reach even of those people who consider getting out of their cars to be a major expedition. The best of the easier walks lie in the Yosemite Valley (described on pages 208–9) and around the giant trees of Sequoia National Park. Longer walks – more properly considered hikes – often branch from the simpler foot-trails, enabling longer and more arduous forays into the rugged environs of the Sierra backcountry. .....■**

Exploring on foot Travelling far from roads and motels, such hikes might take a few hours or a few days (usually necessitating overnight camping at undeveloped sites) to complete, and often connect with longer routes such as the 250-mile **John Muir Trail**, between Mount Whitney and Yosemite Valley, itself part of the enormous Pacific Crest Trail running between Mexico and Canada.

Aside from being a start-point for the John Muir Trail, Yosemite National Park holds many other hikes needing a measure of fitness and determination. Of them, the most rewarding is the eight-mile route to the summit of Half Dome from the Holiday Isles campsite, steep enough in some sections for hikers to require the aid of steel climbing cables fixed to the smooth granite surface.

Many other hikes radiate from Yosemite's Tuolumne Meadows, one of which, the High Sierra Loop Trail, bobbing and weaving around waterfalls, meadows and steep-sided river creeks, is long enough to have six well-equipped overnight huts (advance booking essential) at eight-mile intervals on its course.

The High Sierras After viewing the big trees of Sequoia National Park, drive the 100-mile winding road through the secluded southern section of the park and you will reach Mineral King, a hauntingly quiet valley, 7,500 feet high. Some of the greatest views of the High Sierras – peaceful alpine lakes, lined by fir trees and surrounded by forbidding granite peaks – are within reach of Mineral King on short but often steep trails. The intrepid walker can also join the 50-mile High Sierra Trail here, which affords unmatched high-country views and links with the John Muir Trail.

On the trail in the Sierra Nevada

■ **Guaranteed to stir the soul of the most jaded traveller, the granite cliffs topped by tumbling waterfalls and lake-studded alpine meadows all help to make Yosemite National Park one of the world's most beautiful places. .....■**

208

Do not be surprised to find the waterfalls of the Sierra Nevada – and especially those in Yosemite – more closely resembling dripping taps than the gushing torrents of popular description. The falls are only fully active during the spring, when they are fuelled by melting snow.

El Capitan, a vast granite monolith

When to visit The park can be visited year-round but arriving in spring or autumn avoids the winter snows and the summer's influx of tourists, often causing traffic jams into and out of Yosemite Valley, the park's single most spectacular section. You have not seen Yosemite until you have seen Yosemite Valley, but it is only a seven-mile long section of the 1,000-square-mile park and you should also explore other parts, such as Tuolumne Meadows on the park's eastern side, or Wawona and the Mariposa Grove, south of the valley. Numerous road accidents caused by distracted drivers prove that there is much to admire even from a car window. Simple foot-trails make much more of it accessible, while a network of hiking trails pass through Yosemite's many undeveloped portions, linking with the marathon trans-Sierra treks (see page 207).

Yosemite Valley A natural sculpture on an infinite scale, Yosemite Valley has been filling arrivals with awe since the first non-natives entered it in the mid-19th century. After the valley was carved by glaciers, a lake covered its floor which slowly silted up and became the lush meadow of present times, one dotted with fir trees and enclosed by enormous granite peaks.

The 8,842ft **Half Dome**, its missing half crushed beneath the ice fields, is a vivid indication of the incredible forces that shaped Yosemite Valley. There is a good view of Half Dome, and exceptional views across the valley, from **Glacier Point**, at the top of a 3,200-foot high rock wall on the valley's south side, which is either reached by a winding road or a steep four-mile foot trail. Try to visit Glacier Point at sunset, when Half Dome glows with orange hues, or at night, when moonlight illuminates the valley and millions of stars twinkle above the Sierra Nevada peaks.

From Glacier Point you also get a sense of the mind-boggling scale of **El Capitan** at the valley's western end, the world's tallest exposed granite monolith, rising three times higher than the Empire State Building.

Binocular-wielding visitors are a common sight at El Capitan's foot, hoping to focus on the climbers – almost invisible from the ground – seeking out the challenging peak's few cracks and fissures.

After enjoying the grand views, explore the walking trials. These reach waterfalls, such as **Lower Yosemite Fall** (the more impressive **Upper Yosemite Fall** is at the end of a three-mile uphill hike) and **Bridalveil Falls**, opposite El Capitan. With a day to spare, tackle the longer trek to **Vernal Fall** and **Nevada Fall**, reached via the spray-drenched Mist Trail.

Also on the valley floor, Yosemite Village has shops and services, and the **Indian Cultural Museum**, giving a brief account of Yosemite's Miwok and Paiute Indians. Close by, the stone and concrete of the **Ahwahnee Hotel**, the most up-market accommodation in the park, has slotted neatly into its surrounds since 1927; step inside to peek at the gorgeous dining room and to admire the lounge's sumptuous fireplace.

Tuolumne Meadows Close to the park's eastern entrance but better reached from the west by the vista-rich **Tioga Road**, the vivid greenery of Tuolumne (pronounced 'Twa-LUM-Nay') Meadows – the Sierras' largest alpine meadow – forms a striking contrast to the bald granite peaks all around.

Primarily a base for hardened hikers and experienced climbers, Tuolumne Meadows is also one of the most quietly beautiful sections of the park with plenty to reward a day's rambling.

Wawona and the Mariposa Grove After the crowds and visual drama of Yosemite Valley, Wawona, surrounded by dense forests and bordered by meadows and gushing streams, is the picture of pastoral tranquillity. The white, wood-framed form of the **Wawona Hotel**, opened in 1879 to service stagecoach travellers, adds to the rural charm.

Near the hotel, the **Pioneer Yosemite History Center** remembers, with exhibits and restored buildings, the region's early white settlers. One of them was Glen Clerk, who is credited with the discovery of the **Mariposa Grove**, the thickest of the park's three stands of giant sequoia trees. If you are not visiting Sequoia National Park (see page 201), discover these fascinating trees on the grove's narrated tram tours.

209

Scottish-born John Muir arrived in San Francisco in 1868 and allegedly asked for directions to 'somewhere wild'. Accompanied only by a mule, Muir spent many summers exploring the Sierra Nevada. The eulogistic writings which resulted from these trips, and his tireless efforts to have the Yosemite area put under federal protection, led to the formation of the still-influential Sierra Club, and the creation of Yosemite National Park in 1890 (for more on Muir, see page 81).

High hopes: panning for gold

In 1848, the discovery of gold changed California for ever. Previously a remote farming outpost, California suddenly became the place to be, and for the first (and not to be the last) time its very name exuded the promise of instant and unbridled riches. With no easy links to the rest of the country – the Sierra Nevada mountains, whose hillsides held the gold which the rivers had washed to the lowlands, were then as now a formidable natural barrier – it was not until 1849 when the first huge influx of wealth-seekers arrived; the so-called Forty-niners. Three years on, 100,000 people had settled in the jerry-built wood and brick towns of what was now being called the Gold Country.

The gold-rush fortunes were made by merchants and shopkeepers rather than the hopeful prospectors, however, and many of them wound up as labourers in the company-owned mines which came to dominate the industry as the stocks of river gold were exhausted.

As mining machinery arrived by ship, port towns such as San Francisco and Sacramento flourished, the latter becoming the state capital in 1854. The only Gold Country settlement still of appreciable size, Sacramento lost its prestige when California's influential names departed for the coastal cities, but it makes the most of its history and is slowly shedding the staid image impressed upon it by its army of state bureaucrats.

East of Sacramento The appropriately numbered State Road 49 links many of the smaller Gold Country towns, which pepper a 200-mile long strip – known as the Mother Lode – northwards from Yosemite along the western slopes of the Sierra Nevada mountains. Almost every community here prides itself on preserving its 19th-century buildings which, together with ubiquitous gold mining museums, evoke a potent sense of the rough and ready gold-rush days. The downside is that every town seems uncannily like the last.

California's Far North, separated from the North Coast by the Klamath Mountains and reached by Interstate-5 from the Gold Country, provides greater variety, not with its forgettable towns but with its ravishing scenery: alpine forests, canyons and sparkling rivers, wondrous lava formations at the Lava Beds National Monument and bubbling mud pits, hot springs, and hot gases issuing furiously from the ground at Lassen National Park.

Gold Country

▶ ▷ ▷ **Amador City**

Officially California's smallest city, Amador City is as pretty as a picture and stretches for just one block along State Road 49, holding a handful of cafés, bed and breakfast inns, and art and antique shops.

▶ ▷ ▷ **Angels Camp**

Mines at Angels Camp yielded $19 million worth of gold between 1886 and 1910, but – bizarrely – it is frogs and not precious metal that have brought the town lasting fame. Every May since 1928, the Jumping Frogs Jamboree – in which frogs compete over three measured hops for a $1,000 prize (going to the winning owner, not the champion frog) – has brought tens of thousands of spectators to Angels Camp, and accounts for the frog motifs which appear on many of its buildings.

The frog fixation is actually an expression of the town's literary claim to fame. Legend has it that writer Mark Twain was relaxing in the bar of the Hotel Angels (1227 Main Street) during the 1860s, when he heard the miners' tale about jumping frogs that inspired his first published story. Another writer, Bret Harte, also has links with the town; for more on both scribes, see panel (left).

Besides frogs, Angels Camp can only muster the uninspired crock of mining memorabilia inside the Angels Camp Museum (753 Main Street) to fill travellers' spare minutes.

▶ ▶ ▷ **Auburn**

Thirty miles from Sacramento on Interstate-80, Auburn is fast becoming the state capital's favourite dormitory community. Down the hill from the bland modern town, however, Auburn's cheerful **Old Town** has many restored mid-19th-century buildings – including an 1892 fire station, the state's oldest continuously used post office, a domed neo-classical courthouse and a tiny Chinatown district – battling with restaurants and antique shops (and some rummageable junk stores) for tourists' attention.

The highly commendable Gold Country Museum (1273 High Street) charts Auburn's past with a quality collection of gold mining implements and explanatory displays, backed up with native American items and intriguing pieces from early Auburn's Chinese community.

Near the main museum, the **Bernhard Museum** is a complex of late 1800s buildings intended to replicate Victorian life: you will find a period-furnished home, a working blacksmith's yard, and a former winery now housing an art gallery.

▶ ▶ ▷ **Calaveras Big Trees State Park**

Much less famous nowadays than their counterparts in the Sierra Nevada's national parks, the giant sequoia trees at what became Calaveras Big Trees State Park were the first of their kind to be discovered – by a local settler chasing a bear in 1852 – and were first thought to be the only giant sequoias in the world.

Widespread disbelief greeted press reports of their size

Mark Twain passed through Angel City as part of his grand tour across the western US, which was recorded – as a mix of fact and fiction – in Roughing It, published in 1872. Bret Harte had already gained notoriety as a journalist before taking teaching jobs around Angels Camp, a period which gave rise to sharp, if sometimes whimsical, tales of the lives and life-styles of the booming Gold Country, the first of which was The Luck of the Roaring Camp, published in 1868.

Auburn Old Town's 19th-century elegance

Calavaras Big Trees State Park

(in terms of bulk, giant sequoias are the earth's largest living organisms) and there followed a 'tree rush' of tourists and naturalists to California. The **Big Trees Visitor Center** provides a thorough grounding on the trees, which lie in two sections of the park. The North Grove is looped by a mile-long foot-trail; nine miles south, the less visited South Grove, which requires a bit more walking, holds more than 1,000 sequoias in atmospheric seclusion.

▷ ▷ ▷   **Chinese Camp**

In 1851, one in ten of California's 250,000 miners were Chinese, and 5,000 of them lived in Chinese Camp, nine miles south of Jamestown at the junction of State Road 49 and State Road 120. Not helped by the 'foreigner tax', few Chinese did well out of mining and many went on to provide the labour for the transcontinental railway, before retreating to San Francisco's Chinatown. Nothing remains of Chinese Camp except crumbling brick and adobe buildings, and it is left to a post office and a petrol station to keep the place-name on the map.

The Chinese endured more racism than any other ethnic group during the gold mining days, and there was much disappintment in the non-Chinese community when a 'Tong Wars' battle, which raged here for several hours in 1856, left only four dead.

Drive State Road 49: Jamestown to Placerville

See map on page 210.

Begin in Jamestown, at the Railtown 1897 State Historic Park.
Jamestown's **Railtown 1897 State Historic Park** preserves the engines, carriages and equipment of the Sierra Railway Company, founded in 1897.

From Jamestown, drive three miles east on State Road 49 to reach Sonora.
One of the wealthiest gold-rush towns, **Sonora** continues to thrive, thanks in part to the railway and also to the well-preserved historical buildings in the old section of the town which makes it a much sought-after address.

Continue for four miles on State Road 49 to Columbia State Historic Park.
The outstanding **Columbia State Historic Park** creates an intriguing

Columbia State Historic Park

impression of life in a gold-rush town (see page 215).
Continue for 19 miles on State Road 49 to Angels Camp.
Curiously, **Angels Camp** is the only gold-rush town better known for its frogs than its preserved buildings: writer Mark Twain penned his first published story about them and nowadays a Jumping Frogs Jamboree is held each May (see page 212).

Continue for 11 miles on State Road 49 to San Andreas.
In **San Andreas**, legendary frontier outlaw Black Bart (see panel on page 223) was tried and sentenced in 1883 at the County Courthouse, an immaculately restored building which now serves as the **Calaveras County Historical Museum and Archives**.

Continue for 16 miles on State Road 49 to Jackson.
The seat of tiny Amador County, Jackson holds the **Amador County Museum**, which offers a lively examination of gold mining techniques with working scale models.

Continue for 14 miles on State Road 49, passing Amador City (described on page 212), on the way to Plymouth.
Just outside Plymouth, the **Sobon Estate** is the new name of the D'Agostini Winery, which is one of the oldest wine producers in the state, dug into a hillside in 1856 and open for tastings of its dry and dessert wines.

Continue for 20 miles on State Road 49 to Placerville.
In **Placerville**, once known as Hangtown, the well-lit but chilly innards of the **Gold Bug Mine** can be toured, and the **El Dorado County Museum** stores a vast horde of miners' tools and machinery.

▶ ▶ ▷ Columbia

In 1854, bustling Columbia was pipped by two votes by Sacramento in the race to become California's state capital. Consequently, as soon as its mines closed so too did the town, leaving the 12 square blocks which now form **Columbia State Historic Park**.
The 50 wooden buildings preserved in the park include Columbia's saloon, hotel, schoolhouse and even its dentist's surgery, all staffed by period-dressed guides.

▶ ▷ ▷ Coulterville

Coulterville should be on your itinerary for the engrossing accounts of mining-era life housed in the **North Mariposa County History Center**, inside the community's former Wells Fargo office. Take a walk, too, along Main Street to view the thick-walled adobe buildings of the 1850s, such as the Jeffrey Hotel and the Magnolia Saloon, and the Sun Sun Wo Co Store, a survivor of Coulterville's Chinatown district.

▶ ▷ ▷ Downieville

Flaunting its dubious distinction of being the only mining community to hang a woman, Downieville not only preserves many of its 1850s structures but also keeps a shine on the town gallows. Once a Chinese store and opium den, the Sierra County Museum on Main Street has photographs and knick-knacks.

▷ ▷ ▷ Folsom

More than a quarter of Folsom's 23,000 residents are unhappily enduring what Johnny Cash immortalised in song as Folsom prison blues. Such is the fame of the town's prison that it has its own museum, devoted to crime and its perpetrators. A more orthodox historical stash fills the Folsom Museum. Nearby Lake Folsom has water skiing, swimming and sailing.

A stagecoach is part of the scenery in Columbia

The group of public spirited Downieville citizens who got together in the late 1980s to finance the restoration of their community's most historic landmark – its gallows – rejoiced in the title, The Friends of the Gallows.

■ The romantic image of the lone prospector standing beside a river patiently sifting through a panful of slush in the hope of finding glinting yellow flakes is some way removed from the truth of unearthing gold in California. The real story involved rivers being diverted and dredged, entire hillsides being blown to smithereens, and immense machines keeping whole towns awake at night as they hammered quartz to powder. The same technology that made California rich also inflicted scars across its Sierra foothill landscapes which – a century after the damage was done – are only just starting to heal. .....■

Paying the price for gold fever?

Placer mining Panning was the simplest form of 'placer mining' (the term stemming from the idea of the gold being 'in place' in rivers and streams), the 'placer' scooping up a pan load of gravel from the river bed and carefully removing the lighter material to leave (hopefully) the heavier gold remaining at the bottom. Most of the gold found this way was actually tiny flakes of gold dust which earned the nickname 'color'.

A more sophisticated form of placer mining came with the use of the 'rocker', a long box into which one placer shovelled river bed detritus while a second miner shook the contraption, hoping that gold would be captured by the cleats at the bottom as the dirt passed through.

A further refinement was the 'long tom', a wooden trough about 12 feet long which needed three placers: one shovelling, one mixing, and the third directing a jet of water into the trough. The contents drained out through a 'ripple box', which held any passing gold.

Later, productivity was increased with complex sluice systems, but by the 1850s it was widely accepted that most rivers had yielded all the gold they were going to and attention turned to the gold-bearing Sierra rock.

Hydraulic mining Beginning in the early 1850s, hydraulic mining involved the removal of surface rock from whole hillsides with high-pressure jets of water (using adapted fire-fighting equipment and nozzles weighing a ton) to expose the seams of gold.

Highly productive (although many tons of rock had to be removed to yield a few ounces of gold) but also highly pollutive, hydraulic mining wrecked havoc on the natural landscape, destroying wildlife habitats and clogging rivers with so much mud and gravel that the state's farmland came under threat. Because of such damage, 'hydraulicking', as it was known, was banned in 1884.

Quartz (or hardrock) mining Around the time hydraulic mining commenced, it was discovered that gold was embedded in quartz veins, or lodes (hence the term 'Mother Lode', applied to the whole Gold Country but misleadingly implying that there was a single large lode), vhich occurred throughout the Gold Country.

Jsing dynamite (invented in 1860), holes were blasted nto the hillsides and the first tunnel mines were constructed, often stretching for many miles nderground.

Miners descended into the depths and attacked the juartz lodes with pickaxes and shovels, the quartz hunks they hacked out being carried to the surface on nule-drawn wagons. Mules were also used to turn the *rrastra*, a cumbersome machine of Mexican origin, esembling a large-sized pestle and mortar, which slowly ground the quartz.

he development of stamp mills, enormous machines veighing several tons (and now the prize exhibits of nany Gold Country museums), greatly speeded up the pulverising of the quartz; hammering day and night, the sound of the stamp mills often carried to surrounding owns. Gold was extracted from the pulverised quartz hrough a chemical process, and then, in molten form, it vas poured into moulds to make ingots.

Dredge mining From the 1890s, dredging machines begen gouging up the river beds where the earlier placer niners had worked, depositing the resultant material in uge sluicing machines. The tons of waste which this process created were unceremoniously dumped in any vailable space, often burying vegetation and causing nany rivers to alter their courses. Subject to strict controls, limited dredge mining continues today.

Some people believe the Mother Lode has plenty of gold left to yield and dredge mining and gold panning both have plenty of serious adherents, even today. The pans handed out to tourists at a few spots around the Gold Country, however, are unlikely to produce anything but backache.

217

GOLD COUNTRY

Having danced her way across the US, thrilling audiences with her saucy 'spider dance', Irish-born Lola Montez settled in Grass Valley. Flamboyant and glamourous, Lola's was a bemusing presence to miners but not to Lotta Crabtree, a local six-year-old later to become the highest-earning entertainer in the US, to whom Lola passed on her dancing skills. Leaving Grass Valley after her husband shot her pet bear, Lola underwent a religious conversion and spent the next few years delivering theosophical lectures in Australia and Europe, before dying penniless in New York in 1861, aged 42.

The wealth produced by gold-mining left its mark in the elegant buildings of Grass Valley

▷ ▷ ▷   **Grass Valley**

The biggest and most lucrative mine in California made Grass Valley one of the state's richest communities by the late 1800s. The buildings, a shaft, and many of the machines of the state's most technologically innovative mine – which only ceased operations in 1956 – can be seen at the **Empire Mine State Historic Park**, spread across both sides of State Road 174 a mile east of the town.

Following the closure of the mine, Grass Valley kept itself in the style to which it was accustomed through farming and the lumber trade, and by exploiting the tourist appeal of its many balconied 19th-century buildings – and the restaurants serving 'English-style food, a throwback to the many Cornish miners who settled here.

A less likely settler was Lola Montez, a vivacious European dancer and a former lover of the King of Bavaria (see panel on this page). A replica of her home (at 248 Mill Street) houses the town's tourist office and many mementos of her life.

Elsewhere, the **Grass Valley Museum** (corner of Church and Chapel streets), fills an 1865 schoolhouse with general historical displays, and the **North Star Mining Museum** (intersection of State Road 20 and State Road 49) has detailed exhibitions on mining technology.

▶ ▶ ▷   **Indian Grinding Rocks State Park**

Many generations of Miwok Indians grinding nuts to make flour have left over 1,000 identical *chaw'se*, or mortar cups, indenting a large limestone outcrop at Indian Grinding Rocks State Historic Park, between Amador City and Volcano. Several hundred petroglyphs also mark the rock, and more recent additions to the park are a re-created Miwok Village and a Museum Cultural Center, which describes the use of the *chaw'se* and profiles the 10 tribes native to the area.

▶ ▷ ▷ Malakoff Diggins State Historic Park

Sixteen miles from Nevada City, a massive gash on the side of a mountain caused by hydraulic mining has become a serene expanse of meadows and canyons populated by deer, coyotes and squirrels. A few restored buildings remember the mining settlement here, but it is the extraordinary regenerative abilities of nature that impress most throughout the 3,000-acre park.

▶ ▷ ▷ Mariposa

Most who pass through Mariposa are less interested in the Gold Country than Yosemite National Park, which lies just 30 miles east. If you are one of them, stop off at least long enough to explore the **Mariposa County History Center** (corner of Twelfth and Jessie streets), a rewarding collection revealing plenty about life during the gold-rush times, and featuring a miner's cabin and a lady's boudoir among a group of reconstructed period interiors.

Outside, the lawlessness of the old days is suggested much less by the grand **Mariposa County Courthouse** (5808 Bullion Street) – finished in 1854 and the state's longest serving place of justice – than the nearby Old Mariposa Jail, a grim affair in use until 1960.

Two miles south of Mariposa, the **California State Mining and Mineral Museum** holds ample proof that this region yielded the Gold Country's most spectacular finds, with diamonds and gold nuggets among 200,000 precious pieces.

▶ ▶ ▶ Marshall Gold Discovery State Historic Park

California changed for ever on 24 January 1848, when James Marshall, building a sawmill for landowner John Sutter, chanced upon flakes of gold beside the American River in the settlement of Coloma, commemorated as the Marshall Gold Discovery State Historic Park.

Within a year, 10,000 people were busy with pickaxes and shovels in the vicinity, although they quickly departed as richer veins were discovered elsewhere, leaving Coloma to decline and a disillusioned Marshall to die in 1879 in his cabin, which still stands here.

Among many restored buildings, the park also has a working model of Sutter's Mill and a museum tracing the colossal effect Marshall's find had on the state.

▶ ▷ ▷ Murphys

Named after the two Irish brothers who founded it in 1848, Murphys barely extends beyond its tree-lined Main Street, where the **Murphys Hotel** has stood since 1856, hosting luminaries such as writer Bret Harte and future US president Ulysses S Grant. The clutter of curiosities filling the **Oldtimer's Museum** attests to the mining community's dislike of throwing things away.

North of Murphys off Sheep Ranch Road, a guided tour of **Mercer's Caverns** leads to bizarre limestone formations, and the **Stevenot Winery** has free tastings.

Passed by the state legislature in 1850, the Foreign Miners' License Tax imposed a $20-a-month levy on all miners who were not US citizens. Initially directed at Mexicans – who had staged an uprising against US vigilantes enforcing racist mining codes in Sonora – in practice it came to be only Chinese miners who were subject to the tax. Of the money, $15 went to the state and the rest to the local sheriff.

219

Nevada City, once the state's largest city

▶ ▶ ▷   Nevada City

Like neighbouring Grass Valley, Nevada City benefited from mining to a much greater degree than most Gold Country communities, and is still comfortably off, with much from its past lining its narrow streets.

Serving travellers since 1850, the antique-ridden bar and dining rooms of the **National Hotel** (211 Broad Street) do more to evoke the past than the motley collections of the Firehouse Museum (214 Main Street), inside the town's tall and slender 1861 fire station. More impressive exhibits are to be found at the **Miners' Foundry and Cultural Center** (325 Spring Street), a one-time metalworks turned into a showplace of Victorian arts and crafts.

Only two buildings in the old town do not bear Victorian hallmarks: the art deco Courthouse (on Church Street), and the 1937 City Hall (317 Broad Street).

Keep walking east along Broad Street and you soon reach the **Indian Medicine Rock**, a broad slab of stone where sick members of the Maidu tribe believed they would regain their vigour by soaking up the sun.

▷ ▷ ▷   Plumas-Eureka State Park

Enclosed by rough granite peaks and hillsides streaked green by fir and sugar pine trees, pretty Plumas-Eureka State Park sits above 70 miles of tunnels which belonged to the Sierra Buttes Mining Company. The park office and a well-planned **mining museum** fill the miners' former bunkhouse.

▷ ▷ ▷   Rough And Ready

In an act of drunken bravura and in protest at a miner's tax, Rough And Ready citizens seceded from the US in 1850 (returning two months later), the only town ever to do so. Today, there is no incentive to pause on your way to the **Bridgeport Covered Bridge**, built in 1862 and making a 233-foot span across the Yuba River – the longest such bridge in the US, and in use until 1971.

During April and May, when the melting snow of the High Sierra mountains sends rivers cascading through the foothills, white river rafting comes into its own along the American and Tuolumne rivers. Most Gold Country towns have companies offering guided river runs, which range from white-knuckle beginners' specials to death-defying experts-only trips. Operators include Adventure Connection in Coloma (tel: (916) 626 7385), Sobek Expeditions in Angels Camp (tel (209) 736 4524), and Zephyr River Expeditions in Sonora (tel: (209) 532 6249).

■ **Today, Sacramento may seem an odd choice for state capital but in 1854 it was the gateway to the gold mines with men, machinery and money streaming through it. As California's first fortunes were being made, it was here that the Big Four rose to prominence, and established the power base from which they shaped the state's future. .....■**

Buildings Eclipsing everything around it, the **State Capitol Building** (east end of Capitol Mall), completed in 1874, is not only an impressive example of the neo-classical style that defined US public building for decades, but also, at a cost of $2.5 million, a lasting testament to the incredible wealth of gold-rush California. Inside, several restored offices can be enjoyed on free guided tours, and the state legislature can be witnessed in action.

Sacramento's earliest building, the largely adobe **Sutter's Fort** (2701 L Street), was erected in 1839 by German-born John Sutter as a commercial base for his considerable landholdings. Several reconstructed workshops stand in the fort's grounds, as does the **California State Indian Museum**, making a valiant attempt to chronicle California's 104 native tribes with a fine stock of handicrafts and ceremonial objects.

Beside the Sacramento River, the wooden sidewalks of the Old Town link six blocks of effectively restored 19th-century buildings, the genuine history – revealed by several excellent small museums – sitting slightly awkwardly alongside gift shops and cafés.

Museums The Old Town also boasts the California State Railroad Museum (111 I Street), a dazzling collection of old locomotives and imaginative displays clarifying the crucial role of railways in California's development, and the **Sacramento History Center** (101 I Street), which plots the

<< The 'Big Four' – Charles Crocker, Mark Hopkins, Collis P Huntington and Leland Stanford – were Sacramento businessmen who, in the late 1850s, financed the plans of a railway engineer, Theodore Judah, for a transcontinental railway linking California with the rest of the US. The success of the venture resulted in the Big Four's Southern Pacific Railroad Company enjoying a monopoly of communication links, making them the biggest political power-brokers in state history. >>

growth of the town and its surrounds.

Just outside the Old Town, the Crocker Art Museum (216 O Street) has striking tiled floors and curving staircases, and is claimed to be the West's first art museum.

The Sacramento River

Walk Sacramento

From the State Capitol, described on page 221, walk east along Capitol Avenue, turning left along 28th Street for Sutter's Fort.
Sacramento's earliest building, **Sutter's Fort** is described on page 221.

Walk west along K Street, turning right into 16th Street for the Governor's Mansion.
At 1526 H Street, the 1877 **Governor's Mansion** is now a museum of Victoriana.

Continue west along I Street for the Old Town.
The **Old Town**, with restored buildings and museums, is described on page 221.

Walk through the Old Town for the Towe Ford Museum.
At 2200 Front Street, the **Towe Ford Museum** displays gleaming Ford vehicles from 1903 onwards.

Leave the Old Town, walking east along O Street for the Crocker Art Museum.
The elegant **Crocker Art Museum**, 216 O Street, is described in full on page 221.

<< Born in Germany but living in Switzerland when he went bankrupt, John Sutter arrived in (then Mexican) California in 1839, taking advantage of internecine squabbles to acquire 48,000 acres around the confluence of the Sacramento and American rivers. What might have made him rich beyond his wildest dreams proved to be his downfall. When gold was discovered on his land in 1848, Sutter's workers became gold prospectors overnight, leaving their boss's possessions to rot. By 1852 Sutter was again bankrupt, and died impoverished in 1880. >>

Walk east along P Street, turning left along Eighth Street for the Stanford House.
On the corner with N Street, the **Stanford House** was a home of railway magnate Leland Stanford, one of the Big Four (see above), from 1871.

Walk east along N Street to return to the State Capitol.

▷ ▷ ▷ Sierra City

Evocatively perched in the Sierra foothills beneath towering granite peaks, Sierra City's **Sierra Historical Park** does a tremendous job re-creating the homes and illustrating the life-styles of mining folk. It also does justice to the memory of a local man, James Pelton, who changed the face of Californian mining by devising the Pelton Wheel, which enabled the mines' enormous stamp mills to be powered by small jets of water.

Sonora has maintained its serene charm

223

▷ ▷ ▷ Sonora

The Mexican miners who founded Sonora were driven away by North American settlers before the town became one of the richest gold-rush towns, and later, thanks to the railway, the commercial hub of the entire region. Even now, Sonora is a coveted address, its tranquillity bringing many new residents from the cities. The old section of Sonora is extremely well preserved and many of the town's 19th-century great and good lived in mansions still clustered together along Washington Street. Here, too, is the red and white **St James Episcopal Church**, dating from 1859.

A leaflet detailing the historic homes can be picked up in what used to be the County Jail (158 W Bradford Avenue), now doubling as a tourist office and the **Tuoloumne County Museum**, whose local history exhibits and Old West paintings, fill the former cells.

Wearing a mask and wielding a shotgun, Black Bart (an alias of one Charles Bolton) relieved 28 Wells Fargo stagecoaches of their gold between 1875 and 1883, often leaving his victims with a self-penned poem. Finally traced by, and captured through, a dropped handkerchief, Bart was tried in San Andreas and served five years in San Quentin prison. Following his release he vanished from the public eye – rumoured by some to be receiving a Wells Fargo pension on the understanding that he never robbed from them again.

▶ ▷ ▷ Volcano

A meandering back road (off State Road 88) gives access to Volcano, named for the crater-like landscape in which it sits, which once had a population of 5,000 and a reputation for riotous nightlife. Only a couple of hundred people live here now, and the chief reminder of the halcyon times is the splendid 1864 **St George Hotel**.

Far North

A seven-year period of intermittent eruptions culminated in 1915 when Lassen Peak, California's only active volcano and the southernmost of the Cascade mountain range, threw a cloud of dust seven miles high, tossed out five-ton boulders and smothered the surrounding countryside in a 20-foot deep mud flow.

Lassen Peak, the world's largest 'plug' volcano and one unlikely to erupt again for many decades, sits in Lassen National Park, 50 miles east of Redding, the tallest but by no means the only volcanic peak in a geologically very busy region. It occupies a caldera – or crater – left behind by the collapsing dome of a vast prehistoric volcano.

Along State Road 89, which steers a 30-mile course through the park, the major points of interest are indicated by numbered markers corresponding to explanatory descriptions in a leaflet distributed at the park entrance.

A mile-long trail from the road reaches the park's largest hydrothermal area, **Bumpass Hell**, a steaming cauldron of fumeroles – pressured gases hissing to the surface through gaps in the lava rock – hot springs and bubbling pits of mud. Bringing to life the lunar-like landscape, it is hard to believe that such violent scenes are only mild manifestations of the earth's energies.

The same phenomenon on a less imposing scale is repeated at several points throughout the park, but once your nostrils have had their fill of sulphur gas – the rotten-egg smell which pervades such regions – you should pay attention to the park's meadows, resplendent with midsummer wild flowers and sometimes with grazing deer, and pause by a few of the numerous lakes, often hauntingly still affairs reflecting nearby peaks in their calm surfaces.

Nature's better qualities are also apparent at the **Devastated Area**, where stands of young trees are beginning to reclaim a landscape razed of all vegetation by the mud flows and gases unleashed by the 1915 eruption.

Hiking trails through the park, and to the summit of Lassen Peak, are described on page 226.

▶ ▶ ▷ **Lava Beds National Monument**

Few visitors make the effort to reach Lava Beds National Monument, tucked away in the state's northeast corner, but the reward for those who do is an eerie, often foggy, plateau ridden with volcanic craters, cinder cones and lava tubes formed over 1,000 years ago by cooling magma flows.

Many of the hundreds of lava tubes lie a few feet beneath the ground as cylindrical caves, which can be explored after first borrowing a pair of flashlights from the visitor centre beside State Road 139 at the monument's southern entrance.

Near the visitor centre, exhibits inside the illuminated **Mushpot Cave** aid understanding of the area's geological curiosities, and several unlit caves lie within easy reach on the three-mile **Cave Loop**. If you find their darkness daunting, opt for the guided tours which are conducted daily except Wednesday.

Earthly energy at Bumpass Hell in Lassen Volcanic National Park

Resisting forcible resettlement, a group of Modoc Indians returned to their ancestral lands (what is now the Lava Beds National Monument) in November 1872, turning the area's volcanic formations into a natural line of defence against the US Army troops sent to remove them. The five-month Modoc War which ensued became the only Indian war fought in California. It needed a two-day mortar attack to finally shift the Modoc, following which their chief, Kentipoos (known to whites as Captain Jack), along with three other Modoc leaders, were tried by a military court and executed.

The single road through the monument's desolate landscapes passes many more caves, whose isolation deters all but the most adept explorers (who must get passes from the visitor centre), before reaching the area known as Captain Jack's Stronghold. This was named after a Modoc Indian chief who held out here with 52 tribesmen against 1,000 US soldiers for five months during 1872 and 1873, using the natural terrain as a shield (see panel on page 224).

 ▷ ▷ ▷ **Redding**

Given the alluring natural wonders all around it, it is not surprising that most people only use Redding, the Far North's largest town, for eating and sleeping amid scores of fast-food joints and motels. More cerebral needs are catered for with moderate success by the Carter House Natural Science Museum (48 Quartz Hill Road), providing a taster for the Far North's flora and fauna, and by the Redding Museum and Art Center (1911 Rio Drive), placing temporary local art exhibitions alongside permanent regional historical items, including a large collection of native American basketry.

Pressured gases burst out through crevices in the lava rock at Bumpass Hell

Lassen National Park's extremely volatile weather is a more pressing concern than the likelihood of volcanic eruptions. Temperatures range from cool to very cold, with July and August being the only months dependably free of snow. Whenever you plan to come, check conditions before setting out by phoning the park headquarters on (916) 595 4444.

■ **Only the most devoted city dweller will be able to drive through the landscapes of the Far North and not feel the urge to get out and explore them more closely. In Lassen National Park, and to a lesser extent in the Whiskeytown-Shasta-Trinity National Recreation Area, many miles of hiking trails (none of which require super-human strength) await your footprints.....■**

226

Mount Shasta can only be reached on very steep trails beginning at Ski Bowl and Horse Camp. You will need to set out at dawn to be sure of returning from the majestic (and mysterious, being a setting for many strange occult tales) mountain before nightfall.

Lassen Peak Not surprisingly, the best place for an overview of Lassen National Park is from its highest point, the 10,475ft-high Lassen Peak, reached by a 2.5-mile trail beginning from Marker 22 on State Road 89. A switchback route makes coping with the steep gradient comparatively easy going, but you should allow five hours to reach the top and come back down again, and to savour the sights and the feeling of achievement from the summit.

Other hikes Lassen Peak is a prime objective for many hikers, however, so if you want equally spectacular views and fewer people to share them with, try **Brokeoff Mountain** the second-tallest peak in the National Park, reached along a trail from Marker 2 on State Road 89.
Entering the easterly section of the park on State Road 44 (which, unlike State Road 89, does not cross the park) gives access to the backcountry, ripe for treks of several days' duration, but liable to be snowbound even in the summer.

The best hikes The pick of the shorter hikes in this region is the **Cinder Cone Nature Trial**, starting from Butte Lake, a potentially ankle-twisting trek through loose rock, but passing the aptly named Fantastic Lava Beds and Painted Dunes – multi-coloured lava flows dating from the 1850s.
Much of the **Whiskeytown-Shasta-Trinity National Recreation Area** (see page 227) is geared towards boating rather than walking. The best bets for modest exertion here are the Hirz Bay and Samwell Cave trails, close to Lake Shasta and designed to illustrate local nature and wildlife. Perpetually snow-capped Mount Shasta, 30 miles north of Lake Shasta, is on many hikers' Far North itineraries, but the 14,162-foot-high peak is not to be underestimated, as it is prone to avalanches, rock falls and constantly changing weather.

For the adventurous hiker For longer and more isolated hikes, make for the Clair Engle (also known as Trinity) Lake area, and the **Salmon-Trinity Alps Primitive Area**, with 400 hikeable miles through forests, meadows and canyons, beside waterfalls and beneath glaciated peaks. Be aware that local weather is unpredictable and services are scarce (for information, tel: (916) 246 5338).

▷ ▷ ▷ Shasta

Shasta flourished during the late 1800s on account of the lucrative gold mines which surrounded it. Remains and detailed reconstructions of Shasta's buildings form the **Shasta State Historical Park**, on State Road 299, six miles west of Redding.

▶ ▶ ▷ Whiskeytown-Shasta-Trinity NRA

Covering nearly 250,000 acres, the Whiskeytown-Shasta-Trinity National Recreation Area divides into three sections, each one adjacent to a dam-formed lake. Sailing, windsurfing, and water- and jet-skiing (stocks permitting, most equipment can be hired on arrival) make the lakes, and Whiskeytown especially, intensely busy each summer. Lake Shasta Dam, reached with State Road 155 off Interstate-5, is the area's most spectacular man-made sight and the second-biggest dam in the US. It diverts three rivers to irrigate California's Central Valley farmlands. A film describing the dam's construction is shown at the visitor centre, while crossing the lake on Interstate-5 takes you over the **Pit River Bridge**, the world's biggest double-decked bridge, carrying a railway line as well as the highway.

Turn a visit to Lake Shasta into a day trip by continuing to the **Lake Shasta Caverns**; guided cavern tours commence by boat from O'Brien, on the eastern side of the lake, and feature stalactite and stalagmite formations.

Close to Clair Engle Lake, in the westerly fringes of the recreation area, **Weaverville** has many 19th-century buildings as reminders of its gold prospecting days. During the 1850s, half of Weaverville's population was Chinese, some of whom contributed to the building of the **Joss House**, a Taoist temple decorated with tapestries and ornaments set around a 3,000-year old altar. Now the centrepiece of Joss House State Historic Park, the temple has half-hourly guided tours.

Part of the Whiskeytown-Shasta-Trinity National Recreation Area, the title of Trinity Lake – fed by the Trinity River – was officially changed to Clair Engle Lake to commemorate the state senator who oversaw its damming. Trinity still appears on many maps, however, and is also still in use locally, not least by the resentful residents who formerly owned the land now at the bottom of the reservoir which the dam created.

227

The formidable peak of Mount Shasta

NORTH COAST

```
0    20    40 km
0   10   20 miles
```

Crescent City
Klamath
Redwood National Park
Orick
Trinidad
Hoopa Valley Ind Res
Hoopa
Arcata
Humboldt Bay N W R
Eureka
Fortuna
Ferndale
Grizzly Creek Redwoods S P
Cape Mendocino
Humboldt Redwoods S P
Honeydew
Avenue of the Giants
Weott
Miranda
King Pk 1246m
Garberville
Richardson Grove S P
Standish-Hickey S R A
Round Valley Ind Res
Fort Bragg
Noyo
Jug Handle
Russian Gulch S P
Willits
Mendocino
Albion
Ukiah
Manchester
Point Arena
Manchester St Beach
Clear Lake
Lakeport
Hopland
Gualala
Cloverdale
Geyserville
Healdsburg
Plantation
Fort Ross S H P
Goat Rock
Armstrong Redwoods S P
Jenner
Santa Rosa
Bodega Bay
Petaluma
Pt Reyes Nat Seashore
Novato
Drakes Bay
Bolinas
Muir Woods Nat Mon
Mt Tamalpais S P
Golden Gate Nat Rec Area
SAN FRANCISCO

Klamath
Mad
Eel
Ed
Middle
King Mts

228

A world away from the affluent cities, crowded sands and persistent sunshine of southern California, the state's North Coast – between San Francisco and the Oregon border – is a heavily forested and almost continually damp region, populated by a bizarre mix of unsophisticated lumber workers, marijuana farmers, back-to-nature artists and radical ecologists.

Despite its ample size – accounting for almost a third of the state's Pacific seaboard – the North Coast has always been one of California's most sparsely inhabited and least accessible corners; even today, there are only a couple of viable routes through it. The coast-hugging Highway-1 is the most scenic option but covers just half the region before swinging inland to join Highway-101, which links the inland settlements and the northernmost coastal towns before continuing into Oregon and deep into the Pacific Northwest.

Climate The North Coast's summer temperatures can be searing but fogs regularly block out the heat and, in winter, the area is one of the wettest in the US. Clearly, this is no place to acquire a tan (and typically, the region's best beaches are slivers of sand enclosed by jagged headlands at the end of winding foot-trails) yet it is just this climate which allows the North Coast's most prized feature to flourish: the gigantic coastal redwoods, the tallest trees in the world which are found only here.

There are strands of redwoods within easy striking distance of San Francisco at the Muir Woods National Monument, part of the Golden Gate National Recreation Area, and at Point Reyes National Seashore. But travel further north to Humboldt State Park or the Redwood National Park and you will encounter these incredible trees – their slender trunks often rising for more than 300 feet.

Even if it lacked the redwoods, the North Coast would still be exceptionally strong on natural spectacle. At almost every turn throughout 200 miles of coastline there is a fresh vista to excite, be it wave-sculptured rock arches, gale-tormented bluffs, schools of basking seals, or (at the right time of year) migrating whales.

Gull Rock, on the Pacific Coast

A North Coast small town: Mendocino

Town life Small and separated by long distances, the towns of the North Coast generally provide a sedate accompaniment to the wild scenery around them. Most sprang up during the mid-19th century, when their sheltered bays made perfect landing points for men and machinery destined for the Gold Country, and later grew into busy lumber ports as timber became the region's economic backbone.

Several communities – notably Fort Bragg, half-way along the North Coast – are still dominated by the logging industry, despite the fact that pressure from the environmental lobby has stimulated a re-thinking of tree felling methods (depressingly large sections of the North Coast's forests have been reduced to stumps), part of a widespread reassessment of priorities as the region's other staple local trades, fishing and farming, face decline.

Alternative industry Some landowners in the slumbering agricultural hamlets have sought an alternative source of income by cultivating marijuana. This is no secret to law enforcement agencies but marijuana growing is a money-spinning practice that is proving impossible to curtail, with a particularly productive region around Garberville even earning the nickname, the Emerald Triangle.

Increasingly, though, it is tourism which is seen as the financial future of the North Coast, something which causes commercial interests and conservationists to lock horns with increasing regularity. The battle between the rival factions is clearest at Mendocino, a lovely town with many restored mid-1800s buildings and an artistic flavour that is struggling to maintain its character against a rash of gift shops and bed and breakfast inns.

Elsewhere, larger communities such as Arcata and Eureka pack their charming centres with preserved Victorian homes and they make good bases from which to discover the best of the North Coast's nature. The quirkiest historical sight for miles around, however, is the remnants of a 19th-century Russian fur-trapping settlement at Fort Ross.

One more North Coast curiosity is the notorious San Andreas fault, the line of geological instability that has been responsible for many of California's biggest earthquakes, and which scars the landscape with its presence before moving away beneath the ocean.

▶ ▷ ▷   Arcata

These days a hotbed of radical politics and ecological activism, Arcata was founded as a mining supply base and gained notoriety in 1860 by booting soon-to-be-famous writer Bret Harte out of town for publicising a massacre of Indians.

Numerous Victorian homes and a lovely central plaza bring character to Arcata, and the small town is kept bubbling by the students of the North Coast's only university.

All the sights worth seeing are natural ones: the **Historic Logging Trail** traces the impact of the lumber industry on a section of Arcata Community Forest; landfill sites around **Arcata Bay** have been turned into a wildlife preserve and bird sanctuary; and azaleas, rhododendrons and a host of wild flowers blooming at various times throughout the year, ensure that some colour is always beautifying the 30-acre **Azalea State Reserve**.

▶ ▷ ▷   Bodega Bay

An encouraging first glimpse of the North Coast if you are arriving from the Wine Country and a good base for exploring the Sonoma State Beach (see page 241), Bodega Bay's tall cliffs and sandy beaches look out over the vessels of a declining fishing fleet, whose plaid-shirted workforce are not overly enamoured of the gift shops and boutiques which are spreading through their village.

If Bodega Bay's immense gull population gets on your nerves, it will come as no comfort at all to learn that it was here that Alfred Hitchcock shot his 1963 film, *The Birds*.

▷ ▷ ▷   Bolinas

Just south of Point Reyes National Seashore, Bolinas is so well liked by its residents that they are known to tear down road signs directing traffic to it. As it happens,

To find out if the dietary habits of lumbermen – famed for their gargantuan appetites and their predilection for red meat – have changed over a century, cross Eureka's Humboldt Bay to the Samoa Peninsula and the Samoa Cookhouse, which has been feeding tree fellers (and the general public) since the 1880s. A utensil-stocked museum records the eatery's past, while the main section of the cookhouse still delivers more than ample platefuls to diners at bench tables.

Barbecued oysters – a coastal speciality

Bolinas may be a nice place in which to live but is an entirely uninteresting one to visit. Much more deserving of attention in the area are the birds swooping for fishy snacks at **Bolinas Lagoon**, and the many and various marine creatures inhabiting the tidal pools of **Duxbury Reef**.

▶ ▶ ▷ Eureka

A glut of Victorian residential architecture turns industrialised Eureka, easily the largest town on the North Coast, into an impressive showcase of turn-of-the-century California living. There is no more eloquent example of the style than the **Carson Mansion** (143 M Street), complete with painted window-frames, turrets and towers, built in 1885 by an architect who did not know when to stop.

Using timber to a different end, the **Wooden Garden of Romano Gabriel** (325 Second Street) is an intensely colourful collection of people, plants and symbols carved from disused packing cases with a chain saw. It is either epic folk art or simply a mess – either way, you will kick yourself for missing it.

Eureka's over-the-top architecture

Old Town The downbeat bars and flophouses that have traditionally filled Eureka's dockside area are fast being turned into trendy galleries, boutiques and eateries. These occupy newly painted restored buildings collectively titled the **Old Town** – all a bit contrived and pricey, but none the less the area makes for an enjoyable stroll.

Near by, the **Clarke Memorial Museum** (240 E Street) keeps the dust off myriad exhibits from Eureka's pioneer times, and maintains a ravishing stash of basketry from the Northwest's native American tribes.

By contrast, Eureka's 1853 Fort Humboldt was built to launch attacks on native Americans. At Fort Humboldt State Historic Park (3431 Fort Avenue) only the redwood hospital of the fort's 14 buildings remains upright, and its exhibits – not surprisingly – dwell on logging rather than on genocide.

▶ ▶ ▷ Ferndale

Almost every one of the thousand or so residents of Ferndale, 20 miles south of Eureka, has a well looked after Victorian pile to call home. The few antiques and period furnishings not in daily use are stored inside the **Ferndale Museum** (515 Shaw Avenue), a collection which sets the seal on this wondrous time-locked community.

▷ ▷ ▷ Fort Bragg

You will not find a fort in Fort Bragg but you will find lumber mills and freight yards that diminish the scenic setting of this hard-working coastal town. The Guest House Museum (on Main Street) unfurls an uncritical account of the timber industry, but you are better off opting for a stroll along the two miles of trails weaving through the 17-acre Mendocino Botanical Gardens (18220 N Highway-1), where craggy, wave-lashed headlands vie with blooming wild flowers for your attention.

The cold and choppy waters off the North Coast generally do little to encourage boat tours. An exception is Eureka's sheltered Humboldt Bay, enjoyably cruised on a narrated 75-minute sailing aboard a 1910 ferry, departing from the C Street harbour (for details, tel: (707) 445 1910). Also in Eureka, the Image Tour includes a boat trip as part of a five-hour guided town tour (details from the Chamber of Commerce, tel: (800) 356 6381).

■ **Found only along a slender section of the coast between Big Sur (on the northern half of California's Central Coast) and central Oregon, the tall and comparatively slender coast redwoods (*Sequoia sempervirens*) should not be confused with the slightly shorter and much stockier giant sequoias (*Sequoia gigantea*), which live on the western slopes of the Sierra Nevada mountains. .....■**

Between Fort Bragg and Willits, the Skunk Train – which earned its name from the aromatic qualities of its diesel engine – makes a highly scenic 40-mile trip, crisscrossing the Noyo River and riding on trestles high above redwood groves. Tourists have replaced timber as the main cargo, although the train still makes unscheduled stops to deliver post and supplies to the tiny settlements on its route. Operating twice-daily in summer and daily in winter, the Skunk Train should not be missed.

The tallest trees in the world As a species, the redwoods have been around for 60 million years, and when dinosaurs still roamed the earth they covered large sections of both the North American and European continents. As global weather patterns changed, the redwoods retreated to the US's West Coast, where the heavy rainfall and regular fogs are much to their liking.

Often growing as high as an American football field is long, the coast redwoods are the world's tallest trees – the tallest among them reaching 368 feet – although their lifespan of up to 2,600 years is less than that of the giant sequoias which can live up to 3,400 years. Because of logging, however, many of the trees you will see along the North Coast are comparative youngsters.

Like the giant sequoias, the coast redwoods absorb rainwater through their shallow root systems. Such roots render them unstable in high winds, however, and as a consequence they grow in areas sheltered from ocean breezes and cluster together in tight groves.

With heat-resistant barks, both types of sequoia are able to take advantage of forest fires, dropping their winged seeds to the freshly cleared forest floor, where sunlight is able to reach the sprouting sequoias.

As well as by seeds, sequoias can regenerate in a strange cloning-type process, which enables new trees to grow from fallen branches, stumps or roots, each one bearing the genetic imprint of its progenitor.

The Skunk Train, now mainly tourist transport

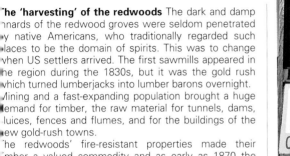

The 'harvesting' of the redwoods The dark and damp innards of the redwood groves were seldom penetrated by native Americans, who traditionally regarded such places to be the domain of spirits. This was to change when US settlers arrived. The first sawmills appeared in the region during the 1830s, but it was the gold rush which turned lumberjacks into lumber barons overnight. Mining and a fast-expanding population brought a huge demand for timber, the raw material for tunnels, dams, sluices, fences and flumes, and for the buildings of the new gold-rush towns.

The redwoods' fire-resistant properties made their timber a valued commodity and as early as 1870 the best of the state's redwood trees had been felled. With no thoughts of reafforestation, commercial logging continued apace for the next 40 years using the highly destructive clear-felling method. This involved an entire hillside or watershed section of forest being sawn down, leaving a desolate stump-strewn landscape where any remaining groves were exposed to erosion and where local wildlife was devastated.

Saving the trees As the lumber industry made fortunes and kept a large contingent of Californians in work – especially so along the North Coast – voices of dissent

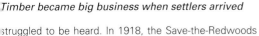

Timber became big business when settlers arrived

struggled to be heard. In 1918, the Save-the-Redwoods League was founded and teamed up with the the Sierra Club to promote awareness of the dangers faced by California's forests. During the 1930s, the Civilian Conservation Corps increased forest protection against fires, diseases and pests, and helped pave the way for 18 of California's forests (including Klamath National Forest on the North Coast) to be given National Forest status. This placed them under the control of the US Forestry Commission, who regulated logging activity.

It is only recently, however, that the environmentalists' (some of whom are colloquially known as 'tree huggers') argument that continued clear-felling will eventually destroy the logging business as well as the forests, has struck home with local commercial interests. Sustained-yield timber harvesting – cutting down no more than the amount grown each year – has now become more accepted as the sensible way ahead.

The various categories of natural areas and historic sites in California can cause confusion, although the differences are quite straightforward. National Forests, National Parks and National Monuments are all federally run from Washington DC (forests by the Forestry Service; parks and monuments by the Department of the Interior). State Parks, State Recreational Areas, State Historical Parks, and the sole State Historical Monument (San Simeon) are administered by California's State Department of Parks and Recreation, based in Sacramento.

THE NORTH COAST

In marked contrast to the US settlers who followed them, the Russians who lived at Fort Ross enjoyed friendly relations with the area's native American tribe, the Pomo, who marked the Russian's departure with a mourning ceremony.

Ravenous carnivores with a taste for the exotic will find their mouths watering just by reading the menus of the North Coast. Particularly in the region's northerly reaches, restaurants are liable to offer delectable morsels such as elk steaks, roasted bear, wild boar and even antelope sausages. Vegetarians who eat fish might console themselves with salmon jerky, a traditional native American creation which involves drying and smoking the fish.

▶ ▶ ▷ Fort Ross

Founded in 1812, Fort Ross was a social centre for a colony of Russians, arriving to grow wheat to supply their countrymen in Alaska and to hunt sea otters for their pelts. Most of the buildings were destroyed after the Russians' departure in 1841, but many, including the exceptional Orthodox Chapel, have been carefully reconstructed and authentically furnished at Fort Ross State Historic Park, beside Highway-1 20 miles north of Bodega Bay.

▷ ▷ ▷ Garberville

When devoted marijuana smokers began forsaking San Francisco for the pleasures of country living, many arrived in Garberville and began cultivating their own patches of the illicit weed. Discovering a booming market for home-grown hemp, Garberville's pioneers became major dealers, buying up large pockets of land and installing elaborate security systems to guard their crops.

It is an open secret that marijuana money contributes substantially to the economy of the tiny town – well endowed with hippie-flavoured bars – which gets most of its visitors during July when top musical names from Jamaica perform at the Reggae on the River rock festival.

▶ ▶ ▷ Golden Gate National Recreation Area

The Golden Gate National Recreation Area (GGNRA) spreads from San Francisco across the Golden Gate Bridge to the southernmost few miles of the North Coast, rubbing shoulders with Stinson Beach (see page 242) and the Port Reyes National Seashore (see page 241).

A network of foot-trails penetrates the GGNRA's Marin Headlands, throwing up exceptional views of San Francisco and the Golden Gate Bridge while traversing an immense acreage of pristine, scrub-covered hillsides to the tops of granite cliffs, buffeted far below by angry ocean waves.

Make for Point Bonita and the half-mile trail which negotiates a tunnel – gouged from the rock by hand in 1877 – and a nerve-tingling rope bridge on the way to **Point Bonita Lighthouse**, in itself less spectacular than the views all around it despite being among the West Coast's earliest beacons; or Rodeo Beach, an impossibly slender strip of sand between the ocean and a wildlife-rich lagoon.

Above Rodeo Beach, the **California Marine Mammal Center** provides treatment for injured seals and sea lions, and informs the public of coastal environmental issues with hands-on exhibits.

▷ ▷ ▷ Green Gulch Farm and Zen Center

From Muir Beach (see page 240), a path climbs to the Green Gulch Farm and Zen Center, founded in the early 1970s to further knowledge of Buddhism and meditation techniques. The centre's organic farm supplies several of the city's top-ranking restaurants. Get tuned in at the free public meditation session held on Sunday mornings (tel: (415) 383 3134).

▷ ▷ ▷ **Gualala**

Claimed by some to have been named after a Spanish rendition of the Norse myth of Valhalla, Gualala is a sleepy lumber town with little to admire beyond the 1903 Gualala Hotel in its centre, and the **Gallery**, which highlights the work of Mendocino area artists who are further celebrated by the Arts in the Redwoods festival held here each August.

Just south, **Gualala Regional Park** encompasses redwoods and beaches, and has a foot-trail to **Del Mar Landing**, a secluded coastal reserve with only the seals basking on the offshore rocks providing company for adventuring humans.

California poppies and onion domes at Gualala

THE NORTH COAST

The five-mile Ecological Staircase Trail at Jug Handle State Park, five miles south of Fort Bragg, makes a geologically fascinating trek across five rock terraces formed by the action of plate tectonics and exposed by wave action. Although only 100 feet separate the terraces, each is 100,000 years older or younger than its neighbour and covered by entirely different vegetation. A final surprise comes at the top, with the stunted and twisted cypress and pine trees of the Mendocino Pygmy Forest.

Drive inland towards the Hoopa Valley and you will be met at Willow Creek by a (supposedly) life-size statue of a Big Foot, the large and hairy ape-like creature which is believed by many to exist in North America's least accessible backcountry areas. Reports of Big Foot activity have come from almost every state (and the beast has long been known to native Americans as 'Sasquatch'), but the majority have originated in this section of California. It was here, too, that the term 'Big Foot' was born in 1958, after a plaster cast was made of unexplained 16-inch long footprints.

▷ ▷ ▷   **Hoopa Valley**

Covering 93,000 acres, the Hoopa Valley Indian Reservation is the largest of its kind in California, but like all Indian reservations it cannot be anything other than a depressing reminder of the wrongs inflicted by white settlers on the country's indigenous peoples. The **Hoopa Tribal Museum**, displays the handicrafts of the Hupa and Yaruk tribes, but many people make the 60-mile drive from the coast simply to attend the Friday and Saturday night bingo sessions; legally, high-stakes bingo can only be played on Indian reservations.

▶ ▶ ▷   **Humboldt Redwoods State Park**

Illuminated by beams of sunlight breaking through towering foliage, the 33-mile long **Avenue of the Giants** winds through a section of the vast Humboldt Redwoods State Park, a 20-million-year old forest harbouring some of the world's tallest trees. Several roadside stops and short walking trails provide a chance to become an insignificant speck at the foot of these 300-foot high green giants.

In spring, the park's Eel River, whose course the avenue follows, is a torrent that brings out the region's daredevil white-water rafters and kayakers. Slowing in summer to an eminently swimmable emerald-coloured stream, the river also has sandy banks well-suited to leisurely picnics.

Hiking trails and long-abandoned lumber roads thread deeper into the park, ascending from the redwood-cloaked lowlands to hillsides covered by strands of fir, where rustic cabins and rough campsites provide for overnight stays.

The Avenue of the Giants, winding for 33 miles through Humboldt Redwoods State Park

Drive The Lost Coast

From the Rockefeller Forest section of Humboldt Redwoods State Park (described on page 236), drive west along Bull Creek Flats Road to join Mattole Road, after 12 miles reaching Honeydew.
The tiny crossroads community of **Honeydew** – where the centre of activity for the single-figure population is the General Store-cum-petrol station – is one of the rainiest spots in the US, with 200 inches falling annually and greatly aiding the local marijuana crop.

From Honeydew, continue on Mattole Road, after eight miles reaching Petrolia.
At the foot of a thickly vegetated valley, eucalyptus-enshrouded **Petrolia** was, in the 1860s, the site of one of California's earliest commercial oil wells; the economic boom which the strike promised was soon thwarted by the remoteness of the region.

From Petrolia, take the bumpy Lighthouse Road to the Punta Gorda headland.
At the **Punta Gorda headland**, a jeep track leads to a disused lighthouse.

Return to Mattole Road and continue north, after six miles passing Cape Mendocino.
Bordered by black-sanded beaches, **Cape Mendocino** is the most westerly point of the continental US and is believed to have been named by 16th-century Spanish seafarers in honour of a Spanish viceroy.

Pass Cape Mendocino and continue on Mattole Road, after 16 miles reaching Ferndale.
An immaculately preserved Victorian village first settled by Swedish dairy farmers, 1,000 inhabitants make **Ferndale** by far the largest settlement on the Lost Coast; it is fully described on page 231.

From Ferndale, continue on Mattole Road for four miles, rejoining Highway-101 10 miles south of Eureka.

▶ ▶ ▷   **The Lost Coast**
Black bears and bald eagles are more common than people within the desolate, deserted landscapes of the Lost Coast, a 30-mile portion of the North Coast south of Eureka, whose dense forests, coastal bluffs and pocket-sized beaches are shielded by the sharp inclinations of the Kings Mountain Range.
The Lost Coast can be sampled lightly by taking Briceland Thorne Road, off Highway-101 near Redway. This route leads to **Shelter Cove,** a tiny coast-hugging community adjacent to a beach at the foot of tall granite headlands, first passing the elk-roamed **Sinkyone Wilderness State Park**, named after the Sinkyone tribe, thought to have inhabited the Lost Coast from 6000BC – a time when abundant food from the sea and from the forest made this North America's most populated place.

Contemplating life in Mendocino

When Californians declare
that they sleep through a
mere 2.3, barely notice a 3.6,
but know exactly what to do
if an 8.9 hits, they are, of
course, quoting Richter
scale measurements of
earthquake magnitudes. Few
of them know, however, that
the man who devised the
Richter scale in 1935,
Charles F Richter, was a 35-
year old seismology
professor at the California
Institute of Technology in
Pasadena.

▷ ▷ ▷ Manchester State Beach

Stretching for several miles beside Highway-1 south of Mendocino State Park, Manchester State Beach is a must-see for beachcombers and hikers, and for hardy campers who do not mind spending a night being buffeted by winds or waking up beside a beach cloaked in fog.

▶ ▶ ▶ Mendocino

Mendocino is delightfully set on a coastal bluff and has a plethora of well-preserved 19th-century buildings dating from its settlement by New England loggers.

A well-deserved reputation as the North Coast's prettiest town frequently causes Mendocino's 1,000 permanent residents to be outnumbered by tourists, who fill a rash of bed and breakfast inns and file ceaselessly through the town's many gift shops.

Crowds aside, Mendocino is very likeable and very easily explored. In decline as a lumber centre, Mendocino's unspoilt beauty proved irresistible to a group of San Francisco artists in the 1950s whose influence lingers on, most notably in numerous galleries and in the arts appreciation programmes of the **Mendocino Art Center** (45200 Little Lake Road).

The **Historical Museum**, inside the 1861 Kelly House (45007 Albion Street), has written and photographic background on most of the town's early buildings. Among these, the 1868 Gothic-style Mendocino Presbyterian Church (44831 Main Street) is still in use, and Mendocino's oldest residence, the 1854 Ford House (Main Street), functions as a visitor centre for **Mendocino Headlands State Park**, four miles south, where an enticing three-mile long clifftop trail reaches a small beach.

San Andreas Fault

■　　The biggest and most destructive earthquake ever to strike California, the 1906 San Francisco earthquake, was caused by the 600- mile long San Andreas fault, the longest of hundreds of geological fault lines which pass through the state, and one which runs for many miles along the North Coast. .....■

The big shake In fact, the 1906 'quake was more powerful along the North Coast than in San Francisco, though the region's moderate level of development meant that damage was only limited to displaced cattle fences and slightly skewed roads. Such damage has long since been rectified, but provided you know where to look – and what look for – the fault line is easy to recognise. At Point Reyes, which was jolted almost 16 feet northwards in the few seconds of the 1906 'quake, the National Seashores' Earthquake Trail follows a section of the fault, and markers indicate some of its effects.

Where the fault lies From Point Reyes, the fault follows the line of Tamales Bay and continues to Bodega Bay, where it passes between Bodega Head and the mainland. Although mostly concealed by sand dunes, the fault's presence here is marked by tell-tale deposits of mixed and crushed rock. The fault continues under the ocean beyond Bodega Head and returns to land just south of Fort Ross, which lost several of its early Russian buildings in the 1906 'quake. Follow the Fort Ross Road inland for a few miles looking for furrows on the hillsides, further evidence of the 1906 'quake.

As it travels just inland from the coast, the fault cuts a dead-straight valley through the hills, causing many streams to change their course. This fact accounts for the Gualala River flowing parallel to the coast for several miles, instead of draining directly into it.

Close to Point Arena, the fault again dips under the ocean. Until recently, experts believed the sharp breaks in the headlands further north around the Lost Coast to be proof of the fault staying close to the shore. A more recent hypothesis, however, suggests that it is only a branch of the San Andreas fault that lies along this part of the coast and that the main line runs some miles off shore, veering westwards under the Pacific.

239

A sample of the earthquake damage suffered in San Francisco

Mount Tamalpais, overlooking Mill Valley

▷ ▷ ▷   Mill Valley

Full of rural charm despite being a San Francisco commuter base, Mill Valley sits on the eastern slopes of Mount Tamalpais. Attracting many of the big city's well-off but liberal souls, the town sports a surprising number of coffee bars, and even stages its own film festival – with the emphasis on independent productions – every autumn.

► ► ►   Mount Tamalpais State Park

A switchback road leads almost to the top of Mount Tamalpais, but you will only feel you have earned the scintillating views – of San Francisco and far inland to the Sierra Nevada mountains – if you have attained the summit after a day's hike from the redwood-filled canyons of Mount Tamalpais State Park. Weather permitting, concerts and performing arts are staged at the park's **Mountain Theater**, where over 3,000 people can enjoy an outdoor show and a stunning natural backdrop.

► ► ▷   Muir Woods National Monument

When San Franciscans feel they are living in a concrete jungle, they head 17 miles northwest to the Muir Woods National Monument, where six miles of trails lead through a dark, cool grove of redwoods. These are not the biggest examples of the North Coast's redwood trees but at over 250 feet high they are unlikely to disappoint; if they do, push on to the slender semi-circular cove holding **Muir Beach**, and mingle with the anglers and birdwatchers.

▷ ▷ ▷   Point Arena

Interrupt the lengthy drive between Bodega Bay and Fort Bragg with a tour of the 1908 **Point Arena Lighthouse** and its museum, which details the many ships which have come to grief off this wild and rugged coastline.

▶ ▶ ▷ Point Reyes National Seashore

The 100-mile coastline of the Point Reyes National Seashore encompasses granite headlands, beaches, dunes and marshes, and reaches inland to hills topped by pine-fringed ridges. Formed by, and still subject to, seismic activity, the area's geological background is outlined at the **Visitor Center**, beside Highway-1, and the adjacent easily walked **Earthquake Trail.**

Longer trails aim to please birdwatchers and beachcombers, and another leads to **Kule Loklo**, a re-created Miwok Indian village. If ocean breezes deter walking, drive to the 1870s **Point Reyes Lighthouse** on the seashore's western extremity.

▶ ▷ ▷ Richardson Grove State Park

A few miles south of Garberville, Richardson Grove State Park has three lush redwood groves and numerous backcountry hikes. But when the summer temperatures send warm air into the otherwise cool groves, the park becomes one of the North Coast's most popular and crowded camping sites.

Close by, the dot-on-the-map settlement of Piercy seeks to lure campers, and any passing traffic on Highway-1, with the optimistically titled World Famous Tree House, a room built 50 feet up a redwood tree, and Confusion Hill, a collection of visual deceits.

▶ ▶ ▷ Sonoma Coast State Beach

Between Bodega Bay and the Russian River hamlet of Jenner, the Sonoma Coast State Beach spans 13 miles of secluded beaches slotted between craggy headlands, many of which have formed sea stacks and arches.

Trails lead to the beaches from Highway-1, and there are connecting paths linking the whole Sonoma coast. Splendid scenery is common to all, yet each beach has its own admirers: fishermen favour **Portuguese Beach; Shell Beach** delights beachcombers, delivering a rich harvest with each receding tide; and the picnic tables at **Rock Point** have provided photogenic picnic locations for many passing tourists.

Best known to Northern Californians for its scores of antique shops, San Anselmo, just north of Mount Tamalpais, lies beneath the hillside stone buildings of the San Francisco Theological Seminary, which in 1992 celebrated 100 years of training Presbyterian Church ministers.

241

Waves batter the northern edge of the Sonoma Coast

THE NORTH COAST

Many places along the North Coast make excellent vantage points to observe the migrating California gray whales, which pass by on their 6,000-mile journey between the Arctic sea off Alaska, where they feed, and the warmer waters off Baja California, where the females give birth. The whales, which weigh up to 40 tons and are thought to use coastal landscapes to navigate, can be sighted at any time from December to July, though the largest numbers are usually visible during March.

 Stinson Beach

Unchallenged as the North Coast's finest and busiest strand, the broad and inviting Stinson Beach sits at the foot of Mount Tamalpais within easy reach of San Francisco, and draws many of the city's frustrated beach bums.

Spared the strong currents that make swimming lethal along much of the North Coast, bathing is a popular pastime here, although many don diver's wet-suits before braving the cool waters. If swimming, or simply sitting in the sun, does not fit your mood, try one of the hikes from the beach to Mount Tamalpais State Park or the Muir Woods National Monument.

Three miles north, the wooded canyons of the **Audubon Canyon Ranch** are cherished by birdwatchers, especially from March to July when egrets and blue herons make their nests in the redwood branches, and visiting hours to this wildlife research centre are extended.

▷ ▷ ▷ **Willits**

Taking the Skunk Train from Fort Bragg (see panel on page 232), you will find yourself 40 miles inland at Willits, a likeable small country community that conserves its energy for regional rodeos. Other than serving wholesome traditional fare in its diners, it offers only the Indian basketry and pioneer-period artefacts of the **Mendocino County Museum** (400 E Commercial Street) for out-of-towners to pass the time before commencing their return journey.

Machinery at Mendocino County Museum

Redwood National Park

■ **Provided you are not sick of the sight of the North Coast's redwood trees by the time you reach it, the Redwood National Park, filling 100,000 acres of California's northwest corner and encompassing four state parks, offers an unrivalled chance to delve among the tall trees and their related flora and fauna, and to strike out across 40 miles of California's utterly untrammelled shoreline. .....■**

Far from the crowds: Smith River, Jedediah Smith State Park,

Take a hike Dozens of short foot-trails lead off Highway-101 (which passes through the park), and longer hiking routes connect the four state parks which form the key sections of the national park.
The southern entrance is close to Orick, where the **Redwood Visitor Center** provides geographical orientation and a wealth of ecological information. Close by, the aptly named **Tall Trees Grove** contains three of the world's tallest trees, including the highest of the lot, the 368-foot Howard Libby Redwood. Its statistics impress most, though; from the ground the tree looks no more enormous than its neighbours.

The park's inland sections Further on, **Prairie Creek State Park** spans a large tract of grassland between the redwoods and the ocean with numerous trails leading to tidal pools and coves. The park's inland sections

<< Jedediah Smith State Park, and indeed the Smith River which runs through it, are named after Jedediah Strong Smith, a New York-born fur trapper who became a California frontier legend in 1826, after making the first non-native crossing of the Sierra Nevada mountains. >>

243

are kept lush and fertile by heavy winter rainfall and its landscapes are at their best at Fern Canyon, a moss-covered floor enclosed by 60- foot high fern walls. The park also boasts a sizeable elk herd; you will see some of them grazing in meadows beside Highway-101, and more can be spotted on the coastal trails. Summer fogs are frequent in the northerly reaches of the national park, especially at **Del Norte State Park**, where the redwood groves reach almost to the shore. Once the fog lifts, seek out the area's main attractions: tidal pools, coves and isolated beaches.

Too far inland to be bothered by fog, **Jedediah Smith State Park** is the least-visited section of the national park yet also one of the most enjoyable. Take the meandering Howland Hill Road, a one-time stagecoach route, and stop at Stout Grove to admire the immense girth of the so-called Stout Tree. Salmon fishermen and canoeists are brought to this park by the Smith River, which has many placid sections ideal for swimming and for taking in the rural tranquillity from sandy banks.

Though better known for its spas, Calistoga also has several notable wineries. Occupying a French-style castle, Château Montelena (1429 Tubbs Lane; tel: (707) 942 5105) produces an award-winning Chardonnay and overlooks Lake Jade, where the formal Chinese gardens, laid out on the banks of the lake, can be hired for picnics. The champagne-making Schramsburg Vineyards (Schramsburg Road; tel: (707) 942 4558), were immortalised in 1880 by Robert Louis Stevenson's book The Silverado Squatters, and an enjoyable cable-car ride is just the start of a tour of Sterling Vineyards (111 Dunaweal Lane; tel: (707) 942 5151).

You will find wineries all over California but only in the Wine Country – beginning 48 miles north of San Francisco and encompassing three separate valleys – is the grape the main attraction of an entire region.

Hot summers, moist winters, fertile volcanic soil – courtesy of the long-extinct Mount St Helena – and heaps of publicity bring hordes of tourists to the Wine Country, whose wineries range from high-tech modern plants to century-old family-run operations in stone buildings. Most of these run tours and tastings, and have become adept at turning know-nothing beginners into (comparative) connoisseurs of California's finest fermentations inside an hour.

State grape Spanish missionaries produced California's earliest wine, but a go-ahead Hungarian named Agoston Haraszthy was the first to bring choice European vine cuttings to the state. Their yield of familiar Mediterranean grapes brought a rush of European vintners to settle the region from the 1880s.

Decades of patient refining were rewarded in the early 1970s when California wines were acknowledged as being among the world's best. Everyone from the Coca-Cola Company to Moët-Hennesey began sinking money into the Wine Country, and the region underwent an unexpected tourist boom.

Among the 200 wineries sited in the Napa Valley, on the Wine Country's eastern edge, are the US's biggest and most prestigious wine producers. Three million wine-thirsty visitors annually beat a path through the compact valley, their cars jamming the main route, State Road 29, between the sprawling town of Napa and the historic spa-resort of Calistoga, on every summer weekend.

Softer options An alternative to the Napa Valley crush is the less congested Sonoma Valley, immediately west, where apple orchards partner the vines on softly sloping hillsides, and where meandering country lanes pass some of the Wine Country's most reputable and longest-established small wineries, while linking amiable rural towns such as the history-laden Sonoma.

On the coastal side of the Wine Country, the Russian River Valley also has its share of smaller wineries. Here, though, the Russian River's sandy banks and thick redwood groves provide appeal beyond wine consuming, and the main community, Guerneville, fully justifies its reputation as a lively resort town.

Château Souverain in Geyserville is one of the many wineries in this area offering tastings

THE WINE COUNTRY

Founded in 1872 as a social
club for San Francisco
newspapermen, and
including socialist writers
such as Jack London and
Ambrose Bierce among its
early members, the
Bohemian Club is now best
known for its July Bohemian
Week. Scores of high-flying
(and exclusively male)
bankers, industrialists,
congressmen, foreign
diplomats, and even ex-US
presidents, arrive at the
club's summer retreat,
Bohemian Grove, a Russian
River Valley redwood grove
near Monte Rio, for seven
days of nefarious activities
behind high-security fences.

Gateway to wining and dining: Château Souverain

Calistoga see page 244

▷ ▷ ▷   Geyserville

Two towers apeing traditional hop kilns on a small hill
just outside Geyserville belong to **Château Souverain**
(400 Souverain Road; tel: (707) 433 8281), whose fame
dominates the village. Besides arriving to sample its
Chardonnay and Cabaret Sauvignon, most Californians
come to Souverain for a gourmet treat in its widely
acclaimed restaurant. By contrast, the J Pedroncelli
Winery (1220 Canyon Road; tel: (707) 857 3531) has
been producing a good cross-section of low-priced
wines since 1904.

▶ ▷ ▷   Guerneville

Carefully preserving its rustic charms, turning canoeing
and kayaking on the Russian River into growth
industries, and keeping its bars and discos jumping into
the small hours, Guerneville (pronounced 'GURN-ville') is
the Wine Country's liveliest resort town, and has
become the weekend place-to-be for a large gay
contingent from San Francisco.

On the edge of town, foot-trails penetrate the dark,
damp groves of the **Armstrong Redwoods State
Reserve**, and continue into the bright open meadows of
the **Austin Creek State Reserve**.

Anyone in Guerneville with a penchant for sparkling
wines should pay a call on the **Korbel Champagne
Cellars** (13250 River Road; tel: (707) 887 2294), which
has been producing them – and excellent brandy – since
1862.

▶ ▶ ▷   Healdsburg

Filled with Victorian homes and prettified by a century-
old tree-lined plaza, Healdsburg, at the northern end of
the Russian River Valley, also has a dozen wineries in its
midsts. If you are tired of tasting wine, you might try
reading about it at the Sonoma County Wine Library
(corner of Center and Piper streets), stocked with more
then 3,000 wine-related volumes, or bone up on it in the
Healdsburg Museum (221 Matheson Street).

Spas and Springs

■ **Bottled and sold throughout the state, sparkling spring water from Calistoga furthers the fame of a Napa Valley town already noted for its mineral-rich spas, which have been earning the respect of dedicated sybarites since the first health-resort was founded here in 1859 by millionaire mormon Sam Brannan. .....■**

Take the waters The cheapest way to find out what all the fuss is about is by taking a dip in the mineral pools at Calistoga Hot Springs Spa (1066 Washington Avenue) or Golden Haven Spa (1713 Lake Street). A more thorough spa session typically costs $20–30 (an extra $15-20 with a massage) and includes a volcanic-mud bath, a soak in a mineral-water whirlpool, a smothering in sweat-inducing blankets, and finally a massage to induce a nirvana-like state of well-being. Purveyors of this relaxing therapy include Nance's Hot Springs (1614 Lincoln Avenue) and Indian Springs (1712 Lincoln Avenue), built around Sam Brannan's resort.

Sam Brannan The founder of Calistoga, Sam Brannan arrived in San Francisco from New York with a boatload of fellow mormons in 1846, who, seeking farm land and religious tolerance, were dismayed to find that California had joined the US just prior to their landing. The 26-year old Brannan published San Francisco's first newspaper and quickly became one of the fledgeling state's wealthiest and most flamboyant figures. His massive investment in Calistoga did not pay off, however, and he spent his final years drunk and destitute in Escondido near San Diego, dying in 1889. Calistoga's more adventurous spas are devising weird – and nearly always wonderful – treatments using herbs, eucalyptus steam, and Japanese-style enzyme baths; one such is the International Spa (1300 Washington Street), soothing souls with the aid of New Age music and environmental art.

<< Five miles west of Calistoga, the Petrified Forest (4100 Petrified Forest Road) is the result of a redwood grove being uprooted and turned to stone by volcanic mud and ash which was spewed out by Mount St Helena. >>

Old Faithful Geyser Another way to enjoy the legacy of the area's volcanic activity is simply by looking at it. A mile north of Calistoga, the Old Faithful Geyser (1299 Tubbs Lane), heated by an underground river, sends a high-pressure jet of boiling water 60 feet skywards every 30 or 50 minutes (depending upon seismic activity in the region).

The Old Faithful Geyser, producing natural energy near Calistoga

THE WINE COUNTRY

Drive Calistogo-Clear Lake Loop

See map on page 244.

Drive 10 miles north from Calistoga on State Road 29 for Robert Louis Stevenson State Park.
On the site of Silverado, a disused mining camp, author Robert Louis Stevenson and his wife honeymooned during 1880 in what is now **Robert Louis Stevenson State Park**, whose 3,000 undeveloped acres include a trail to the summit of Mount St Helena.

Continue seven miles north on State Road 29 for Middletown.
Middletown marks the half-way point of the former Calistoga-Lakeport stagecoach route, which State Road 29 follows. Immediately east of the town on Butts Canyon Road, the **Guenoc Winery** was once owned by English actress Lillie Langtry.

Continue for 15 miles on State Road 29 to the Anderson Marsh Historic Site, just north of Lower Lake.
At the **Anderson Marsh Historic Site**, 10,000-year old sites of native American habitation have been discovered; another section of the 1,000-acre site is a wildlife refuge, protecting bald eagles among many other species.

Clear Lake State Park

<< Robert Louis Stevenson spent part of his honeymoon in a miners' cabin on the slopes of Mount St Helena, and was so impressed that he used it as the model for Spyglass Hill in *Treasure Island* >>

From Lower Lake, continue on State Road 29 to Clear Lake State Park.
Set on land still bearing evidence of native American occupation, **Clear Lake State Park** is popular with anglers who hunt the catfish and perch in the waters of the park's misnamed volcanic lake.

Continue on State Road 29 for 10 milesto Lakeport.
Besides the usual exhibits, **Lakeport's County Historical Museum** holds a glittering cache of locally grown diamonds.

Continue for nine miles on State Road 29, turning east on to State Road 20 at Upper Lake and driving for 21 miles to State Road 53.
Quiet lakeside villages punctuate the drive east from Upper Lake.

From the junction with State Road 53, drive nine miles south on State Road 29 to Lower Lake, continuing for 32 miles to return to Calistoga.

▶▷▷ **Oakville**

Nervous newcomers who do not know their Chardonnay from their Pinot Noir should take the highly instructive (and free) tasting and tour winding through the underground passages of Oakville's **Robert Mondavi Winery** (7801 St Helena Highway; tel: (707) 963 9611); this tasting is one of the best of its kind in the Wine Country.

Along the road, a geodesic dome covers the workings of the reputable De Moor Winery (7481 St Helena Highway; tel: (707) 944 2565), as well as the winery's visitor centre.

▶▶▷ **Petaluma**

Long famed for its poultry and dairy farms, Petaluma now sets the pace for snail rearing, being the site of the only commercial snail farm in existence in the US, whose products are disseminated to discerning palates the world over.

In the town itself, however, snails are less in evidence than the carefully maintained totems of smalltown America circa 1950s. It is no surprise that nostalgia movies such as *American Graffiti* and *Peggy Sue Got Married*, looking back to the post-war era, used Petaluma's streets as backdrops.

Pre-dating the golden age of Americana, the town's early 1900s commercial strip, which is set along the banks of the Russian River, has undergone a tidy restoration, and what no longer remains of turn-of-the-century Petaluma outdoors can still be found indoors, on display inside the **Historical Library and Museum** (20 Fourth Street).

Early days There is evidence of still earlier times on a hillside across Highway-101, where the **Petaluma Adobe State Historic Park** holds the well-restored 1836 two-storey adobe building which was at the centre of one of Mexican California's largest land holdings, a vast rancho with which General Mariano Vallejo – the founder of Sonoma – established himself among the province's rich and powerful.

▷▷▷ **Rutherford**

Several of the Napa Valley's major wine producers lie close to the hamlet of Rutherford and offer novice-friendly tours. The **Rutherford Hill Winery** (200 Rutherford Hill Road; tel: (707) 963 9694 or (707) 963 9694), is a winery which welcomes beginners and which, like most of its rivals, ages its wine in caves, though these particular underground tunnels are claimed to have the distinction of being the biggest such system in the world.

Château tasting Wine enthusiasts who happen to be claustrophobic might prefer to visit the ivy-covered stone chateau, complete with stained-glass windows, housing **Inglenook Vineyards** (1919 St Helena Highway; tel: (707) 969 3363), where a lengthy tour of the wine-making process concludes with a drawn-out 'sensory evaluation' – the wine snob's phrase for a tasting.

Petaluma, guardian of a golden age of small town America

A popular accompaniment to wine drinking, dry and nutty Monterey Jack, California's native cheese, was first produced in 1892 on dairy farms close to Monterey under the control of an unpopular Scottish migrant called David Jacks. Since then, the Sonoma Valley has became a significant cheese-producing area, with the Sonoma Cheese Factory (2 West Spain Street) and the Petaluma Cheese Factory (7500 Red Hill Road) both giving tours of the manufacturing process – and dispensing bite-sized free samples.

FOCUS ON *Wine*

■ **Verdant its valleys may be, but only teetotallers visit the Wine Country for its scenery. For everyone else, a trip through the region begins and ends with a glass in their hand and, given the large number of winery tours and wine tastings on offer, it is a glass that should be held a lot more knowledgeably at the completion of a trip than at the start. .....■**

250

The larger wineries have daily tours and tastings for which reservations are sometimes necessary, but some of the smaller wineries only open for a few hours a week, so always phone ahead to check the details.

A round of drinks Most tours and tastings are free although some wineries have implemented charges (typically, $1 a glass, or $5 for a half-hour session) to dissuade those seeking free inebriation; unlike the European tradition, wine in California is swallowed after being tasted.

Tour one of the major producers first, such as Robert Mondavi in Oakville, for a look at the wine-making process and for a broad introduction to the state's wines. Later, move on to the more specialist small wineries, whose produce will only reveal its subtleties to the initiated drinker.

Grape stuff California's wine types are known by their grape: the main whites include Chardonnay, Chenin Blanc, Gewurztraminer, Riesling and Sauvignon (or Fumé) Blanc; the main reds are Cabernet Sauvignon, Merlot, Pinot Noir and Zinfandel.

The extremely versatile Zinfandel also appears as White Zinfandel, actually a pinkish-hued 'blush' wine, a result of the grapes' skins being removed during the fermentation process.

Sparkling wine, or champagne (though it is generally bad form to use this term for a product that does not come from France), is also found in the Wine Country, and some of the more interesting sparkling-wine producers use the traditional Méthode Champenoise, when fermentation is carried out in the bottle rather than in casks.

Tasting by train Known locally as the 'swine train' for the noise it makes rumbling through the valley, with the aim of easing traffic congestion, the Napa Valley Wine Train, pulling restored Pullman cars, makes a three-tour sojourn between Napa and St Helena, stopping at selected wineries and serving highly priced gourmet food. The basic return-trip fare charges meals as an extra and the train, environmental considerations aside, is hard to beat if you only have half a day to see the Wine Country (for further information tel: (800) 427 4124 or (800) 522 4124.

Wine tasting tips There may be hundreds to choose from, but it is a good idea to limit your winery visits to three or less on any single day. Every wine that you sample affects the taste buds and red wines tend to coat the tongue which is not at all conducive to determining a wine's subtleties of flavour.

For best appreciation, you should also stick to either whites or reds at a tasting. If the temptation proves too much, however, begin with whites, move on to reds and rosés, follow these with dessert wines and, finally, try the sparkling wines.

Young wines Do not feel cheated if your host produces a recent wine to sample. Owing to climate differences, vintages count for far less in California than they do in Europe, though certain wines are noted as being exceptionally good in certain years. The final verdict on a wine's qualities is down to personal choice, although there are well-established stages in judging a wine.

Step by step tasting First look closely at the wine to judge its colour. All wines should be free of clouding; whites should have a yellow to golden shading; rosés should be pink, possibly with an orange hue; reds should have a purple hint and may vary in tone from a light crimson to a rich ruby.

Secondly, swirl the wine to release its fragrance, or 'nose' – something which results from a combination of the 'aroma', supplied by the grape, and the 'bouquet', which comes from the wine-making process.

Thirdly, sip the wine and roll it around the tongue to determine texture and balance. Flavours are a complex field, and range from a Chardonnay's dry fruitiness to a Zinfandel's zippy spiciness.

At tastings, never feel embarrassed at revealing your ignorance to the host. California's vintners are keen for appreciation of their products to spread, and respond much better to the genuine interest of a beginner than the witless comments of the wine pseud.

Gathering to taste and discuss the fruit of the vine at the Robert Mondavi Winery in Oakville

While most Californian grapes are clearly of European origin, the roots of Zinfandel are shrouded in mystery. A Black Zinfandel wine appeared on the US's East Coast in 1838, and Zinfandel grapes were first grown in California 20 years later, but where the grapes actually come from is uncertain. The son of Agoston Haraszthy, the state's earliest vintner, falsely claimed that his father was the first to import them (but did not say where from), and more recently experts have variously cited southern Italy, Slovenia, and even California itself, as the true home of Zinfandel.

251

The Church of One Tree in Santa Rosa

When you tire of looking at it through the bottom of a wine glass, you can view the Wine Country from above, wafting across the valleys in a balloon. Prices start at around $125 for an hour, and many flights touch down in some scenic spot for a champagne picnic. Numerous widely advertised companies run flights, among them Bonaventure Balloon Company (tel: (800) 243 6743); Napa Valley Balloons (tel: (800) 253 2224); and Sonoma Thunder (tel: (800) 759 5638).

▶ ▶ ▷ St Helena

Ten miles south of Calistoga, St Helena sits fortuitously at the heart of the Napa Valley, cashing in on its passing visitors with up-market restaurants and craft shops.

One person who passed through St Helena was impoverished writer Robert Louis Stevenson who, having married Fanny Osbourne in 1880, honeymooned north of the town in what is now Robert Louis Stevenson State Park. Occupying a special wing of the St Helena Public Library (1490 Library Lane), the **Silverado Museum** celebrates the Stevenson connection with manuscripts and memorabilia.

▶ ▷ ▷ Santa Rosa

Levelled by the 1906 earthquake, Santa Rosa has made a dramatic comeback. It is now the fastest growing Wine Country community. The restored 1920s buildings of Railroad Square and the pre-earthquake rail terminal in Railroad Park, allow the town's residents discover something of their community's roots, but Santa Rosa does a better job remembering two former inhabitants. The Church of One Tree (492 Sonoma Avenue) – not the base of a tree-centred religion but built entirely from a redwood felled in 1875 – contains the **Ripley Memorial Museum**, devoted to local man Robert Ripley, whose cartoon strips – recounting strange and exotic phenomena – were massively popular from the 1920s.

Self-taught horticulturalist Luther Burbank arrived in Santa Rosa in 1875 armed with 10 Burbank potatoes, early examples of what was to be a lifetime's devotion to developing vegetable, fruit and plant hybrids. The **Luther Burbank Home and Memorial Gardens** (415 Steele Lane) preserves Burbank's Greek Revival-style abode, and the gardens where his creations evolved.

▷ ▷ ▷ Sebastopol

Americans know Sebastopol for its reddish-yellow Gravenstein apples, grown here and celebrated by April's Apple Blossom Festival. Otherwise, the area is notable for its dry wines, particularly Pinot Noir, best sampled at the **Dehlinger Winery** (6300 Guerneville Road; tel: (707) 823 2378).

■ **Besides harbouring a winery at every turn, the Sonoma and Napa valleys boast a formidable grouping of state parks. Combining historic and scenic interest, the parks also provide a head-clearing pick-me-up for anyone who has overdone the wine tasting.....■**

Inspirational country A prolific writer, and the first millionaire author in the US, Jack London eulogised over the Sonoma Valley in his 1913 book, *Valley of the Moon*. At the time he had already put into practice the return-to-nature way of living which its pages advocated, turning a large track of grassy hillside beneath Sonoma Mountain into an experimental farm, and building the 26-room Wolf House for himself and his wife.

His ranch is now **Jack London State Historic Park**, at the bucolic hamlet of Glen Ellen, just west of Sonoma. Only the ruins of the fire-destroyed Wolf House remain, but the park's House of Happy Walls Museum is well-stocked with mementos of London's far from peaceful life (see panel on this page).

At the northern end of the Sonoma Valley Hiking and horse-riding trails crisscross the 5,000-acre **Annadel State Park**, rising from meadows and marshes into steep-sided canyons. Even more rugged terrain fills **Sugarloaf Ridge State Park**, 14 miles east of Santa Rosa, where wine-induced lethargy will quickly be forgotten after a brisk hike over chaparral-covered ridges on the way to the summit of Bald Mountain.

Just north of St Helena in the Napa Valley, a ramble through the **Bale Grist Mill State Historic** Park (3801 St Helena Highway) turns up a restored 19th-century water mill, built for an English ships' surgeon who became a prominent Napa Valley landowner after his vessel ran aground at Monterey in 1837.

Immediately south Greater hiking opportunities are presented by **Bothe-Napa Valley State Park**, whose trails pass through strands of coastal redwoods. One leads to the remains of the valley's earliest church and to a pioneer-era graveyard, where several members of the ill-fated Donner party (see page 200) lie buried.

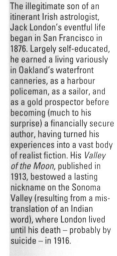

The illegitimate son of an itinerant Irish astrologist, Jack London's eventful life began in San Francisco in 1876. Largely self-educated, he earned a living variously in Oakland's waterfront canneries, as a harbour policeman, as a sailor, and as a gold prospector before becoming (much to his surprise) a financially secure author, having turned his experiences into a vast body of realist fiction. His *Valley of the Moon*, published in 1913, bestowed a lasting nickname on the Sonoma Valley (resulting from a mis-translation of an Indian word), where London lived until his death – probably by suicide – in 1916.

253

THE WINE COUNTRY

 Sonoma

With a history far in excess of its contemporary importance, Sonoma's many restored adobe buildings provide an evocative window on the turbulent decades that saw California switch from Spanish to Mexican and finally to US rule. A host of bed and breakfast inns make the small town a good base for exploring the Wine Country, though Sonoma itself is easily covered by a half-day walk.

Surrounded by historic hotels, Sonoma's eight-acre **plaza** was constructed in 1835 and is the largest in California. On its south side is **Sonoma City Hall**, dating from 1906 and presenting a symbol of early US authority in the town. The **Bear Flag Monument**, on the plaza's northeast corner, commemorates the 1846 hoisting of the Bear Flag, denoting an independent California Republic. Across Spain Street, on the corner with First Street East, is the much-restored **Mission San Francisco de Solano**. Founded in 1823, this was the last and most northerly of California's Spanish missions. It also saw service as a saloon, a warehouse and barn; a small museum tells its story.

At 285 First Street West, the **Historical Museum**, reached across Depot Park from First Street East, mounts changing temporary exhibitions on local heritage themes. The main buildings of **Sonoma State Historical Park** are across First Street West: several important structures form this far-flung park, among them two former homes of General Mariano Vallejo, wealthy rancho owner and the founder and first mayor of Sonoma, and the Sonoma Barracks, whose storming by US cavalrymen in 1846 was part of the Bear Flag Revolt – briefly turning California into an independent republic.

The Buena Vista Winery, two miles outside Sonoma

Guerneville stages the Russian River Jazz Festival and the Russian River Rodeo every September, and in March, the bizarre Slug Festival; Healdsburg's Harvest Hoedown marks September; Petaluma hosts the World Wristwrestling Championships in October; and Sonoma holds Living History Days during May and October.

Domaine Chandon Winery, in Yountville

On the outskirts, the **Buena Vista Winery** (18000 Old Winery Road; tel: (707) 938 1266), founded by the colourful Hungarian, Agoston Haraszthy (remembered as the 'father' of Californian wine making), in 1857 is the oldest winery in the state.

▶ ▷ ▷ Ukiah

Native American culture has a decidedly low profile throughout the Wine Country, a fact which makes the **Grace Hudson Museum and Sun House** (431 Main Street) all the more welcome. It houses lyrical studies of Pomo Indians by painter Grace Carpenter Hudson and her husband's extensive ethnographical collections. Remarkably, this outstanding collection crops up in what is a run-of-the-mill lumber town, with only tastings and tours at the Parducci Wine Cellars (501 Parducci Road; tel: (707) 462 9463) providing other diversion.

▶ ▷ ▷ Yountville

A rural counterpart to sprawling Napa, 14 miles south, pleasant Yountville became a stop on the wine-tourists' circuit in 1986 following the opening of **Domain Chandon** (W California Drive; tel: (707) 944 2280) by the top-bracket champagne and brandy producers, Moët & Hennessy. Tours describing the champagne-making process are free, but you have to pay to sample a glass. Next door to Domain Chandon, the **Armistice Chapel Museum** holds a surprisingly interesting stock of historic military miscellanea. Also in town, the Napa Valley Show (at the Vintage 1870 shopping centre, 6525 Washington Street) involves a fair-to-middling slide show capturing the Napa Valley's seasonal moods.

Used during the 1800s to carry cinnabar from mines at Mount St Helena to the river docks in Napa, the Silverado Trail crosses the east side of the Napa Valley and makes for a quieter passage than the busy State Road 29, to which it mostly runs parallel. Complementing the peaceful mood, several tourable and rarely crowded small wineries line the trail.

Arranging a Trip
Flights and Packages

Competition between tour operators specialising in US holidays and transatlantic airlines is fierce and you are well advised to shop around for the best deal.

Package holidays, involving any combination of flights, accommodation and car hire and widely advertised in travel agents' brochures, can save legwork once you have arrived, but will not necessarily be the cheapest or most interesting way to see the Golden State.

If you are booking a flight independently, take advantage of the reduced fares regularly offered during quiet periods (autumn and spring) by the major airlines – American, British Airways, United and Virgin – which fly non-stop between London and California (the least costly flights from Europe to the US are via London), or use a discount ticket agent. Being under 26 or a student will bring further reductions.

Three US airlines - **Continental**, **Delta** and **Northwest** – have services from London to California via other US cities, which allows for greater choice as to where you land in California – many small towns are well served by domestic flights.

The majority of scheduled non-stop international flights land at Los Angeles; fewer touch down at San Francisco. Some charter airlines fly direct to San Diego or Oakland (for San Francisco) from London and regional UK airports.

Arriving in California
Visas, Immigration and Customs

Citizens of the UK, Canada and New Zealand need a full passport to visit the US, but do not need a visa. It is necessary, however, to fill out the visa-waiver form issued on the plane. Citizens of Eire and Australia do need visas. Passengers will also be given customs and immigration forms to complete. These will present no difficulties if you are visiting the US on holiday; if you are planning to live and/or work in the US you will need proof that you can do this legally.

If travelling with a major airline, it is likely that an immigration check (a computer check of passengers' names against those of known miscreants) will be carried out when you check in. A sticker will then be attached to your passport to speed your passage through immigration control when you land. On arrival, your passport will be stamped and part of the immigration form will be fixed to your passport; this is only removed when you leave.

Duty-free allowances include a quart (just under a litre) of alcoholic spirits or wine and 300 cigarettes or 50 cigars. Among things not permitted into the US are meat, fruit and plants.

Banks

California's banks usually open Monday to Thursday 10.00–15.00hrs, Friday 10.00–17.30hrs. Major branches may also open Saturday 10.00–13.00hrs.

Bed and Breakfast Inns

California's most atmospheric lodgings, the bed and breakfast inns, are commonly restored Victorian homes with a small number of antique-filled guest rooms with private or shared bathrooms. Unlike at hotels and motels, bed and breakfast guests are encouraged to mingle, and breakfast itself is normally a hearty affair served around a large table. Prices per room range from $45 to $150, depending on location and facilities.

The **California Office of Tourism** (see Maps and Tourist Information) publish the free *Bed and Breakfast Inn Directory*, and reservations can be made through an agency such as Merican Bed & Breakfast, 16 Village Green, Suite 203, Crofton, Maryland 21114 (tel: (301) 261 0180).

Camping

Most of California's 285 state parks have well-equipped campsites costing $10-12. Places can be reserved up to eight weeks in advance through **MISTIX**, PO Box 85705, San Diego, CA92138-5705 (tel: (1 800) 444 7275). Larger state parks may also have very basic

TRAVEL FACTS

hikers' campsites ($2-6) on the backcountry trails.

For information on camping in National Parks, such as Yosemite, which again vary from large sites with full facilities to rough plots in the wilds, contact the **Western Region Information Office**, National Park Service, Fort Mason, Building 201, San Francisco, CA 94123 (tel: (415) 556 0560).

In addition, there are many privately run campsites throughout the state. One of the larger operators is the **California Travel Parks Association**, PO Box 5648, Auburn, CA 95604 (tel: (916) 885 1624).

Car Rental

Car rental companies – all the major international names and smaller local firms with links to European operators – have desks at the airports (and offices throughout the state). Here, you can collect a pre-booked car or hire on the spot. Driving is legal with a valid licence of most European countries or with an International Driving Licence. Prices between car rental companies vary little but it is usually cheaper to arrange car hire before arrival in the US. Do not neglect to read the small print, particularly if you are intending to leave California from a different city from where you arrived (some companies do not allow for this and you might incur extra charges). Be aware, too, of the Collision Damage Waiver (CDW), a compulsory form of insurance that can add to costs. Without booking ahead, anyone under 25 and/or without a credit card may have problems hiring a car.

Children

Rarely in California will children be regarded as objects of disdain. Hotels and motels will usually provide a crib or extra bed in the parents' room for under 12s at no extra charge, and restaurant staff are likely to appear with games, the children's menu and – if required – a high chair. The state has much that will amuse children: Disneyland is just the most famous of a number of theme parks; many museums provide hands-on exhibits; and the state's parks and forests (and their wildlife) can make an excellent introduction to the natural world.

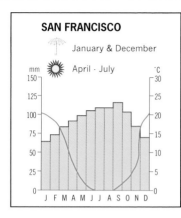

SAN FRANCISCO

January & December

April · July

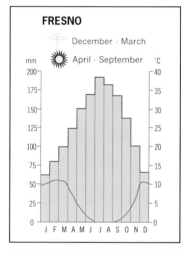

FRESNO

December · March

April · September

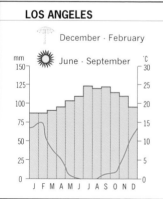

LOS ANGELES

December · February

June · September

Climate and Clothing

The common perception of California as a sun-drenched paradise applies only to the southern section of the state, and even here there are variations: humidity-free San Diego ranges from mild to warm; Los Angeles can be hot and sticky in summer, warm but potentially wet during the winter; inland, the baking deserts are off-limits to humans throughout the summer and are hot during the rest of the year.

In the north, San Francisco's temperatures are mild, but persistent fog can mean a cool start to even the sunniest day; further north along the coast, expect more fog and colder, damper conditions; inland, the Gold Country can be scorching in summer while the higher elevations of the Sierra Nevada region are welcomingly mild – in winter, snow covers the mountains and their immediate surrounds.

If you are travelling widely around the state you should pack with varying climates in mind. Californian dress is always casual, but bare feet and swimsuits are not acceptable in public buildings and the most elegant restaurants require formal attire. The national and state parks, and much of the undeveloped coastline, are best seen by walking, so bring suitable footwear.

Crime

Theft of money and valuables from your room is easy to avoid simply by handing them over to the staff for safe keeping. Being robbed in the street is statistically very unlikely but does happen, usually to people who are have been careless enough to make things easy for the robber – by carrying easily snatched handbags or having wallets sticking out of their back pockets.

Lost travellers' cheques are relatively easy to replace (read the instructions when you buy the cheques), but replacing a stolen passport is much harder and begins with a visit or phone call to your country's nearest consular office (those in San Francisco and Los Angeles are given in the regional gazetteer).

Straying into dangerous areas of

The San Francisco Police Department – the 'Smokey Bears'

cities is another potential hazard. San Francisco is fairly (but not completely) safe, San Diego slightly less so, and Los Angeles much less so; local advice is worth heeding.

Disabled Travellers

California leads the US in providing facilities for the disabled traveller. All public buildings have to be at least partially wheelchair accessible and wheelchair users will find city public transport equipped with 'kneeling' buses, and (in San Francisco) lifts to the underground BART system.

US trains and airlines are obliged to provide services for the disabled if requested, and **Amtrak** (the US train service) has earned a reputation for doing this well. Though less comfortable than the trains, Greyhound buses are more frequent and allow a companion to travel free provided you have a doctor's certificate. Car rental companies can arrange vehicles with hand controls provided they receive advance notice; all Californian public car parks have disabled spaces.

For information on travelling in California contact the Information Center for Individuals with Disabilities, Fort Point Place, 1st Floor, 27–43 Wormwood Street, Boston, MA 02210 (tel: (617) 727 5540).

Driving

With petrol costing as little as $1 a gallon and public transport (see page 264) far from comprehensive, you will save money and time by touring California by car.

California's roads fall into several categories depending on who pays for their upkeep. The Interstates and US Highways are part of the federally run road network; State Highways and State Roads tend to be smaller and are financed by the state government; much less often you will be travelling on County Roads – typically winding lanes through isolated rural areas.

Except for some minor routes, the roads are of a high standard with petrol (or gas) stations easy to find in all but the most secluded or inhospitable regions.

Distances are always given in miles, traffic travels on the right, and overtaking is permitted on the inside lanes of Interstates, where there is a 55mph speed limit (in some sections there is also a minimum limit). Lower speed limits are indicated in built-up areas. On-the-spot fines can be imposed for speeding and a very dim view is taken of drinking and driving. If you belong to a motoring organisation, check its links with the California State Automobile Association (tel: (213) 741 3111 - Los Angeles) or the Automobile Club of Southern California (tel: (415) 565 2012 - San Francisco), who may offer services to affiliates.

California crabs

Eating

One of the greatest pleasures of the Golden State is eating, which can be done extremely well and extremely cheaply. Your biggest problem could simply be succumbing to temptation and over-indulging, although the potential for gluttony is balanced by a well-established trend towards healthy eating. Even some of the state's major fast-food outlets, McDonalds being just one, offer fat-free or low-fat alternatives to their burgers and french fries.

Traditional American coffee shops and diners are found in every community and don't stay in business long if they do not deliver good food at good prices. Most offer gigantic breakfasts for around $5, washed down by as much coffee as you like for the price of a single cup. For lunch, they serve sandwiches (actually a whole hot meal) and salads (actually a whole cold meal) for $6-8. Many coffee shops and diners close after lunch, but some provide substantial dinners for $10–12.

For just a few dollars more, slightly classier **restaurants** offer more variety, particularly for lunch and dinner, and utilise the best of California's abundance of natural produce: the state's farms yield an incredible range of fruit and vegetables while the ocean and the well-stocked rivers make seafood and freshwater fish a prime feature of many menus, alongside the ubiquitous steaks and ribs.

Ethnic food is vital part of the culinary scene. **Mexican** food is extremely inexpensive and easy to locate – and a lot tastier and healthier than you will find in Mexico itself – as is **Chinese**, **Japanese** and **Italian** fare.

Of late, the state's adventurous eaters have been acquainting themselves with **Korean** and **Vietnamese** food in a growing band of low-cost restaurants that reflect the ethnic background of California's newest settlers.

At the top end of the scale are the gourmet restaurants, whose chefs are the leading practitioners of California cuisine: an ever-inventive manipulation of local produce to create attractively presented and nutritionally balanced meals - worth a $25–50 splurge at least once.

Electricity
The US electrical supply is 110–115 volts (60 cycles) and appliances use two-prong plugs. European appliances are designed for 220 volts (50 cycles) and can only be used with an adaptor. These can be bought before leaving (though first make sure the adaptor is suitable for the US) or in the US.

Festivals and Events
From county fairs to frog racing, thousands of festivals and special events take place in California each year. The pick of the bunch is in the regional gazetteer. For a (very long) full list, contact the **California Office of Tourism** (see Maps and Information).

Gay and Lesbian Travellers
California in general and San Francisco in particular are welcoming places for gay and lesbian travellers. Gay and lesbian bars, clubs, accommodation and information centres are well established in the major cities, and gays and lesbians are unlikely to encounter open public hostility anywhere except in the most out-of-the-way places.

Health and Insurance
It is essential, though not compulsory, to have insurance when you travel anywhere in the US. Besides the obvious benefits of compensation for stolen articles and disrupted travel, being insured will guard against an astronomical bill if you are unfortunate enough to need medical treatment.
If you need to see a doctor, find one by looking under 'physicians' in the phone book; some hospitals in major cities have casualty departments, but if you are dealing with a serious injury call an ambulance by dialling the emergency number, 911.

Holidays
Banks and all public offices will be closed on all the following holidays, and shops may be open on some of these days: New Year's Day (1 January), Martin Luther King's Birthday (third Monday in January), Lincoln's Birthday (12 February), Washington's Birthday (Monday before 22 February), Memorial Day (4th Monday in May), Independence Day (4 July), Labor Day (1st Monday in September), Columbus Day (12 October), Veteran's Day (11 November), Thanksgiving Day (4th Thursday in November), Christmas Day (25 December).
In addition, Good Friday is a half-day holiday and Easter Monday is a full day holiday.

Hotels and Motels
The major American mid-range hotel chains (usually $55–85 a night), such as Holiday Inn, Howard Johnson, Travelodge and Vagabond, are heavily represented in California and conform to a good level, offering double beds, colour TVs, private bathrooms and in-room phones as standard.
Such hotels are rarely the best value choice, however. Many smaller hotels and motels – including budget-priced chains such as Hampton Inn, Days Inn, and Motel 6 ($28–45) – often offer the same things as the pricier hotels, minus room service and other non-essential frills.
Thousands of small, owner-run motels are likely to have even lower prices ($22–35), especially during quiet periods when the rooms would otherwise be unoccupied. Although you should always check the room before booking in, bargain-priced motels nearly always offer perfectly acceptable accommodation and include in-room phones, private bathrooms and TV.
Prices are quoted per room rather than per person, so two people sharing will obviously pay half what a single traveller might; single rooms are non-existent, although a reduction of a few dollars on the double rate might be offered to a lone traveller. Three people sharing

can often add an extra bed to a double room for $10–15 above the regular rate.

It is possible to save money by buying prepaid vouchers for the major chain hotels before arriving in the US, although these schemes are often less reliable than they seem. Most participating hotels only set aside a few rooms for voucher holders and will turn you away (or offer rooms at regular prices) if these are full.

Besides the standard sales tax (see below), some areas impose a 'bed tax' of 5-15 per cent on the standard room charge.

Maps and Tourist Information

Almost every community has a Visitors' Bureau or Chamber of Commerce equipped to provide tourists with free maps, leaflets and information. These are usually signposted and their addresses are always in the phone book. Most keep regular business hours; those in major cities are often open at weekends, too.

Information on, and reliable maps of the whole state are provided by the **California Office of Tourism,**which is based at 1121 L Street, Suite 103, Sacramento, CA 95814 (tel: (916) 322 2881).

Money and Currency Exchange

Before arriving in the US, make sure you convert your spending money to US dollar travellers' cheques, which can be used as cash all over the country in shops, hotels, restaurants and so on.

Foreign currency can be changed in some banks and at a small number of exchange bureaux, but rates and commissions are never good. Credit cards should be carried, too; these are a standard form of payment for major expenses such as car hire and accommodation, and are also an indication that you are a credit-worthy person.

The US currency you will be handling most frequently are the identical looking notes: $20, $10, $5 and $1; and the variously sized coins: 25¢ (a 'quarter'), 10¢ (a 'dime'), 5¢ (a 'nickel') and 1¢ (a 'penny').

CONVERSION CHARTS

FROM		MULTIPLY
Inches	Centimetres	2.54
Centimetres	Inches	0.3937
Feet	Metres	0.3048
Metres	Feet	3.2810
Yards	Metres	0.9144
Metres	Yards	1.0940
Miles	Kilometres	1.6090
Kilometres	Miles	0.6214
Acres	Hectares	0.4047
Hectares	Acres	2.4710
Gallons	Litres	4.5460
Litres	Gallons	0.2200
Ounces	Grams	28.35
Grams	Ounces	0.0353
Pounds	Grams	453.6
Grams	Pounds	0.0022
Pounds	Kilograms	0.4536
Kilograms	Pounds	2.205
Tons	Tonnes	1.0160
Tonnes	Tons	0.9842

MEN'S SUITS

UK	36	38	40	42	44	46	48
Rest of Europe	46	48	50	52	54	56	58
US	36	38	40	42	44	46	48

DRESS SIZES

UK	8	10	12	14	16	18
France	36	38	40	42	44	46
Italy	38	40	42	44	46	48
Rest of Europe	34	36	38	40	42	44
US	6	8	10	12	14	16

MEN'S SHIRTS

UK	14	14.5	15	15.5	16	16.5	17
Rest of Europe	36	37	38	39/40	41	42	43
US	14	14.5	15	15.5	16	16.5	17

MEN'S SHOES

UK	7	7.5	8.5	9.5	10.5	11
Rest of Europe	41	42	43	44	45	46
US	8	8.5	9.5	10.5	11.5	12

WOMEN'S SHOES

UK	4.5	5	5.5	6	6.5	7
Rest of Europe	36	37	39	39	40	41
US	6	6.5	7	7.5	8	8.5

Language

When California joined the Union in 1850, Spanish was spoken as a mother tongue by two-thirds of the state's population. It was only with the influx of English-speakers from the east during the Gold Rush that the language lost its predominance. Now, after 100 years, Spanish is once again a widely spoken language in California. Spanish-speakers are concentrated in the most densely populated third of the state: over a quarter of the population of Los Angeles, America's second largest city, are Hispanic Americans. Many face discrimination and prejudice. Controversy has raged about education provision in Spanish schools and the rights of Spanish-speakers. Despite opposition from Civil Rights groups, Californians voted in a state-wide referendum to

make English their official language. A Spanish-speaker can easily understand Mexican Spanish. The main difficulty is in vocabulary: Mexican Spanish has been much enriched by words from Nahuatl, the language of the Aztec Empire. Here is a very basic vocabulary to help you in Hispanic restaurants.

al mojo de ajo	fried with garlic in butter
cafe	coffee
cerveza	beer
el guacamole	avocado purée
el jitomate	tomato
el licuado de agua	fruit juice with water
el licuado de leche	fruit juice with milk
el refresco	soft drink
empanizado	fried in breadcrumbs
la botana	appetiser la carne de res beef
la cena	dinner
la cochinita pibil	spicy pork Yucatan-style
la comida	lunch
la comida corrida	set menu
la crepa	pancake
la cuenta	the bill
la papa	potato
la torta	roll with meat, lettuce, avocado, cream
las puntas de filete	thin slices of beef (sometimes in a sandwich)
las enchiladas suizas	tortilla filled with chicken and covered with cooked cheese and cream
las carnitas	small pieces of grilled pork
las crepas con cajeta	pancakes with sweet sauce
las papas francesas	chips/french fries
los tamales	dumplings
los totopos tacos	dips
pescado	fish
vegetariano	vegetarian
verduras	vegetables

Mission Beach Broadwalk

Nightlife

To discover the best of the nightlife – be it cinema, live music, discos or bars – look for the free local newspapers distributed in bookshops, bars, restaurants, or just piled up on street corners. Each community has at least one and they are dependable and opinionated sources of what's on information.

Post Offices

All towns have post offices and most are open Monday to Friday 08.30–17.00hrs, Saturday 08.00–12.00hrs.

Public Transport

It is possible to see most of California without a car, but public transport is decidedly thin outside of the cities and non-existent in many country and coastal areas.
There is a very limited train service connecting San Francisco, Los Angeles and San Diego; a more common form of long-distance travel is Greyhound buses, but the Greyhound service can be expensive.
However, costs over very long journeys might be reduced with an Ameripass ticket, which offers unlimited Greyhound travel over a fixed period - from four to 30 days. Bear in mind that the buses often fall hours behind schedule and bypass much of the state's finest scenery. With the exception of San Francisco,

which has an excellent public transport network, getting around cities without a car is also problematic – though not impossible, provided you study the local timetables carefully.
When using city buses, take care not to miss your stop and unwittingly stray into dangerous areas (this is especially important after dark); the driver will always be ready to give advic e.

Sales Tax

A state sales tax of up to 8.5 per cent is added to the marked price of everything sold in California's shops.

Shops

Shops in California span everything from gigantic city shopping malls to country stores beside rural crossroads. Opening hours vary, but are usually Monday to Saturday, 09.00–17.30hrs.

Sports

While California's spectator sports enjoy a high profile and regularly fill TV screens, more popular are participant sports, which range from surfing and scuba-diving to skiing and white-river rafting. Details are given in the appropriate section of the regional gazetteer.

Taxis

Taxis can be hailed in the street though it is more common to phone for one; many companies are listed (under 'taxicabs') in the Yellow Pages. Hotels and motel lobby staff will usually phone a taxi for you. Fares are reasonable, averaging around $1.80 a mile.

Telephones

Found on the street, in hotel lobbies, bus stations, bars, restaurants and, indeed, in most public buildings, California's public telephones almost always work and, by European standards, are cheap. Local calls cost only cents (the phone has slots for quarters, dimes and nickels, which should be inserted before dialling), although calls further afield can be very costly.

To phone out of the US dial 011 and then your country code: Australia 61; Eire 353; New Zealand 64; UK 44. Emergency calls (dial 911) and calls to the operator (dial 0) or the international operator (dial 1 800 874 4000) are free.

Time
California uses Pacific Standard Time, three hours behind the US's East Coast, eight hours behind the UK and nine hours behind the rest of Western Europe. Australia is between 16 and 18 hours later than California; New Zealand is 20 hours later.

Tipping
After using restaurants, bars or taxis, leave a tip of 15–20 per cent of the bill. If a hotel porter carries your luggage, tip 50¢–$1 per bag.

Toilets
Called 'rest rooms' or 'bathrooms', California's public toilets are plentiful and free, but are generally found inside public buildings rather than on the street.

Wine and Beer
International recognition draws many visitors to sample the produce of California's Wine Country, but also worth investigating are the state's native beers. San Francisco's Anchor Steam Beer has gained worldwide acclaim and there are many micro-breweries creating exceptionally good brews that knock for six the weak and tasteless mass-market American beers.

Women Travellers
All visitors to California are the potential victims of crime but women, especially those travelling alone, are particularly at risk. The common precautions for reducing danger in cities, such as taking a taxi rather than public transport at night and being wary of the uninvited interest of strangers, should be employed.

On the positive side, it is quite common in the cities for women to go out unaccompanied to bars, restaurants and nightclubs; any unwanted attention in such places can usually be seen off with a verbal rebuff.

Most cities have some women-only accommodation and a range of women's groups – and a rape crisis hotline – which are listed in the phone book.

Youth Hostels, YMCAs and YWCAs
Youth hostels and a small number of comparable YMCAs and YWCAs are scattered throughout California and, at $7-10 a night, are by far the least costly form of accommodation. Most hostels have small, shared rooms (usually six to eight beds in each) and a few single and double rooms (around $25), and simple cooking facilities. A three-night limit operates when the hostel is fully booked, as is very likely during the summer.

Further information can be obtained from any YH office in Europe or by contacting **American Youth Hostels**, PO Box 67613, Washington, DC 20013–7613 (tel: (202) 783 6161).

Views of California

30¢ + Tax

DIRECTORY

SAN FRANCISCO

Accommodation

Expensive

The Fairmont Hotel, 950 Mason Street (tel: (415) 772 5000). An élite hotel in élite Nob Hill and a survivor of the 1906 earthquake: the marble-pillared lobby is just the start.

Hotel Griffon, 155 Steuart Street (tel: (415) 495 2100). Classy accommodation on the Embarcadero waterfront; guests get free use of the adjoining fitness centre.

Mark Hopkins Hotel, 1 Nob Hill (tel: (415) 992 2055). Now owned by the Intercontinental chain but retaining individuality.

The Miyako, 1625 Post Street (tel: (415) 922 3200). A discreet and luxurious retreat in Little Tokyo that is a blending of Japanese and Western ideas.

San Francisco Marriott, 777 Market Street (tel: (800) 228 9290). Opposite the Convention Center; opened in 1989.

Tuscan Inn, 425 North Point (tel: (800) 648 4626). The pick of the hotels in strongly touristed Fisherman's Wharf: warmly furnished rooms, personable staff, and a complimentary wine hour.

Moderate

Abigail Hotel, 246 McAllister Street (tel: (800) 553 5575). Delightfully old fashioned and stuffed with mementoes from earlier days, when it catered for visiting theatre companies; budget weekly rates.

Alamo Square Inn, 719 Scott Street (tel: (415) 992 2055). Bed and breakfast in an atmospheric rambling Victorian building with fabulous views; in a fast-improving area between Haight-Ashbury and Pacific Heights.

The Alexander Inn, 415 O'Farrel Street (tel: (800) 253 9263). Compact and stylishly furnished; a good choice in a central area.

Days Inn at the Wharf, 2358 Lombard Street (tel: (800) 556 2667). The least costly of the chain motels close to Fisherman's Wharf.

Edward II Bed & Breakfast Inn, 3155 Scott Street (tel: (1 800) 473 2846). The finest four-poster beds and whirlpool baths to be found in Pacific Heights; price includes a glass of sherry in the adjoining bar.

Holland Motel, 1 Richardson Avenue (tel: (415) 922 0810). Run-of-the-mill motel but nicely located for Fisherman's Wharf, and reasonably priced.

Hotel Diva, 440 Geary Street (tel: (415) 885 0200). Striking modern Italian design and a VCR in each room.

Hotel Essex, 684 Ellis Street (tel: (415) 474 4664). Pleasant, well placed and good value.

Hotel Union Square, 114 Powell Street (tel: (415) 397 3000). Well-known hotel of the 1930s, stylishly revamped; complimentary croissants and herbal teas.

The Inn San Francisco, 943 Van Ness Avenue (tel: (800) 359 0913). A historic Mission district mansion converted into a charming small hotel; complimentary breakfast buffet.

The King George, 334 Mason Street (tel: (415) 781 5050). Pleasant if unspectacular rooms in the heart of Downtown; serves 'English-style' afternoon tea to piano accompaniment.

Laurel Motor Inn, 444 Presidio Avenue (tel: (800) 552 8753). Unspectacular but good value; distanced from the strongly touristed areas.

Lombard, 1015 Geary Street (tel: (415) 673 5232). Stylish, modestly sized hotel with a fabulous roof-top terrace and a range of services that belie its competitive rates.

Pacific Bay Inn, 520 Jones Street (tel: (800) 445 2631). An inviting option close to Downtown, with warm décor and attentive staff.

The Pickwick, 85 Fifth Street (tel: (415) 421 7500). Up-and-coming hotel in the increasing fashionable SoMa district; still good value despite steadily rising prices.

Raphael Hotel, 386 Geary Street (tel: (415) 986 2000). Unexceptional but brightened by friendly staff; useful Downtown location.

The San Francisco Marriott Hotel

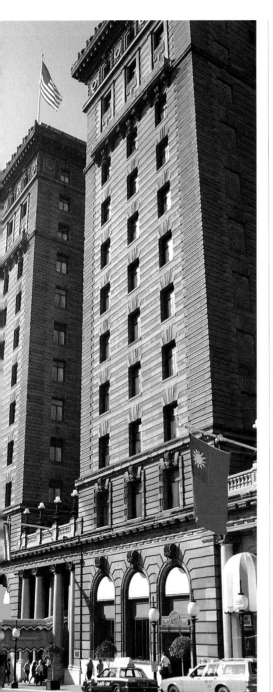

DIRECTORY

The Red Victorian, 1665 Haight Street (tel: (415) 864 1978). A 1904 structure with stress-relieving décor, a meditation room, in-house masseurs and healthy breakfasts – a true San Francisco experience.
Stanyan Park Hotel, 750 Stanyan Street (tel: (415) 751 1000). Elegantly renovated and facing Golden Gate Park; the room rate includes breakfast.
Washington Square Inn, 1660 Stockton Street (tel: (415) 981 4220). Antique-laden bed and breakfast accommodation in a prime North Beach setting; price includes afternoon tea and biscuits, and evening wine and cheese.

Budget
18th Street Guest House, 3930 Eighteenth Street (tel: (415) 255 0644). Very cheap and atmospheric hostel; provides a complimentary breakfast daily and hosts weekly barbecues in summer.
Central YMCA, 220 Golden Gate Avenue (tel: (415) 885 0460). Plain single and double rooms in an uninteresting neighbourhood, but a solid budget option for men and women.
Embarcadero YMCA, 166

Embarcadero (tel: (415) 392 2192). By far the nicest of the city's YMCAs; men and women welcome.
European Guest House, 761 Minna Street (tel: (415) 861 6634). Cosy low-cost option in dodgy part of the Mission District; an easy-going, youth-orientated mood and a mix of dormitory beds and double rooms.
Geary Hotel, 610 Geary Street (tel: (800) 828 2880). Fairly drab and depressing but clean and safe, and the cheapest hotel in Downtown.
Globetrotters Inn, 225 Ellis Street (tel: (415) 7346 5786). Easy-going backpackers' hostel with dormitory beds and a well-equipped kitchen.
Grant Plaza, 465 Grant Avenue (tel: (800) 472 6805). Tremendous value in the centre of Chinatown, with small but thoughtfully decorated rooms and a stained-glass dome on the top floor.
Hotel One, 1087 Market Street (tel: (415) 861 4946). Dirt cheap, no-frills hotel in a central location; often offering special deals to cut its rates still further.
Hotel Sheehan, 620 Sutter Street (tel: (800) 848 1529). A converted YMCA building

with large but not pricey rooms; also has an Olympic-sized swimming pool and a gymnasium for guests' free use.
International Guest House, 2976 23rd Street (tel: (415) 641 1411). Aimed at backpacking students, with dormitory bunk beds and a few private rooms.
Obrero Hotel, 1208 Stockton Street (tel: (415) 989 3960). A great find wedged between bustling Chinatown and the lively North Beach: the staff are helpful, the rooms are adequate, and the complimentary breakfasts are substantial.
Sam Wong Hotel, 615 Broadway (tel: (415) 781 6836). A small, cheap and cheerful hotel in bustling Chinatown.
San Francisco International Hostel, Building 24, Fort Mason (tel: (415) 771 7277). Massive youth hostel with maximum stays of three nights in summer, five nights in winter.
San Francisco Summer Hostel, 100 McAllister Street (tel: (415) 621 5809). A summer option in Downtown, with dormitory beds, laundry facilities and a friendly atmosphere.
San Remo Hotel, 2237 Mason Street (tel: (415) 776 8688). Comfortable, if spartan rooms and shared bathrooms; good value in a good location.
Sutter Larkin Hotel, 1048 Larkin Street (tel: (415) 474 6820). The bare necessities at a very low price in a handy Downtown spot.
Women's Hotel, 642 Jones Street (tel: (415) 775 1711). Basic rooms exclusively for women in the seedy (but small) Tenderloin neighbourhood.

Fisherman's Wharf, San Francisco

The North Beach area, San Francisco

Eating

Expensive

Asuka Brasserie, 1625 Post Street (tel: (800) 533 4567). Combines traditional Japanese cookery with Californian culinary innovations to produce visually stunning, as well as sensationally tasting, meals.

Café Majestic, 1500 Sutter Street (tel: (415) 776 6400). California cuisine in an ultra-elegant, classically furnished dining room.

Crown Room, 950 Mason Street (tel: (415) 772 5131). Extravagant lunch and dinner buffets to be consumed while gazing across the city from the top-floor skyroom of the very posh Fairmont Hotel.

Greens, Building A, Fort Mason (tel: (415) 771 6222). State-of-the-art gourmet-vegetarian eating, using ingredients grown on a Zen Buddhist farm across the bay in Marin County.

La Follie, 2316 Polk Street (tel: (415) 776 5577). Outstanding French food in a refreshingly unstuffy setting; options include a five-course dinner designed to reveal the chef's individual talents.

Moderate

An Hong Phu-Nhuan, 808 Geary Street (tel: (415) 885 5180). Tempting Vietnamese dishes at fair prices.

Bahia, 41 Franklin Street (tel: (415) 626 3306). Choice Brazilian and South American fare in an over-the-top tropical setting.

Bayon, 2018 Lombard Street (tel: (415) 922 1400). Surprisingly affordable gourmet-class French and Cambodian cooking; dinner only.

Blue Light Café, 1979 Union Street (tel: (415) 922 5510). Southwestern cuisine, spicy and predominantly meat-based.

The Buena Vista, 2765 Hyde Street (tel: (415) 474 5044). One of the few good-value places in the Fisherman's Wharf area; a good selection of basic breakfasts and lunches but more famous for its Irish coffee.

Calzone's, 430 Columbus Avenue (tel: (415) 397 3600). Wood-fired pizzas with a variety of inventive, exotic toppings.

Cha Cha Cha, 1805 Haight Street (tel: (415) 386 5758). A small and lively spot that pulls a diverse crowd for its (predominantly) Cuban lunches and dinners at reasonable prices.

The Élite Café, 2049 Filmore Street (tel: (415) 346 8668). Wide selection of good quality cajun and creole dishes.

Fog City Diner, 1300 Battery Street (tel: (415) 982 2000). Disguised as a 1950s diner complete with neon lights and stainless steel fittings, but the food is creative – and affordable – California cuisine.

Gaylords, 1 Embarcadero Center (tel: (415) 397 7775). One of a chain of unremarkable Indian restaurants but with a good value fixed-price lunch buffet.

Gold Spike, 527 Columbus Avenue (tel: (415) 421 4591). A North Beach institution on account of its gluttonous six-course Italian dinners,

The Good Earth, 1865 Post Street (tel: (415) 771 0151). A fine array of omelettes, soups, and meat and fish dishes, all made from fresh ingredients and prepared to emphasise the natural flavours. Bland setting, though.

Judy's Café, 2268 Chestnut Street (tel: (415) 922 4588).

DIRECTORY

In San Francisco coffee is taken seriously: it's a meal in itself

Hunger-busting omelettes and sandwiches munched by a trendy Marina District crowd.

Lefty O'Douls, 333 Geary Street (tel: (415) 982 8900). Straightforward American cuisine: immense sandwiches, juicy burgers, sizzling steaks and more.

Limbo, 299 Ninth Stret (tel: (415) 255 9945). An arty crowd and a healthy menu that will delight vegetarians while also providing carnivores with plenty of choice.

Little Thai, 2348 Polk Street (tel: (415) 771 5544). Wonderful yet under-acknowledged place in which to indulge in a tempting assortment of cleverly concocted Thai dishes.

Max's Diner, 311 Third Street (tel: (415) 546 6297). Ample platefuls of traditional American fare – meatloaf, turkey sandwiches, burgers, milkshakes and much more – dished up in a 1950s-style diner.

The New San Remo Restaurant, 2237 Mason Street (tel: (415) 673 9090). Open nightly for low-cost five-course Italian dinners featuring the chef's specials.

North Beach Pizza, 1499 Grant Street (tel: (415) 433 2444). Always busy and famous all over town for its expertly made pizzas, available with a long list of toppings.

Perry's, 1944 Union Street (tel: (415) 922 9022). Large portions of traditional American food in a famed Pacific Heights rendezvous.

The Pine Crest, 401 Geary Street (tel: (415) 885 6407). Somewhat over-priced Downtown diner open around the clock for very simple, very stodgy coffee shop fare.

Yang Sing, 427 Battery Street (tel: (415) 362 1640). Not cheap but among the best dim sum restaurants in the city; always busy.

Budget

Bohemian Cigar Store, 566 Columbus Avenue (tel: (415) 362 0536). Great place to interrupt a tour of the North Beach; the *focaccia* sandwiches are a knockout.

Café Caravan, 1312 Chestnut Street (tel: (415) 441 1168). Good value locals' diner with fast and friendly service.

Caffè Trieste, 601 Vallejo Street (tel: (415) 392 6739). A long established Italian coffee house legendary for its espresso and its live opera on Saturday afternoons.

Dottie's True Blue Café, 522 Jones Street (tel: (415) 885 2767). Health-conscious diner food – making special use of fresh fruit and cereals – in a Downtown location.

Eats, 50 Clement Street (tel: (415) 752 8837). Open for breakfast and lunch and serving mammoth portions of fast, cheap and very succulent food.

El Toro Taqueria, 598 Valencia Street (tel: (415) 431 3351). Popular fill-up stop for down-to-earth Mexican food.

Gum Tong, 675 Jackson Street (tel: (415) 788 5393). Remarkably low-priced Chinatown restaurant.

Hamburger Mary's Organic Grill, 1582 Folsom Street (tel: (415) 626 5767). Great burgers, loud music and an eye-catching clientele.

Hang Ah Tea Room, 1 Hang Ah Street (tel: (415) 982 5686). A fine place to sample inexpensive *dim sum* amid a crowd of Chinatown regulars.

La Cumbre, 515 Valencia Street (tel: (415) 863 8205). Cafeteria-style outlet for simple but delicious low-cost Mexican favourites.

Muffin Classics, 1400 Haight Street (tel: (415) 861 1789). Mouthwatering array of freshly baked goods and plenty of what its name suggests.

New Dawn, 3174 16th Street (tel: (415) 553 8888). A very San Francisco twist on the traditional coffee shop, with crazy décor and anything-goes ambience but proffering stomach-filling breakfasts and lunches.

St Francis Candy Store, 2801 24th Street (tel: (415) 826 4200). Wonderful, long-established provider of sandwiches and frothy milkshakes.

Salvadoreno, 535 Valencia Street (tel: (415) 431 6554). Salvadorean bakery offering plenty of scope for assembling picnics.

San Francisco Bar-B-Cue, 1328 Eighteenth Street (tel: (415) 431 8956). Spicy meat dishes prepared Thai style.

Tad's, 120 Powell Street (tel: (415) 982 1718). Good spot for cheap breakfasts; also does burgers, soups and sourdough bread.

Village Pizza, 3348 Steiner Street (tel: (415) 931 2470). A budget-priced hunger killer in an expensive area; pizza sold whole and by the slice.

THE BAY AREA

Accommodation

Expensive

Claremont Resort Hotel and Tennis Club, Ashby and Domingo avenues, Oakland (tel: (510) 843 3000). An extensively refurbished 1916 mansion set within landscaped grounds in the Oakland hills; saunas, swimming pools and jacuzzis.

Moderate

Cowper Inn, 705 Cowper Street, Palo Alto (tel: (415) 327 4457). Bed and breakfast in a comfortable 19th-century house.
The Hensley House, 456 N Third Street, San José (tel: (408) 298 3537). Tiny but luxurious 1884 house offering bed and breakfast.

Budget

Hidden Villa Ranch Hostel, 26870 Moody Road, near Los Gatos (tel: (415) 941 6407). Limited number of beds on a working farm; fills quickly and is closed June, July and August.
Motel 6, 4301 El Camino Real, Palo Alto (tel: (415) 949 0833). Part of the nationwide budget chain of plain but functional motels.
Motel 6, 2560 Fontaine Road, San Jose (tel: (408) 270 3131). See comment above.
Sanborn Park Hostel, 15808 Sanborn Road, Saratoga (tel: (408) 741 9555). A lovely rustic youth hostel, formerly a hunting lodge

Eating

Expensive

Chez Panisse, 1517 Shattuck Avenue, Berkeley (tel: (510) 548 5525). The birthplace of California cuisine and as innovative and popular as ever.

Moderate

Frankie, Johnny, and Luigi's Too, 939 El Camino Real, Palo Alto (tel: (415) 967 5384). Earns the favour of locals, including many Stanford students, for its delectable pizzas.
The Good Earth, 185 University Avenue, Palo Alto (tel: (415) 321 9449). Only healthy, natural ingredients are used to whip up omelettes, salads and sandwiches; also has a counter for take-away

Seals Guard Pier, in Monterey

muffins.
Quoc Te, 155 E San Fernando Street, San José (tel: (408) 289 8323). Very well priced Chinese and Vietnamese dishes with the accent on seafood.

Budget

Blondie's Pizza, 2340 Telegraph Avenue, Berkeley (tel: (510) 548 1129) Chewy, tasty pizza by the slice; always crowded.
The Blue Nile, 2525 Telegraph Avenue, Berkeley (tel: (510) 540 6777). Absurdly cheap East African food, ideal for vegetarians and anyone seeking a culinary bargain.
La Taqueria, 15 S First Sreet, San José (tel: (408) 287 1542). Very edible Mexican fare in an unpretentious setting.

DIRECTORY

CENTRAL COAST NORTH

Accommodation

Expensive

Highlands Inn, on Highway-1 four miles south of Carmel (tel: (800) 538 9525). Where singer Madonna honeymooned: every room has an ocean view.

Moderate

Carmel Village Inn, Ocean Avenue and Junipero Street (tel: (408) 624 3864). Good value for pricey Carmel, with comfortable rooms and nice grounds.

Château Victorian, 118 First Street, Santa Cruz (tel: (408) 458 9458). Bed and breakfast near the beach.

The Jabberwock, 598 Laine Street, Monterey (tel: (408) 372 4777). Bed and breakfast inn with an Alice-in-Wonderland theme.

Budget

Hotel St George, 1520 Pacific Avenue, Santa Cruz (tel: (408) 423 8181). Very laid-back; very cheap.

Motel 6, 2124 Freemont Street, Monterey (tel: (408) 373 3500). By just a few dollars, the cheapest in town; early booking essential but plenty of alternatives along this motel-lined street.

Motel 6, 1010 Fairview Avenue, Salinas (tel: (408) 758 2122). The least expensive of two of this bland but dependable motel chain in Salinas.

Eating

Expensive

Pacific's Edge, at the Highlands Inn on Highway-1 four miles south of Carmel (tel: (408) 624 3801). Scintillating ocean views and fabulous food from a menu which varies according to what is in season.

Moderate

Hog's Breath Inn, San Carlos and Fifth streets, Carmel (tel: (408) 625 1044). Steaks and seafood are the speciality but the attraction for many is the owner, actor Clint Eastwood.

India Joze, 1001 Center Street (tel: (408) 427 3554). Inspiring mix of Indian and Indonesian fare given the California treatment.

Rappa's, Fisherman's Wharf, Monterey (tel: (408) 372 7562). Fresh seafood and a lively, congenial atmosphere.

Budget

Kathy's Restaurant, 700 Cass Street, Monterey (tel: (408) 647 9540). Open for breakfast and lunch; best for chunky omelettes and sandwiches, ideally consumed from the patio tables.

Rosita's Armory Café, 231 Salinas Street, Salinas (tel: (408) 424 7039). Mexican eatery popular with locals for its low-cost breakfasts and lunches.

Tuck Box, Delores and Seventh streets, Carmel (tel: (408) 624 6365). Shepherds pie, Welsh rarebit and scones are some of the offerings in this shoebox-sized restaurant.

Zachary's, 819 Pacific Avenue, Santa Cruz (tel: (408) 427 0646). Fine value American breakfasts and lunches served with delicious home-made breads.

Coastal beauty at Morro Bay

CENTRAL COAST SOUTH

Accommodation

Expensive

El Encanto Hotel, 1900 Lausen Road, Santa Barbara (tel: (805) 687 5000). Ordinary rooms inside the 1927 Spanish-style main building, but more appealing are the small cottages dotting the expansive grounds.

Moderate

Adobe Inn, 1473 Monterey Street, San Luis Obispo (tel: (805) 549 0321). Run of the mill motel converted into a stylish bed and breakfast .
Inn on the Beach, 1175 Seaward Drive, Ventura (tel: (805) 652 2000). All rooms with beach-facing balconies; complimentary breakfast, wine and cheese.
Keystone Motel, 540 Main Street, Morro Bay (tel: (805) 772 7503). The pick of the town's mid-range motels.
Santa Barbara Inn, 901 Cabrillo Boulevard, Santa Barbara (tel: (805) 966 2285). Plush, relaxing.

Budget

Motel Inn, 2223 Monterey Street, San Luis Obispo (tel: (805) 543 4000). Became the

world's first motel in 1925; these days it is just one of many lining the main approach road to the town's centre.
Motel 6, 442 Corona del Mar, Santa Barbara (tel: (805) 464 1392). Santa Barbara's only budget-priced beds.

Eating

Expensive

The Palace Café, 8 E Cota Street, Santa Barbara (tel: (805) 966 3133). An award-winning mixture of Cajun and Caribbean cuisine; open evenings only.

Moderate

Paradise Café, 702 Anacapa Street, Santa Barbara (tel: (805) 962 4416). Plain but good American cooking in a simple setting.
Rose's Landing Restaurant, 725 Embarcadero, Morro Bay (tel: (805) 772 4441). Deservedly popular seafood restaurant with a view over the bay and the massive Morro Rock.

Budget

Chocolate Soup Restaurant, 980 Morro Street, San Luis Obispo (tel: (408) 624 3801). Enticing assortment of soups and sandwiches during the day and a no less alluring choice of chef's dinner specials available in the evening.
Dorn's Original Breakers Café, 801 Market Street, Morro Bay (tel: (805) 772 4415). Unsurpassed for inventive breakfasts, also a likely lunch and dinner stop.
J K Frimple's, 1701 State Street, Santa Barbara (tel: (805) 569 1671). Down-to-earth coffee shop with wide-ranging menu.
Joe's Café, 536 State Street, Santa Barbara (tel: (805) 966 4638). Always an eager crowd for the large helpings of meat and fish dishes.
La Marina Cantina, 1567 Spinnaker Drive, Ventura (tel: (805) 658 6077). Wonderful inexpensive Mexican food overlooking the harbour.

LOS ANGELES

Accommodation

Expensive

Beverly Hills Hotel, 9641 Sunset Boulevard (tel: (310) 276 2251). One movie-world legend that everyone has heard of, but the service will not be great unless the staff have heard of you.
L'Ermitage, 9291 Burton Way (tel: (800) 424 4443). The place to bask in luxury Beverly Hills style; every room is a suite and complimentary caviar and strawberries are served each afternoon.
Loews Santa Monica Beach Hotel, 1700 Ocean Avenue (tel: (310) 458 6700). An architectural showpiece hotel beside the ocean and Santa Monica Pier.
New Otani Garden Hotel, 120 S Los Angeles Street, Downtown (tel: (800) 252 0197). In the Little Tokyo section of Downtown; try the Japanese-style rooms for maximum value.

Moderate

Bel Air Summit Hotel, 11461 Sunset Boulevard, West Hollywood (tel: (800) 352 6680). Uninspiring façade but the sleek, ultra-modern design makes for a memorable stay.
Beverly Crest Motel, 125 S Spaulding Drive (tel: (310) 274 6801).Unprepossessing but tucked close to Beverly Hills.
Beverly Terrace Hotel, 469 N Doheny Drive (tel: (800) 421 7223). A personable Beverly Hills base at a price that will not frighten.
Del Capri Hotel, 10587 Wilshire Boulevard (tel: (310) 474 3511). Homely and good value in expensive Westwood; most rooms have kitchenettes.
Figueroa Hotel, 939 S Figueroa Street, Downtown (tel: (800) 331 5151). Relaxed hotel with an appealing Spanish look.
Highland Gardens Hotel, 7047 Franklin Avenue (tel: (213) 850 8536). Good facilities on a central but mostly residential Hollywood street.

DIRECTORY

Holiday Inn, 1755 N Highland Avenue (tel: (213) 462 7181). Unexciting but dependable mid-range chain hotel within walking distance of most Hollywood sights.

Holiday Inn Westwood Plaza, 10740 Wilshire Boulevard (tel: (800) 235 7973). Part of the dependable nationwide chain; handy for exploring Westwood and Beverly Hills.

Hollywood Roosevelt, 700 Hollywood Boulevard (tel: (213) 466 7000). Steeped in Hollywood tradition but the rooms are less impressive than the lobby; adequate but ordinary.

Huntley House Hotel, 1111 Second Street, Santa Monica (tel: (800) 556 4012). Reliable high-rise close to the beach; aim for a room which offers a view of the ocean.

Jamaica Bay Inn, 4175 Admiralty Way, Marina Del Rey (tel: (310) 823 5333). An agreeable small hotel removed from the hurly-burly of the city, beside a palm-fringed beach.

Le Parc, 733 West Knoll Drive, West Hollywood (tel: (310) 855 8888). Quiet, low-key elegance in a residential street and a fashionable neighbourhood.

Los Angeles West Travelodge, 10740 Santa Monica Boulevard (tel: (800) 255 3050). One of the functional nationwide chain, but reasonably priced for the area and boasting a pool.

Shangri-la Hotel, 1301 Ocean Avenue, Santa Monica (tel: (310) 394 2791). Unmistakable art deco delight which has been carefully restored to its original 1930s style; all rooms overlook Santa Monica Bay.

The Sovereign at Santa Monica Bay, 205 Washington Avenue (tel: (800) 331 0163). Major renovation turned this 1920s Santa Monica landmark into a plush but not unaffordable place to stay.

Budget

Academy Motel, 1621 McCladden Place (tel: (213) 465 1918). Safe and secure, and close to pulsating Hollywood Boulevard.

Cadillac Hotel, 401 Ocean Front Walk (tel: (310) 399 8876). Low-cost shared or private rooms beside lively Venice Beach.

Crest Motel, 7701 Beverly Boulevard (tel: (800) 367 1717). Clean, tidy and quiet, and surprisingly low priced for its West Hollywood/Beverly Hills location.

Kent Motel, 920 S Figueroa Street (tel: (213) 626 8701). Functional, no-frills Downtown motel.

Los Angeles International Hostel, 3601 S Gaffrey Street, Building 613, San Pedro (tel: (310) 831 8109). Some way from the centre

of LA life but handy for the South Bay area and airport.

Hastings Hotel, 6162 Hollywood Boulevard (tel: (213) 464 4136). Easily the least expensive option in central Hollywood; an unnerving neighbourhood by night.

Motel de Ville, 1123 W Seventh Street, Downtown (tel: (213) 624 8474). Garish décor but adequate, no-frills rooms.

Orchid Motel, 819 Flower Street (tel: (213) 626 5855). Attractive budget option in the centre of Downtown.

Park Plaza Hotel, 607 Park View Street (tel: (213) 384 5281). Small, plain rooms in an art deco megalith overlooking MacArthur Park; an unsafe area by night.

St Moritz Hotel, 5849 Sunset Boulevard (tel: (213) 469 2174). Austere but encouragingly cheap hotel

in the heart of Hollywood.

Santa Monica International Hostel, 1436 Second Street, Santa Monica (tel: (310) 393 9913). Large, modern hostel in a safe and enjoyable area.

Share-tel International Hostel, 20 Brooks Avenue, Venice (tel: (310) 392 0295). Popular backpackers' beachside accommodation with small, shared rooms.

Eating

Expensive

Citrus, 6703 Melrose Avenue, West Hollywood (tel: (213) 857 0034). For food and design, the most creative restaurant in LA.

Spago, 8795 Sunset Boulevard, West Hollywood (tel: (310) 652 4025). Be it with exotic gourmet pizzas or mouthwatering pasta dishes, Spago has been setting LA's culinary standards for years — reservations should be made weeks ahead.

Valentino, 3115 Pico Boulevard, Santa Monica (tel: (310) 829 4313). World-class Italian food and a long and diverse list of exceptional daily specials.

Moderate

Authentic Café, 7605 Beverly Boulevard, West Hollywood (tel: (310) 939 4626). Classy and inventive southwestern cooking; always popular with discerning diners.

Café Blanc, 3706 Beverly Boulevard, Hollywood (tel: (213) 380 2829). Highly successful and highly imaginative blending of French and Japanese cuisine.

Café Habana, 7465 Melrose Avenue, West Hollywood (tel: (213) 655 2822). Highly-rated Cuban food that draws discerning diners and some of LA's most fashionable faces.

Café Mambo, 707 Heliotrope Drive, Hollywood (tel: (213) 663 5800). Spicy Latin and Caribbean fare and a laid-back atmosphere.

California Pizza Kitchen, 330 S Hope Street,

Downtown (tel: (213) 626 6216). Mouthwatering pizzas with a host of dreamy toppings and a wide choice of salads.

City, 180 S La Brea Avenue, West Hollywood (tel: (213) 938 2155). Endlessly inventive main lunch courses and a host of devilish desserts; dinner is in the super-pricey bracket.

Dar Maghreb, 7651 Sunset Boulevard, Hollywood (tel: (213) 876 7651). Morocco re-created Hollywood-style complete with belly dancers, but the food is reasonable and comes in large amounts.

East Indian Grill, 345 N La Brea Avenue, West Hollywood (tel: (213) 938 8844). Fiery combinations of Indian and California cuisine.

El Cholo, 1121 S Western Avenue, Wilshire District (tel: (213) 734 2773). Award-winning Mexican food in a restaurant once patronised by Hollywood's biggest names.

Mon Kee, 679 N Spring Street, Chinatown (tel: (213) 628 6717). Justifiably busy Chinese eatery specialising in seafood.

Nowhere Café, 8009 Beverly Boulevard, West Hollywood (tel: (213) 655 8895). Excellent wholefood restaurant that will thrill the tastebuds and keep you healthy.

The Original Sonora Café, 445 S Figueroa Street, Downtown (tel: (213) 624 1800). Not cheap, but some of the best southwestern cooking you are likely to find in California.

Orleans, 11705 National Boulevard, near Beverly Hills (tel: (310) 479 4187). Top-rated cajun and creole dishes served in a relaxed atmosphere.

Pacific Dining Car, 1310 W Sixth Street, Wilshire District (tel: (231) 483 6000). Succulent ribs and steaks in a room kitted out as a luxury railway dining carriage; open 24 hours, the breakfasts are also worth sampling.

Red Sea, 1551 Ocean Avenue, Santa Monica (tel: (310) 394 5198). Excellent Ethiopian food and helpful staff to guide unfamiliar diners through the menu.

Budget

Barney's Beanery, 8447 Santa Monica Boulevard, West Hollywood (tel: (213) 654 2287). Burgers, chilli and imported beers in poolhall-cum-eatery-cum-bar.

Canter's, 419 Fairfax Avenue, West Hollywood (tel: (310) 651 2287). New York-style deli that has been serving generous portions of everything for decades.

Clifton's Brookdale Cafeteria, 648 S Broadway, Downtown (tel: (213) 627 1673). Help yourself to meat, vegetables and desserts from a vast array of steaming trays, then pay per item at the till.

Gorky's, 1716 N Cahuenga Boulevard, Hollywood (tel: (213) 463 7576). Inexpensive Russian dishes offered 24 hours a day.

The Gumbo Pot, at Farmer's Market, 6333 W Third Street (tel: (213) 933 0358). Tempting Cajun and Creole food in eat-and-run setting.

Home Café, 859 N Broadway, Chinatown (tel: (213) 624 6956). Hole-in-the-wall Chinatown stop for noodles and soup.

Hot Wings, 7011 Melrose Avenue (tel: (213) 930 1233). Chicken wings, sandwiches and other snacks at the lowest prices to be found on this trendy shopping and eating strip.

The Pantry, 877 S Figueroa Street, Downtown (tel: (213) 972 9279). Run-of-the-mill coffee shop food but the best value in Downtown – and always open.

Philippe's, 1001 N Alameda Street, Downtown (tel: (213) 462 7181). Since 1918 has been serving wholesome American food to diners at shared wooden bench tables.

Pinks Famous Chili Dogs, 711 N La Brea Avenue, Hollywood (tel: (213) 931 4223). Burgers, hot dogs and chilli dishes in what has become (inexplicably) an LA fast-food legend.

Positively Fourth Street, 1215 Fourth Street, Santa Monica (tel: (310) 393 1464). Great selection of take-away salads, pastas and soups to devour while exploring Santa Monica.

Vickman's, 1228 E Eighth Street, Downtown (tel: (213) 622 3852). Spartan coffee shop providing hearty breakfasts and all manner of home-baked delights.

The Beverly Wilshire

DIRECTORY

AROUND L A

Accommodation

Expensive

The Disneyland Hotel, 1150 W Cerritos Avenue, Anaheim (tel: (800) 854 6165). The official Disneyland hotel, every bit as themed as the famous park itself and with almost as much innocent amusement.

The Ritz-Carlton Huntington Hotel, 1401 S Oak Knoll Avenue (tel: (818) 568 3900). A 1907 Pasadena landmark restored to its grandeur and elegance.

Surf and Sand Hotel, 1555 S Coast Highway, Laguna Beach (tel: (800) 524 8621). Fully equipped luxurious rooms, most with balconies overlooking the ocean.

Moderate

Casa Malibu, 22752 Pacific Coast Highway, Malibu (tel: (310) 456 2219). One of the few places to stay in Malibu; quiet, comfortable and usually busy.

Doubletree Hotel, 191 N Los Robles Avenue, Pasadena (tel: (800) 528 0444). Smart and stylish, and ideally placed for seeing Pasadena.

Howard Johnson's Motor Lodge, 1380 S Harbor Boulevard, Anaheim (tel: (800) 654 2000). With its plush landscaped grounds, an almost unrecognisable link in the nationwide mid-priced chain; within easy walking distance of Disneyland.

The Inn at the Park, 1855 Harbor Boulevard, Anaheim (tel: (714) 750 1811). Large and comfortable, and close to Disneyland, with a positive attitude towards children.

Seacliff Motel, 1661 S Coast Highway, Laguna Beach (tel: (714) 497 9717). Unpretentious motel with the best rates in this otherwise very costly town.

Zane Grey Hotel, 199 Chimes Tower Road, Santa Catalina Island (tel: (714) 510 0966). Former home of the western writer and the island's most atmospheric hotel.

Budget

Anaheim Angel Inn, 1800 E Katella Avenue, Anaheim (tel: (800) 358 4400). Motels are plentiful all around Disneyland; this is consistently among the cheapest.

Colonial Inn Youth Hostel, 421 Eighth Street, Huntington Beach (tel: (714) 536 3315). Well placed for the busy local beach and easily reached by bus from LA's airport.

Econo Lodge, 1203 E Colorado Boulevard, Pasadena (tel: (818) 449 3170). Helpful staff raise the appeal of this functional low-rate hotel.

Fullerton Hacienda Hostel, 1700 N Harbor Boulevard (tel: (714) 738 3721). Tiny hostel just five miles from Disneyland – book early.

Sunset Inn, 1000 S Euclid Avenue, Fullerton (tel: (800) 445 4045). Simple, reliable motel sited between Disneyland and Knotts Berry Farm.

Eating

Expensive

Fresco, 514 S Brand Boulevard, Glendale (tel: (818) 247 5541). Draws fussy eaters from all over LA to its world-class Italian menu.

Kitayama, 1012 Bayview Place, Newport Beach (tel: (714) 725 0777). Caringly prepared and presented Japanese cuisine, with a leaning towards seafood and exquisite sauces.

Moderate

Alice's, 23000 Pacific Coast Highway, Malibu (tel: (310) 456 6646). Offers well-cooked American food and a view of the ocean.

Armstrong's Seafood Restaurant, 306 Crescent Avenue, Santa Catalina Island (tel: (714) 510 0113). Freshly caught swordfish and mahi-mahi among the mesquite-grilled delights.

The Cottage, 308 N Pacific Coast Highway, Laguna Beach (tel: (714) 494 3023). Well-prepared, very well-priced food served throughout the day in a dining room filled with intriguing locally found antiques.

Gladstone's 4 Fish, 17300 Pacific Coast Highway, Malibu (tel: (310) 454 3474). Fine, fresh sea fare combined with ocean views and, at dinner, memorable sunsets.

Inn of the Seventh Ray, 128 Old Topanga Canyon Road, Topanga Canyon (tel: (310) 455 1311). Californian flower power lives on in this long-running and rightly popular health food restaurant.

Parkway Grill, 510 S Arroyo Parkway (tel: (818) 795 1001). Scintillating fresh salads and a mouthwatering selection of pizzas and pastas, plus quality fish and meat dishes and a well-stocked California wine cellar.

Budget

The Busy Bee, 306 Crescent Avenue, Santa Catalina Island (tel: (714) 510 1983). Simple but filling breakfasts and lunches served at patio tables.

Green Street, 146 Shopper's Lane, Pasadena (tel: (818) 577 7170). Good range of all-American favourites, several notches above the standard coffee shop.

Lawry's, California Center, 570 W Avenue 26, Glendale (tel: (818) 225 2491). Refined Mexican food served cafeteria-style and devoured on a landscaped patio – sometimes with mariachi musicians for company.

Nui Ngu, 10528 McFadden Avenue, Garden Grove, Orange County (tel: (714) 775 1108). An inexpensive Vietnamese diner worth seeking out.

Rose City Diner, 45 S Fair Oaks Avenue, Pasadena (tel: (818) 793 8282). Excellent 1950s-style diner with substantial breakfasts, lunches and dinners – and complimentary bubblegum.

Ruby's, Balboa Pier, Newport Beach (tel: (714) 675 7829). Art deco diner at the end of the pier; great location and milkshakes but the food is average.

SAN DIEGO

Accommodation

Expensive

Hotel Del Coronado, 1500 Orange Avenue (tel: (619) 522 8000). A wooden architectural marvel, steeped in history and reeking of grandeur.

U S Grant Hotel, 326 Broadway (tel: (800) 334 6957). A characterful hotel that has been pampering presidents and celebrities for many years.

Moderate

Beach Front Motorlodge, 707 Reed Avenue (tel: (619) 483) 7670). Compact rooms but an unbeatable location for enjoying Mission and Pacific beaches.

Hotel St James, 830 Sixth Avenue (tel: (619) 234 0155). Smart but not large rooms in an appealingly restored building.

Hotel San Diego, 339 W Broadway (tel: (800) 824 1244). High-class lodgings in a fully renovated Downtown landmark.

La Jolla Cove Motel, 1155 Coast Boulevard (tel: (619) 459 2621). Fine base for discovering La Jolla.

La Pensione Hotel, 1654 Columbia Street (tel: (619) 232 3400). Clean and quiet with a European flavour.

Loma Lodge, 3202 Rosecrans Street (tel: (619) 222 0511). One of the better value motels on the Point Loma peninsula.

Padre Trail Inn, 4200 Taylor Street (tel: (619) 297 3291). Popular, medium-sized motel near the Old Town.

Budget

Downtown Inn Hotel, 660 G Street (tel: (619) 238 4100). Remarkably low rates for welcoming rooms.

Jim's San Diego, 1425 C Street (tel: (619) 235 8341). Hostel accommodation aimed at backpackers, with complimentary breakfast and a weekly barbecue.

The Maryland Hotel, 630 F Street (tel: (619) 239 9243). Basic but clean, with a useful central location.

Pickwick Hotel, 132 W Broadway (tel: (619) 234 0141). Drab but cheap on Downtown San Diego's main street.

Point Loma Hostel, 3790 Udall Street (tel: (619) 223 4788). Friendly hostel with small, shared rooms; perfectly sited for the local beach but some miles from the city centre.

YMCA, 500 W Broadway (tel: (619) 232 1133). Big and rather soulless but offering simple rooms for men or women at a bargain rate amid the up-market Downtown hotels.

YWCA, 1012 C Street (tel: (619) 239 0355). Exclusively for women; dormitory beds or small, private rooms. In a slightly seedy section of Downtown.

Eating

Expensive

George's at the Cove, 1250 Prospect Street (tel: (619) 454 4244). Justly acclaimed for its creative seafood dishes and divine pastas.

Grant Grill, U S Grant Hotel, 326 Broadway (tel: (619) 239 6808). Long favoured by the city's powerbrokers; a large selection of meats and seafood, but best known for its mock turtle soup and meal-in-themselves salads.

Moderate

Anthony's Fish Grotto, 1360 N Harbor Drive (tel: (619) 232 5103). Extensive range of succulent seafood served overlooking the harbour.

Bayou Bar & Grill, 329 Market Street (tel: (619) 696 8747). Fine cajun and creole dishes to set your tastebuds alight.

La Gran Tapa, 611 B Street (tel: (619) 234 8272). Mesmerising choice of *tapas* dishes; excellent paella served nightly.

Old Town Mexican Café y Cantina, 2489 San Diego Avenue (tel: (619) 297 4330). Always packed, but endure the queues for the best Mexican food in the Old Town area.

Red Onion, 3125 Ocean Front Walk (tel: (619) 488 9040). A party atmosphere, Mexican food in large amounts and delicious fruit margaritas.

The Spot, 105 Prospect Street, La Jolla (tel: (619) 459 0800). Gourmet-standard cuisine, spanning steaks, seafood and pizzas.

Budget

Broken Yolk, 1851 Garnet Street (tel: (619) 270 0045). Immense range of omelettes at next-to-nothing prices.

El Indio, 3695 India Street (tel: (619) 299 0333). Good quality Mexican fare in a fast-food setting.

Grand Central Café, 500 W Broadway (tel: (619) 234 CAFE). Wholesome American fare and many daily specials on offer inside the enormous YMCA building.

Hob Nob Hill, 2271 First Avenue (tel: (619) 239 8176). Dependable, family-run coffee shop that has been feeding San Diegans for decades.

Ingrid's Cantina, 818 Fifth Avenue (tel: (619) 233 6945). Chunky breakfast omelettes, and tasty chilli dishes and burgers served into the small hours.

Old Columbia Brewery & Grill, 1157 Columbia Street (tel: (619) 234 2739). Meat and seafood dishes in large portions; beer brewed on the premises.

Wonder Sushi, Level Three, Horton Plaza (tel: (619) 233 5300). A fabulous array of inexpensive sushi and other tasty Japanese dishes.

277

DIRECTORY

Lake Tahoe

THE DESERTS

Accommodation

Expensive

La Quinta Golf and Tennis Resort, 49499 Eisenhower Drive, La Quinta (tel: (619) 564 4111). A finely restored 1926 Spanish-style resort complete with luxury villas spread across several acres.

Moderate

Furnace Creek Ranch, Death Valley (tel: (800) 622 0838). Fairly charmless but a prime base for touring Death Valley.
Hampton Inn, 1590 University Avenue, Riverside (tel: (714) 683 6000). Part of an expanding nationwide chain noted for being good value.
Holiday Inn Palm Mountain Resort, 155 S Belardo Road, Palm Springs (tel: (619) 325 1301). Well located near the social centre of Palm Springs.

Budget

Motel 6, 666 S Palm Canyon Drive, Palm Springs (tel: (619) 325 6129). The larger of two Motel 6s in town and the most liable of them to have space.
Tiki Palms Hotel, 2135 N Palm Canyon Drive, Palm Springs (tel: (619) 327 5961). Homely and well run with good rates

Eating

Expensive

Cuistot, 73111 El Paseo, Palm Desert (tel: (619) 340 1000). California cuisine that pleases the palates of the desert communities' wealthiest residents.

Moderate

Flower Drum, 424 S Indian Canyon Drive, Palm Springs (tel: (619) 323 3020). Classy cuisine from five regions of China served beside an indoor waterfall.
La Casuelas Terraza, 222 S Palm Canyon Drive, Palm Springs (tel: (619) 325 2794). Gorge on well-prepared Mexican food on the micromist-cooled patio.
Hank's Fish House, 155 S Belardo, Palm Springs (tel: (619) 778 7171). Fresh seafood is the speciality; also has a popular oyster bar.

Budget

Elmer's Pancake and Steakhouse, 1030 E Palm Canyon Drive, Palm Springs (tel: (619) 327 8419). Pancakes and waffles galore at prices to incite gluttony.
Kitty's Country Kitchen, 109 S Palm Canyon Drive, Palm Springs (tel: (619) 320 7855). No-nonsense American fare – liver and onions, meatloaf and more – served throughout the day.
Louise's Pantry, 124 S Palm Canyon Drive, Palm Springs (tel: (619) 325 5124). Simple coffee shop favourites in shed-sized diner.
The Wheel Inn, near Cabazon exit of Interstate-10 (tel: (619) 849 7012). Open round-the-clock for large helpings of stodgy truck drivers' fare; complete with Country & Western jukebox.

SIERRA NEVADA

Accommodation

Expensive

Ahwahnee Lodge, Yosemite Valley (tel: (209) 252 4848). A 1927 creation in local stone and concrete slotting perfectly into beautiful natural surrounds.

Moderate

Truckee Hotel, Commercial and Bridge streets, Truckee (tel: (916) 587 4444). An 1886 structure, handy for exploring Lake Tahoe; most rooms without baths.
Giant Forest Lodge, Sequoia National Park (tel: (209) 565 3381). Cosy but far from luxurious; rooms.
Wawona Hotel, Mariposa, Yosemite National Park (tel: (209) 252 4848). Charming Victorian hotel nicely distanced from the park's busiest sections.

Budget

Bishop Elms Motel, 233 E Elm Street, Bishop (tel: (619) 873 8118). The least inexpensive choice in this motel-laden town.
Kings Inn, Second Street, Lee Vining (tel: (619) 647 6300). Small and friendly, and the least costly option close to Mono Lake.
Motel 6, 2375 Lake Tahoe Boulevard, Lake Tahoe (tel: (916) 542 1400). The cheapest for miles; be sure to book well ahead.
Motel 6, 473372 Main Street, Mammoth Lakes (tel: (916) 934 6660). A rare cut-rate alternative to the ski resorts; always busy.

Eating

Expensive

Ahwahnee Dining Room, Yosemite Valley (tel: (209) 372 1000). Formal dining in a grand setting.

Moderate

Giant Forest Lodge Dining Room, Sequoia National Park (tel: (209) 565 3314). Indulgent dinners to round off a day of forest exploration.
Whiskey Creek, Highway-203 and Minaret Road, Mammoth Lakes (tel: (619) 934 2555). Mainly popular

for its steaks and ribs but also doing imaginative things with seafood and sauces.

Wolfdale's, 640 N Lake Boulevard, Lake Tahoe (tel: (916) 583 5700). Scrumptious vegetarian meals.

Budget
Jack's Waffle Shop, 437 N Main Street, Bishop (tel: (619) 872 7971). Solid rather than refined nourishment on offer 24 hours a day.
Rosie's Café, 571 N Lake Boulevard, Lake Tahoe (tel: (916) 583 8504). Sandwiches, soups and burgers served with a smile.
Squeeze In, Commercial Row, Truckee (tel: (209) 587 9814). Every imaginable type of omelette, plus pizzas and a large range of sandwiches.
Village Cafeteria, Giant Forest Village, Sequoia National Park (tel: (209) 565 3314). Unpretentious, filling fare taken in the company of tree lovers and dedicated hikers

A slower pace in Old Sacramento

GOLD COUNTRY
Accommodation
Expensive
Delta King Riverboat Hotel, 1000 Front Street, Sacramento (tel: (916) 444 5464). Rooms aboard a 1927 riverboat moored beside the Old Town.

Moderate
Bear Flag Inn, 2814 I Street, Sacramento (tel: (916) 448 5417). Bed and breakfast in a peachy Craftsman-style bungalow from 1910.
National Hotel, 211 Broad Street, Nevada City (tel: (916) 265 4551). Believably claims to be the oldest hotel in the West, operating since 1856.
Ryan House, 153 S Shepherd Street, Sonora (tel: (209) 533 3445). Competitively priced bed and breakfast in a mid-19th-century miner's home.

Budget
Central Motel, 818 16th Street, Sacramento (tel: (916) 446 6006). Well priced and a useful location.

Gold Rush Home Hostel, 1421 Tiverton Avenue, Sacramento (tel: (916) 421 5954). On the outskirts with just four beds – book well ahead.
Sierra Motel, 816 W Main Street, Grass Valley (tel: (916) 273 8133). No-frills lodgings in the centre of town.
Sonora Inn, 160 S Washington Street, Sonora (tel: (916) 532 7468). Comfy rooms in the Spanish-style main building; cheaper, plainer accommodation in the annexe.

Eating
Expensive
Lautrec, Lehmann's Plaza, Sacramento (tel: (619) 973 0403). Classic French food, admired and devoured by food critics and state politicians alike.

Moderate
Americo's Trattoria Italiana, 2000 Capitol Avenue, Sacramento (tel: (916) 442 8119). Delicious pastas and sauces.
City Hotel Dining Room, Main Street, Columbia (tel: (209) 532 1479). French cuisine in a gold-rush era setting.
Murphys Hotel Restaurant, Main Street, Murphys (tel: (209) 728 3444). Exotic dishes such as calves' liver and frog's legs alongside the more usual meat-based American fare.

Budget
524, 524 Twelfth Street, Sacramento (tel: (916) 446 6147). Generous helpings of fiery Mexican food.
Europa, 275 S Washington Street, Sonora (tel: (209) 532 9957). Earthy, coffee shop staples served around the clock.
Juliana's Kitchen, 1800 L Street, Sacramento (tel: (916) 444 0187). Wide selection of low-priced Middle Eastern meals and snacks.
Marshall's, 203 Mill Street, Grass Valley (tel: (916) 272 2844). Has the town's tastiest examples of the local delicacy: Cornish pasties.

279

NORTH COAST

Accommodation
Expensive

Eureka Inn, Seventh and F streets, Eureka (tel: (707) 442 6441). Tudor-style mansion with elegant, spacious rooms and attentive staff.

Moderate

Carson House Inn, Fourth and M streets, Eureka (tel: (707) 443 1601). Bland but comfortable motel.
Grey Whale Inn, 615 N Main Street, Fort Bragg (tel: (707) 964 0640). Four-storey redwood mansion that served as the local hospital until 1971.
MacCallum House, Albion Street, Mendocino (tel: (707) 937 0289). Homely bed and breakfast in an 1882 house with some

original fittings.
Plough and Stars Country Inn, 1800 27th Street, Arcata (tel: (707) 822 8236). An intimate farmhouse offering bed and breakfast – and games of croquet.

Budget

Broadway Motel, 1921 Broadway, Eureka (tel: (707) 443 3156). Rock-bottom rates; clean, basic rooms.
Driftwood Motel, 820 N Main Street, Fort Bragg (tel: (707) 964 4061). Not fancy but close to everything.
Fairwinds Motel, 1674 G Street, Arcata (tel: (707) 822 4824). A bargain in this surprisingly expensive town.

Eating
Expensive

Café Beaujolais, 961 Ukiah Street, Mendocino (tel: (707) 937 5614). Also serves moderately priced breakfasts and lunches, but it is the more expensive dinners that demonstrate creative flair.

Moderate

Ferndale Café, 606 Main Street, Ferndale (tel: (707) 786 4795). Good quality, basic American meals

Eureka streets

served all day.
O Bento, 739 Tenth Street, Arcata (tel: (707) 826 2064). Offers Japanese and Eastern European food produced to an impressive standard.
Wharf Restaurant, 780 N Harbor Drive, Fort Bragg (tel: (707) 964 4283). Steaks and salads, but seafood is the speciality of this good value harbourside eatery.

Budget

Bob's Breakfast Café, 1039 Fourth Street, Eureka (tel: (707) 443 4788). Low-priced breakfasts and lunches, and a booming jukebox.
Egghead Omelettes of Oz, 356 N Main Street, Fort Bragg (tel: (707) 964 5005). Cosy, relaxed diner delivering plenty of what its name suggests – and much more.
Luna's, 1134 Fifth Street, Eureka (tel: (707) 445 9162). Very edible, very cheap Mexican food.
Main Street Deli, 40450 Main Street, Mendocino (tel: (707) 937 5031). Watch the crowds go by while grazing on sandwiches or simple breakfasts.

WINE COUNTRY

Accommodation

Expensive

Sonoma Mission Inn and Spa, 18140 Sonoma Highway, Sonoma (tel: (800) 358 9022). Luxury rooms, gourmet dining and a fully equipped health spa set within rolling acres.

Moderate

Brannan Cottage Inn, 109 Wapoo Avenue, Calistoga (tel: (707) 942 4200). Highly rated bed and breakfast in 1860 cottage built by a legendary California pioneer.

Mount View Hotel, 1457 Lincoln Avenue, Calistoga (tel: (707) 942 6877). A restored 1917 art deco showpiece with a swimming pool and a lavish breakfast spread supplied.

Sonoma Hotel, 110 Spain Street, Sonoma (tel: (707) 996 2996). Antique-filled establishment facing the town's historic plaza.

Budget

Calistoga Inn, 1250 Lincoln Avenue, Calistoga (tel: (707)

942 4101). A great deal by Wine Country standards, with cosy rooms and a complimentary breakfast.

Motel 6, 2760 Cleveland Avenue, Santa Rosa (tel: (707) 546 1500). A Wine Country rarity of genuinely cheap, if uninspiring, accommodation.

Swiss Hotel, 18 Spain Street, Sonoma (tel: (707) 938 2884). Tiny, atmospheric adobe building, centrally placed.

Eating

Expensive

Auberge du Soleil, 180 Rutherford Hill Road, Rutherford (tel: (707) 963 1211). Delectably prepared and presented nouvelle French and California cuisine in rural location.

Moderate

Calistoga Inn Restaurant, 1250 Lincoln Avenue (tel: (707) 942 4101). Varied range of classy meat and seafood dishes; outdoors eating in summer.

Mustards Grill, 7399 St Helena Highway, Yountville (tel: (707) 944 2424). Delicious grilled morsels in

a California cuisine style.

Tra Vigne, 1050 Charter Oak Avenue, St Helena (tel: (707) 963 4444). Excellent Italian food in a gorgeous vine-covered building.

Budget

Boskos, 1403 Lincoln Avenue, Calistoga (tel: (707) 942 9088). Freshly made pasta and tempting desserts.

Ma Stokeld's Pie Shop and Village Pub, 464 First Street, Sonoma (tel: (707) 935 0660). Succulent pies and pasties with California quirks.

St Helena Coffee Shop, 61 Main Street, St Helena (tel: (707) 963 3235). Spartan, but providing fair-priced simple breakfasts and lunches.

Sonoma Cheese Factory, 2 Spain Street, Sonoma (tel: (707) 996 1931) More than 100 home-made cheeses for your picnic.

281

Buena Vista Winery, Sonoma Mission

Index

INDEX

285

INDEX

INDEX/ACKNOWLEDGEMENTS

Acknowledgements

The Automobile Association would like to thank the following photographers, libraries and associations for their assistance in the preparation of this book. ROBERT HOLMES (© AA Photo Library) took most of the pictures, with the exception of: CALIFORNIA DEPT OF PARKS AND RECREATION 97 Monterey area beach 200 Pools across the meadows LOS ANGELES CONVENTION AND VISITORS BUREAU 18/9 Beach boy MARINE WORLD 87 Elephants, dolphin MARY EVANS PICTURE LIBRARY 22 Native Americans and Jesuit missionaries, Native American and 23 Mission San Diego 26 Prospector 28 Earthquake 29 Cartoon POPPERFOTO 16 Charles Manson 30 Gentlemen of Paramount 32/3 Police and demonstrator 85 Education course REX FEATURES 132 Beach boys 133 The Doors ROYAL GEOGRAPHIC SOCIETY 20 Map SPECTRUM COLOUR LIBRARY Cover Lone Cypress 75 Fireworks 97 Fruit 102 Oil platforms 128/9 Hollywood sign 137 University of California 202/3 Sierra Mountain lake 207 Kaweah River, Mount Whitney Trail 239 Earthquake damage 243 Smith River WALT DISNEY CO 160 Sleeping Beauty's Castle ZEFA PICTURE LIBRARY (UK) LTD Back flap Hollywood neon sign 6 Hollywood sign 136 LA Westwood Village 144 Hard Rock Café 145 Sunset Boulevard 148 LA Airport 149 Yellow cabs 162 Catalina Island 164 LA Freeways and skyline 175 Mission Bay 201 Sequoia tree 228 Gull Rock 257 Los Angeles Harbour AA PHOTO LIBRARY contributions from Harold Harris and Barrie Smith.